Visual SourceSafe 2005 Software Configuration Management in Practice

Best practice management and development of Visual Studio .NET 2005 applications with this easy-to-use SCM tool from Microsoft

Alexandru Serban

PUBLISHING

BIRMINGHAM - MUMBAI

Visual SourceSafe 2005 Software Configuration Management in Practice

First published: February 2007

Production Reference: 1090207

Published by Packt Publishing Ltd.
32 Lincoln Road
Olton
Birmingham, B27 6PA, UK.

ISBN 978-1-904811-69-5

www.packtpub.com

Cover Image by www.visionwt.com

Credits

Author

Alexandru Serban

Reviewers

Alin Constantin

Dragos Brezoi

Jean-Baptiste Lab

Development Editor

Cristian Darie

Technical Editor

Saurabh Singh

Editorial Manager

Dipali Chittar

Project Manager

Patricia Weir

Project Coordinator

Abhijeet Deobhakta

Indexer

Bhushan Pangaonkar

Proofreader

Chris Smith

Layouts and Illustrations

Shantanu Zagade

Cover Designer

Shantanu Zagade

About the Author

Alexandru Serban is the founder and CEO of Unievo, a new software development company.

Previously, he worked as a .NET Software Architect with Softwin and Microsoft on extending Visual Studio for enterprise infrastructure projects. In 2004, he co-authored *Pro .NET 1.1 Network Programming*, Second Edition.

Alexandru has been driven by the computer revolution ever since he can remember. Now he plans to be a part of it.

When not planning to take over the word, he likes to drive and travel, in the summer to the sea and in the winter to the mountains, where he hits the slopes with his snowboard.

About the Reviewers

Alin Constantin graduated from the Faculty of Automatic Control and Computers of the Politehnica University of Bucharest in 1997. He worked at Crinsoft S.R.L., developing hotel management and user interface automation software. Then in 1999 he joined Microsoft. For almost 7 years he focused on developing Visual SourceSafe and source control integration in Visual Studio.

Dragos Brezoi started programming to create an application for processing and adding extra effects to his guitar's sound. Several years later, he got a Masters Degree in Computer Science from the Politehnica University of Bucharest, and is now researching for a Ph.D. in Advanced Automatics. Dragos worked for several years in the industrial automation field as a programmer for PLC and DSP programming to SCADA, OPC, and DCS solutions. Dragos co-authored *GDI+ Custom Controls with Visual C# 2005* (Packt Publishing, 2006), and he currently works for Motorola TTPCom Product Group (Denmark), developing a next-generation embedded software framework.

Jean-Baptiste Lab discovered computers at the age of 12, when he started writing demos in assembly to impress his friends. After a scientific-oriented basic education, he obtained a B.Sc. in Computer Science at Portsmouth University, UK in 1998, and went on to achieve an M.Sc. in Mathematics and Computing at the University of Besancon, France. Expatriated in Denmark, Jean-Baptiste has been working in the mobile phone industry since 2001, touching various fields spanning from GSM Protocol Stack simulation to software architecture, build systems, and configuration management.

Table of Contents

Preface

Software Configuration Management (SCM) is one of the first skills a serious developer should master, after becoming proficient with his or her development tools of choice. Unfortunately this doesn't always happen because the subject of SCM is not commonly taught in academic or company training.

Although software is not a material thing, as you cannot touch it, smell it, or taste it, building software can be as complex as building physical things such as cars or planes, if not more so. The main difference between the two worlds lies in the limitations you confront. In the world of developing software there are no physical limitations — the only limit is your imagination.

However, all this freedom can have a downside. A good TV commercial once stated "Power is nothing without control" — if you do not control it wisely, it may start working against you. When developing software, you need to have a manageable team development effort, track and maintain the history of your projects, sustain parallel development on multiple product versions, fix bugs, and release service packs while further developing the applications.

This is where the concept of Software Configuration Management (SCM) comes into play, dealing among other things with source code versioning, tracking development evolution, building, and releasing. Putting it in simple terms, SCM is about getting the job done safer, faster, and better.

While trying to keep the theory to a minimum, this book starts by teaching you what SCM is, why it is important, and what benefits you get by using it, either by working individually or by being part of a team. You will find this part very valuable if you're new to the concept of SCM, because you will be setting your base for understanding what happens in the rest of the book.

Then the book concentrates on the Microsoft Visual SourceSafe 2005 SCM tool and the best practices used to manage the development and evolution of Visual Studio .NET 2005 applications. You will learn the theory by going through a journey, in which we will actually develop a new application, starting from designing its specifications and ending with releasing it and completing the Software Development Lifecycle (SDLC).

You will learn how the SCM concepts are applied by Visual SourceSafe 2005 by developing *Orbital Hotel*, a Service-Oriented Application hotel reservation system. You will learn how to use the team cooperation features in Visual SourceSafe 2005 with the help of John and Mary, two fictional team members who have been assigned to implement various project components.

The end of the book deals with SourceSafe administration tasks. It describes SourceSafe database creation, management, and maintenance, how to secure the database, how to create users and assign user rights, and how to manage projects and project settings.

Additional material on how to customize SourceSafe to suit your development style is available at `http://www.packtpub.com/visual-sourcesafe-2005/book`. You can visit Orbital Hotel online at `http://orbitalhotel.alexandruserban.com/`.

I hope you will find this book a great resource about Visual SourceSafe 2005, and I hope you will enjoy reading it as much as I enjoyed writing it!

What This Book Covers

Chapter 1 teaches you the basic terminology and concepts used in the SCM world, and how SCM integrates in the Software Development Lifecycle.

Chapter 2 introduces you to Microsoft's SCM tool for small and medium teams: Visual SourceSafe 2005. You'll learn what this product is made of, and what new features and improvements it has over the previous versions.

Chapter 3 introduces Orbital Hotel, a hotel-reservation system application, which will be used in the next chapters as a case study for developing Visual Studio applications with SourceSafe. We will see what the best structure for Visual Studio solutions is when working under Source Control.

Chapter 4 discusses the various ways you can add a software project to the SourceSafe database. This is the first step you'll take when starting to develop an application under Source Control.

Chapter 5 covers the Source Control operations used daily in our development activities. We'll set up a new workspace and get the solution from the SourceSafe database. Then, we will add new files to the solution, check them in, examine their history, and get latest versions. We will also explore the team-cooperation models and see what are the differences between them, their advantages and disadvantages, and operations such as item comparison, undoing changes, file merging and pinning, and conflict resolution.

Chapter 6 teaches you how to access the SourceSafe server through the intranet or the Internet, in order to perform the necessary Source Control tasks. If you don't have an internet connection at the remote location, or if the local SourceSafe server is temporarily down, you can work *offline*, provided you already have the solution files on your remote machine. When a connection to the database becomes available again, you reconnect to the SourceSafe database and synchronize the changes. Depending on the database configuration and the Visual Studio plug-ins you use while reconnecting, there are some scenarios to consider for avoiding data loss. We will examine the possible scenarios that can lead to data loss and see how to avoid such situations.

Chapter 7 teaches you how to manage the software development lifecycle using SourceSafe. In the evolution of software products there are many milestones. We will see how to manage them using SourceSafe so that we can reproduce their specific configurations when needed. We will also talk about the build process and how a periodical build can catch integration problems early on. We will take a brief look at white-box and black-box tests and how they help in ensuring final product quality. Last but not the least, we will see how to maintain multiple product versions to be able to release service packs while continuing development towards the next versions.

Appendix A covers the installation steps for Visual SourceSafe 2005 and the configuration for remote access.

Appendix B describes how to perform SourceSafe database administration tasks such as creating and securing databases, managing database and Windows users, creating shadow folders, and configuring the services for the SourceSafe plug-ins in Visual Studio.

Appendix C discusses how to perform maintenance tasks on SourceSafe databases such as undoing user checkouts, changing the team version control model, locking, archiving, restoring, and running database maintenance tools.

Additional material on Customizing Visual SourceSafe 2005 is available at `http://www.packtpub.com/ sourcesafe/book`.

What You Need for This Book

To follow this book you need Visual SourceSafe 2005, and Visual Studio .NET 2005 Standard edition or above.

Who This Book is For

This book is for .NET developers, testers, and configuration managers who:

- Use Visual Studio .NET 2005 for building software
- Want to use software configuration to manage their products in day-to-day activities
- Want to improve their efficiency by learning to use the best practices with SourceSafe
- Want to install, manage, and configure Visual SourceSafe 2005 for optimal operation

The book doesn't assume previous experience with any software configuration tool and is a great resource for people who want to start learning about this subject.

Conventions

In this book, you will find a number of styles of text that distinguish between different kinds of information. Here are some examples of these styles, and an explanation of their meaning.

There are three styles for code. Code words in text are shown as follows: "In the third page we have to specify the LAN network path to the database shared folder that contains the `srcsafe.ini` file."

A block of code will be set as follows:

```
/// <summary>
/// Updates the room database with the information in the room
/// parameter
/// </summary>
/// <param name="rooms">The RoomDataTable object containing
/// the information to be updated</param>
public void UpdateRooms(RoomDS.RoomDataTable rooms)
{
    throw new System.NotImplementedException();
}
```

Any command-line input and output is written as follows:

```
selfssl.exe /N:CN=vss.alexandruserban.com /T /V:365
```

New terms and **important words** are introduced in a bold-type font. Words that you see on the screen, in menus or dialog boxes for example, appear in our text like this: "The path can be entered manually or by using the **Browse** button to browse the network for the specific path."

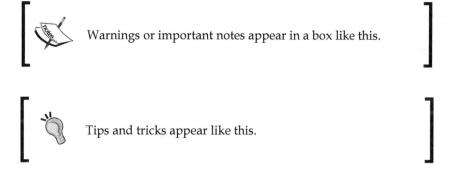

Warnings or important notes appear in a box like this.

Tips and tricks appear like this.

Reader Feedback

Feedback from our readers is always welcome. Let us know what you think about this book, what you liked or may have disliked. Reader feedback is important for us to develop titles that you really get the most out of.

To send us general feedback, simply drop an email to feedback@packtpub.com, making sure to mention the book title in the subject of your message.

If there is a book that you need and would like to see us publish, please send us a note in the **SUGGEST A TITLE** form on www.packtpub.com or email suggest@packtpub.com.

If there is a topic that you have expertise in and you are interested in either writing or contributing to a book, see our author guide on www.packtpub.com/authors.

Customer Support

Now that you are the proud owner of a Packt book, we have a number of things to help you to get the most from your purchase.

Downloading the Example Code for the Book

Visit http://www.packtpub.com/support, and select this book from the list of titles to download any example code or extra resources for this book. The files available for download will then be displayed.

The downloadable files contain instructions on how to use them.

Errata

Although we have taken every care to ensure the accuracy of our contents, mistakes do happen. If you find a mistake in one of our books—maybe a mistake in text or code—we would be grateful if you would report this to us. By doing this you can save other readers from frustration, and help to improve subsequent versions of this book. If you find any errata, report them by visiting http://www.packtpub.com/support, selecting your book, clicking on the **Submit Errata** link, and entering the details of your errata. Once your errata are verified, your submission will be accepted and the errata are added to the list of existing errata. The existing errata can be viewed by selecting your title from http://www.packtpub.com/support.

Questions

You can contact us at questions@packtpub.com if you are having a problem with some aspect of the book, and we will do our best to address it.

1

Controlling the Evolution of Software Products

On April 30, 1999, a Titan IV B rocket carrying a military satellite into orbit was launched from Space Launch Complex 40 at Cape Canaveral Air Station, Florida. The flight performance of the Titan solid rocket motor and the core vehicle was nominal. However, the vehicle began experiencing instability about the roll axis during the first burn. This instability was greatly magnified during the upper stage second main engine burn, resulting in uncontrolled vehicle tumbling. As a result of these anomalous events the satellite was placed in an unusable low elliptical final orbit instead of an intended geosynchronous orbit. After several days of satellite life-saving effort by Air Force and satellite contractor personnel the satellite was declared a complete loss by the acting secretary of the Air Force on 4 May 1999.

The investigation into this accident concluded that the cause was due to a failed software development, testing, and quality assurance process. This process did not detect and correct a software engineer error in a manual entry of a constant value of a roll rate filter, which is the value initially entered in the Inertial Measurement flight software file. The value should have been entered as 1.992476, but was entered as 0.1992476. The incorrect roll rate filter constant zeroed any roll rate data, resulting in the loss of roll axis control, which then caused loss of yaw and pitch control.

What could have been done to prevent the problem? The answer to this question points to lack of organization and control in the software development process.

Why did the software engineer need to manually type the constant value into that file? Well, it turns out that the original file provided by the Control Dynamics group was somehow lost and he had to recreate it from scratch. While human error can be considered as a factor, the primary cause of this one billion dollar disaster was the accidental loss of the original file.

You can view the full story on the Internet at:

`http://sunnyday.mit.edu/accidents/titan_1999_rpt.doc`

This one-billion dollar disaster could have been avoided if the software development team had used a **Software Configuration Management** (**SCM**) system that stored all the files safely from accidental loses. However, SCM can do much more than that.

What is Software Configuration Management?

While the rest of this book is focused on the Microsoft Visual SourceSafe 2005 tool, this first chapter is neutral to any SCM tool. In this chapter you will learn the basic terminology and concepts used in the SCM world. If you are already familiar with these concepts you can skip this chapter, although I would still suggest you take a quick look.

First, let me tell you the story of my first interaction with SCM tools and principles. It was during my first job. I was hired along with one of my friends by a small company that had just opened its new software development department. We were the first developers and we had to build an ERP system. All we knew was to write (spaghetti) code. They told us what the application should do and that was it. We were all on our own to make it happen (sounds familiar?). So we scratched our heads and started to write the code. It wasn't long until we needed to work on the same files. We scratched our heads again and came up with a state-of-the-art source management system — manually copying the files from one another. When one person finished the work on a file it was like, "Hey dude, you can take the file now. Oh wait, I must make a backup in case you mess it up." It was like that for a couple of days until we got sick and tired of all the file backups. We had to do something about it.

Then we saw in the Visual Studio suite something called Visual SourceSafe. We told ourselves, "Hey, this thing has something to do with the source files. Let's see what it does!", and installed SourceSafe on our machines. The rest is history. We were now able to work together but independently, without manual file backups, sticky notes, and all that hassle. We never got the chance to experience what would have happened if a third developer had come in before SourceSafe and we had to exchange files between all three of us. It probably wouldn't have been as disastrous as the Titan case but still a serious problem. We thus resolved the source management problem. Now we had to build the ERP system. But that's another story.

SCM was invented to resolve problems of this kind and many more. During the early days of software engineering, the impact of the rapid increases in computer power and the complexity of the problems that could be tackled resulted in the so called "software crisis". This was characterized by an inability to develop software on time, within budget, and within requirements. As a result new ideas, principles, and practices had to be developed. The Software Configuration Management concepts were born.

Software Configuration Management appeared as a solution to software problems, when it was clear that programming does not cover every aspect in software engineering and there was a need for predictability in software development. In this context we can define Software Configuration Management as follows:

> Software Configuration Management is the discipline of managing how software is *modified* and *built* through techniques including *source code control, revision control, object build tracking*, and *release construction*. SCM involves identifying the configuration of the software at given points in time, systematically *controlling changes* to the configuration, and maintaining the integrity and traceability of the configuration throughout the *software development lifecycle*.

As you can see from its definition, Software Configuration Management aggregates several different concepts and techniques. You may be familiar with some of them as they can work on their own. But as the whole is more than the sum of its parts; SCM is more than all these techniques used independently.

So, let's start with... the end. What is the software development lifecycle?

The Software Development Lifecycle

The **Software Development Lifecycle (SDLC)** represents the process used to develop a software system, starting with its conception and ending with its termination.

When developing any software system we adopt a development model. There are many development models, each having its advantages and disadvantages, but one way or another they all employ a succession of basic development phases as follows:

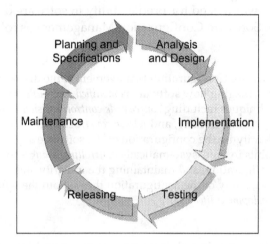

Planning and Specifications: Every activity must start with a plan. Failing to plan is planning to fail. The degree of planning differs from one model to another, but it's very important to have a clear understanding of what we are going to build by creating the system's specifications.

Analysis and Design: In this phase we analyze and define the system's structure. We define the architecture, the components, and how these components fit together to produce a working system.

Implementation: This is the development phase. We start code generation based on the system's design using compilers, interpreters, debuggers to bring the system to life.

Testing: As different parts of the system are completed, they are put through a series of tests. Test plans and test cases are used to identify bugs and to ensure that the system is working according to the specifications.

Releasing: After the test phase ends, the system is released and enters the production environment.

Maintenance: Once in the production environment, the system will suffer modifications as a result of undetected bugs or other unexpected events. The system is evaluated and the cycle is repeated.

SCM provides the way to control the software development lifecycle, allowing for a greater degree of software management being one of the core components in the software development process.

Let's see how SCM helps us control the development lifecycle.

Software Configuration Management Concepts

In order to control the software development lifecycle, SCM employs a series of concepts and techniques. We will take a look at some of these key concepts and techniques, what they are, and how they work. In this section you will learn about the following:

- *Resource Management*: Managing source code files, project files, documents, images, etc., in a central area commonly called *repository*, *database*, or *depot*.

- *Workspaces*: Providing a private work area for each project participant, separate from the other participants (architects, developers, testers, etc.).

- *Resource Versioning*: Maintaining different resource versions as the project evolves using file *revisions* stored as *file deltas*.

- *Cooperation Support*: Managing the interaction between the project participants using operations like *check out*, *check in*, and *merge*.

- *History Management*: The ability to view, manage, and mark resource versions using *labels*.

- *Build* and *Release Management*: The ability to manage project builds and releases in order to ensure that the configuration for the resources used in the builds is marked, known, and reproducible.

- *Parallel Development*: The ability to work in parallel on more than one project version by *branching* multiple *codelines* and later *merging* them.

Let's discuss each of these topics, one at a time.

Resource Management

In order to build any system, you need resources. When you build a house, you need bricks, cement, roof, windows, doors, and so on. The same concept applies to software systems. Your resources, however, will consist of *source code files, image files, configuration files,* and so on (depending on your project type).

Managing resources is an essential aspect in building any kind of system. When it comes to software, these resources must be *identified* and *organized* in a way that provides flexibility as well as security. We can achieve this organization by storing the resources in a *managed area*. This area is commonly referred to as a **repository**, **database**, or **depot** where every resource of the project resides.

The Repository

The **repository** is the place where all the source code files, images, documents, configuration files, and all the software components concerning the project are stored. In a traditional way, they are organized in a hierarchy of logical files and folders, a virtual file system tree. Security is also enforced because the repository provides a *single point of access* for everything the project needs in order to be successfully built.

The following figure represents a simplified repository structure:

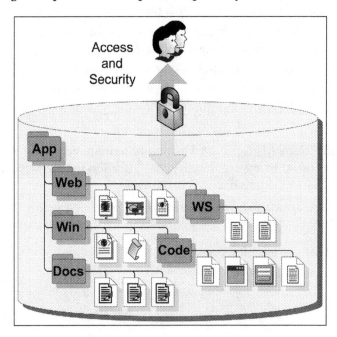

Typically we create a new repository when we start development on a new product. We create a base project structure and add it to a new repository. The logical repository structure matches the project structure.

Some of the main reasons to have a central repository are:

- Easy sharing among users.
- Easy management: The assets kept in the repository are stored in a single place where they are easy to control, back up, and restore.
- Security: Provides strict access control for the items in the repository.
- Logging: The ability to maintain logs of user activity in the repository.

The best physical location of the repository is on a dedicated server machine as this simplifies repository management and security, and gives an optimal performance. To ensure the maximum operation uptime and disaster recovery, the server should be equipped with:

- A **Redundant Array** of **Independent Disks (RAID)** to prevent disastrous disk failure cases.
- Redundant power supplies to prevent power loss in the case of power supply failure.
- An **Uninterruptible Power Supply (UPS)** in case of an environmental power loss.

While RAID systems and UPS are fairly cheap nowadays, if you cannot afford such configuration it is wise to think of other methods of ensuring repository safety. Users sometimes make the mistake of thinking their source code is a hundred percent safe once it has been added to a source control management repository. Creating disk backups of the repository is a smart choice and a must when RAID configurations are not used.

Different SCM systems store the repository using files on the server's file system, a database system, or a hybrid between these two. Apart from the actual resources, a repository must keep resource metadata, or data about the resources such as file history. The metadata grows side by side with the resources in the repository and adds to its size.

Having only one repository may seem a good idea. However keeping many unrelated projects in one repository can have an impact on performance. Many SCM systems are capable of managing multiple distinct repositories. To obtain maximum performance it's better to store resources that belong to different products using different repositories.

Many SCM systems also have remote user support. Remote users can access the repository from thousands of miles away through the Internet using different protocols. However, exposing the server on the Internet presents a high security risk. To protect the server from Internet threats, a firewall must be configured to allow only authorized connections.

So far we have a place to store our software projects. But we need a place to work and develop our projects, and to test our new ideas that might or might not work. For that purpose, SCM systems have **workspaces**.

Workspaces

While the repository is stored in a central area on the server machine, its users (developers, testers, etc.) work individually on different machines. The SCM system has to provide a workspace area for each of them and be able to synchronize the workspace with the repository when this is required. Different SCM systems name this workspace differently: *working folder*, *working directory*, *sandbox*, *view*, *enlistment*, etc.

The purpose of the individual workspace is to provide users with an area where they can work separated from the repository and to isolate each user from the others. This is done in order to prevent one user's changes from affecting the others while they are working. Users make changes to the workspace content, adding, modifying, and deleting files without the worry that they might affect the repository or anybody else for that matter.

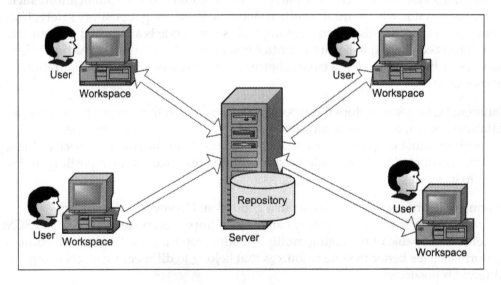

To synchronize the workspace with the repository, SCM systems have basic commands that perform actions to:

- `Add` (used to add new files or folders to the repository)
- `Get` (used to copy files or folders from the repository to the workspace)
- `Save` (used to save back the changes from the workspace to the repository)

The actual names for these commands differ from one SCM tool to another but all have them.

The repository starts as an empty storage area for the new product. After creating a basic organization of the project, we add it to the repository using the `Add` command. This operation adds our initial project structure to the repository from which other users can `Get` it.

The workspace starts as an image of the repository at a given point in time on the users' machines, having no real new value. They use the `Get` command to obtain the contents of the repository.

In contrast with the repository, a workspace can get very messy. Tying to implement a new feature or trying to fix a bug can lead to the contents of the workspace failing to even compile. Maybe the changes that at first seemed a good idea don't seem such a good idea after a while. All those changes can simply be discarded and the workspace be recreated from the repository. If, however, the changes are functional, then the workspace suddenly acquires value. As soon as this happens we want to make sure we save these changes in the repository where they are safe and everybody else can see and use them.

Best Practice

Do not let the workspace acquire too much value. Instead, synchronize the changes to the repository as often as possible.

While storing the projects to the latest resource versions, the repository has what a simple storage server doesn't. It has a timeline, a way to keep a record of resource history — *resource versioning*.

Resource Versioning

A fundamental feature of the repository is its ability to store all the versions of the resources it contains. During the development process, resources in the repository change and evolve as the project evolves. Resources are modified, renamed, and moved from one folder to another, new resources are added, and others are deleted. All these operations are part of the day-to-day work. The repository keeps track of these operations and provides the ability to view its state at any time in the past. It remembers every operation ever performed. If we wish we can view, compare, and restore any old resource version. Unfortunately it cannot provide us with a view of the future, but that's where we come into play, right?

Resource changes are stored by the repository as **revisions**.

Revisions

Each time a resource is *changed* and *saved* back to the repository, a *revision* is created. Thus, a resource evolves as a succession of revisions, usually referred to by successive numbers such as 1, 2, 3 or 1.1, 1.2, 1.3 etc.

There are two modes of keeping revisions. One is called *per-file* revision numbering, where every resource has independent revision numbers. Consecutive revisions have different contents.

Another revision mode uses *global* revision numbering. For each resource change, the entire folder structure is updated with a new revision number regardless of the fact that other resources haven't changed. In this mode, consecutive revisions of a file may, or may not have different contents.

The following figure shows a resource that has evolved over the course of five revisions:

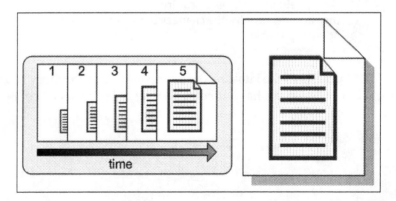

The repository keeps every revision with the ability to retrieve any one of them.

But how does the repository keep resource versions? One simple solution would be
to keep a copy of every version of a resource. While this solution is very simple, it
has a major disadvantage: as time passes, these copies occupy more and more disk
space. This makes repository management harder, lowers performance, and
is inefficient.

For example, let's say we have a 1MB file stored in the repository. This may be
a document specifying project specifications. Every once in a while we alter this
document by making small changes to it. Every revision we create will be about the
same size, so after four changes this file could take as much as 5MB. And this is just
for one file.

Usually, only a small part changes between successive revisions, so two successive
revisions differ only by a small percentage. A cleverer idea would be to save only the
difference between the two revisions.

Deltas

The difference between the two revisions is called a **delta**. Keeping only the delta and
not having redundant information allows us to use the storage space very efficiently
and increase performance. When getting a resource version, the deltas will be applied
against a base version and the resource will be reconstructed at that point in time.

Using deltas, after four small changes, our 1MB document will not take as much as
5MB anymore, adding just the space to save the deltas.

The following figure shows how the latest resource version is constructed using the
base version and the *forward deltas*:

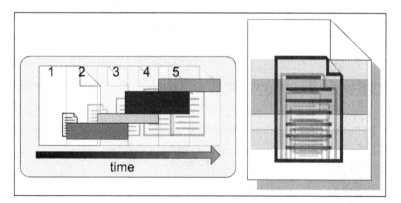

This approach helps in retrieving old versions very fast, but as we retrieve newer
versions, more and more deltas have to be combined resulting in greater overhead.
As most of the time we retrieve the latest version, we have to deal with this overhead
every time.

To overcome this, another approach is to keep the latest file version and use *reverse deltas*. Older versions are kept as differences of newer versions. The latest version is always available and the overhead associated with combining deltas is eliminated:

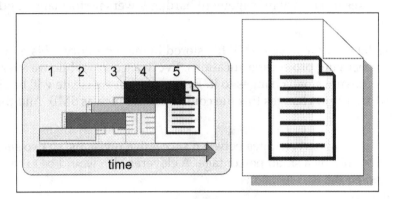

For best performance, these two approaches can be combined using forward and reverse deltas, by keeping a full version after a number of consecutive deltas. Retrieving a certain version means that deltas are applied against the nearest full version.

The repository uses deltas for other operations like renaming resources and moving them between folders. These operations have to be remembered because they are a part of the history. Getting the state of a project at a point in time means these operations have to be remembered and applied when this is necessary.

Until now, we have seen how the SCM system manages to isolate users from affecting one another. But, if we look at a bigger picture, these users form a team that should work together on the product development. The SCM system also has to be able to manage how users work together.

Cooperation Support

Cooperation support is an essential SCM feature because software development is usually done by a number of participants working in a team. While team members work in a personal workspace, they must be able to collaborate in a congruent way while minimizing conflicts, like the need to work on the same repository resources.

Let's imagine a situation in which you need to work on a source code file to fix a bug. You get the file and work on it in your private workspace. At the same time, your teammate Lisa needs to modify the same file. She gets the file and starts to modify it. After you finish your work, you save the file back to the repository, happy to have fixed the bug. Later, when Lisa finishes her changes as well, she saves the file too, overwriting your changes.

When two or more users need to work on the same resource from the repository, the SCM system must be able to handle this situation and prevent one user from accidentally overwriting other user's changes. This is an essential requirement. Without this support, team collaboration would be a very hard if not an impossible thing to accomplish.

In order to manage cooperation support, SCM systems employ several mechanisms, providing commands like:

- Check Out
- Modify/Edit
- Check in
- Merge
- Commit/Submit
- Undo Check Out

Before we explore the cooperation models, let's take a look at these operations and understand their specifics. SCM tools can support all of them or only a subset as some of them accomplish the same operation. The difference is the cooperation model and the context in which they are used.

Check Out

When we want to get a resource from the repository with the purpose of making changes to it, we perform a **check-out** operation on that resource. This indicates that we will change the contents of the resource and the SCM system will mark the resource in the repository to indicate to the other users that the specified resource is being used.

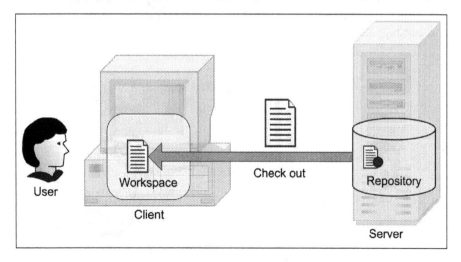

Depending on the cooperation model used, a check-out operation can lock the resource in the repository so other users cannot change it or it can only mark it as being used, allowing others to still change it. We will learn more about this in the *Cooperation Models* section.

When we need to modify multiple related resources, a check-out operation will be performed for every resource we need to change.

Modify/Edit

This is the action of making changes to the resources in our workspace, including working on source code files, configuration files, documents, etc.

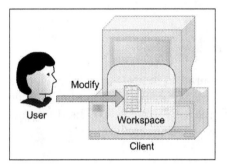

This is where we edit our project's resources and perform the necessary work.

Check In

This operation ends a check-out operation. After we've modified the resources, we must save them back to the repository. This is accomplished using a **check-in** operation. This indicates to the SCM system that the modified resources need to be saved and reintegrated into the repository.

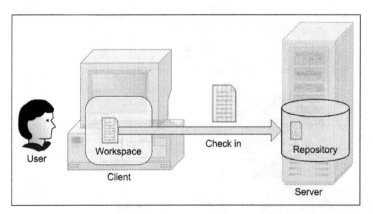

Not all SCM systems require checking out a resource before modifying it. For such systems, the `check in` command is replaced by `Commit`/`Submit` and is used to push changes from the workspace to the repository.

Best Practice

Every resource change can and should be associated with a comment that explains what was modified and why. SCM tools provide a special area for these comments when checking files in. Give a detailed explanation about what was changed and why, as it will help in easily identifying bugs and other issues.

After the check-in operation, the SCM tool will save the modified resources back to the repository and if necessary remove their lock so other users can modify them.

At this point, we must be careful not to *break* the repository state by checking in code that will not build and affect the entire team when they get the latest changes.

As we saw in the *Resource Versioning* section, checking in files creates file revisions in the repository and generates deltas that add to the files history.

Best Practice

When using multiple resources, in order not to break the repository state by checking in only parts of the changes, group the related changes together and save them to the repository in one operation. Also, do not begin to work on several issues at the same time and avoid checking out files that you are not sure you will need. Only check out files when you need them.

To support logical grouping of operations, some SCM tools use the notion of a change set. A **change set** represents a grouping of changes in multiple resources that must be made all at the same time. These may constitute a bug fix, a new feature, or any other set of related changes.

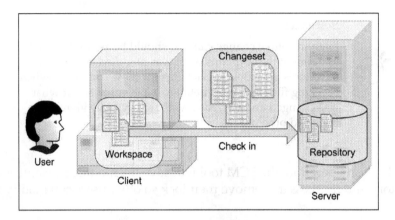

To ensure that all grouped changes are submitted to the repository in one operation, some SCM tools use atomic transactions. An **atomic transaction** is an operation in which either all changes are made or, if any one of them cannot be made, none are made. This ensures the repository is not updated with only half the changes but with all the changes at once, ensuring its integrity.

Merge

Let's imagine that one user, Alex, needed to work on a source code file. When he began to work, he checked out version 3 from the repository. While he was working, John, another user also checked out the same version and began working (in this case the SCM tool's configuration allows multiple users to check out the same resource).

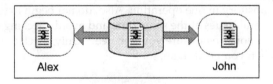

Let's say John finishes the work before Alex does and checks in the file into the repository. Now, the repository contains a new revision for that file, version 4.

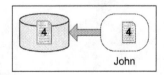

After Alex finishes making his changes he wants to save them. But now he is not saving the file after version 3, which he got when he began to work, but against version 4 which contains new changes.

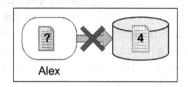

These changes have to be integrated in Alex's file before he can check in his work. The SCM system has to provide a way to handle this situation. The solution is a file **merge**. **Merging** is the process by which we create a new version (revision) of a file, based on the other two file versions.

These file versions started with a common ancestor, in our case version 3. Alex needs to check in his changes and while doing so he has to integrate John's changes into his file, otherwise he would overwrite John's changes. He needs to merge his file against the latest version in the repository.

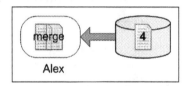

There are two ways to perform a merge operation:

- Automatic merge
- Manual merge

An automatic merge is attempted by the SCM system. If it doesn't detect any *conflicts*, the automatic merge will succeed and Alex can then verify the new merged version, make sure it is working, and save it to the repository.

Best Practice

Always verify the contents of the merged file before saving it to the repository. This ensures that you will not break the project build.

Conflicts occur when changes made in one file overlap the changes made in the other. Usually this is caused by making changes to the same line numbers in the file. In this case an automatic merge cannot be performed.

A manual merge leaves Alex with the responsibility of conciliating changes. For this purpose SCM systems have specialized tools called *three-way merge* tools, that present in a graphical user interface the three file versions that must be merged. These file versions are: the latest file version in the repository (in our case version 4), the file containing Alex's changes, and the base file version for these two files (in our case version 3) into which Alex must merge the changes to construct the final version. The tool shows the conflicts found between the latest file version and Alex's version. Alex can choose the way he wants to resolve them having the ability to edit the resulting merged file. For file merging to be successful, all conflicts must be resolved.

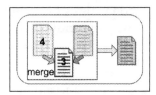

After resolving all the conflicts and creating the merged file we have to make sure the file is working (doesn't break the build). We can finally check it in into the repository where it would create a new revision (in our case version 5).

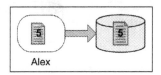

In this example Alex only needed to merge his changes into a file that was newer by only one version. But if Alex took longer to make his changes, the repository could have been updated with more new versions. The longer he took to make his changes the greater the possibility for the file in the repository to be updated with several versions. Instead of merging his changes into version 4, he would have had to merge them into let's say version 10. This increases the possibility of merge conflicts that he must resolve.

Best Practice

When using file merge, we must integrate our changes as often as possible to avoid merging conflicts.

We can also stay up to date with the repository version of a file by periodically getting the file from the repository and merging it into our workspace file. This way we can resolve possible conflicts incrementally and we can incorporate the repository changes into our changes along the way.

The merging operations using this approach can be applied on text files. They can also be applied on binary files by using merge tools that are capable of merging them. Many SCM tools have the possibility of specifying custom merge tools for different files. If there are no tools available for merging binary files, then these files cannot be merged and they should never be changed by multiple users at the same time.

Commit/Submit

This operation's results are similar to the check-in operation. The difference is that usually this operation ends a series of changes started without a check-out operation and which are saved using an atomic transaction as we will see shortly in the *Cooperation Models* section.

Undo Check Out

If for some reason we checked out something by mistake or we decide we no longer want to check in some or all of our changes, we can use the Undo Check Out command. This undoes the check out restoring the repository to the state it was before we performed the check out and deletes the changes in our workspace. However, we have the option of undoing the check out in the repository while keeping the changes in our workspace.

We saw what operations SCM tools employ to manage user cooperation. Let's take a look now at the cooperation models and the commands that are associated with them.

Cooperation Models

To manage user cooperation, SCM systems employ two main cooperation models:

- Check Out-Modify-Check In
- Modify-Merge-Commit

The fundamental difference between these two models is the degree of control versus the freedom they offer.

The Check Out-Modify-Check In model emphasizes more control and most of the time requires a connection to the repository, especially when checking out and checking in the resources. It may or it may not allow multiple users to modify resources at the same time.

The Modify-Merge-Commit model is more relaxed when it comes to repository availability, requiring a connection only when committing the changes back to the repository. However, more freedom means more risk of conflicts.

Check Out-Modify-Check In

The **Check Out-Modify-Check In** model has two sub-models of operation:

- Exclusive Check-Out Model
- Multiple Check-Out Model

The **Exclusive Check-Out** Model uses a pessimistic concurrency scheme characterized by a *Lock-Modify-Unlock* mode of operation. It allows *only one* user at a time to modify a resource. Typically, our workflow activity when using this model is an iteration of these three operations:

1. *Check out*: When we need to make changes to a resource, we begin with a check-out operation during which:

    ° Depending on the settings or the SCM tool's characteristics, the resource is copied from the repository into the workspace using a Get command to ensure we are working on the latest version, otherwise the resource is checked out using the version from our workspace.

    ° A *lock* operation is performed on the resource in the repository to prevent other users from checking out the file while we are using it.

    ° The resource in our workspace is prepared for writing and marked as checked out.

Other attempts by other users to modify the same resource will fail as the resource is specifically locked.

 While using this mode, we should exclusively check out only the required resources and for limited periods of time, as other users will not be allowed to work on them if required.

2. *Modify*: We modify the contents in the resource. We must test the changes to ensure that the changes do not break the project build.

3. *Check in*: After we are done with making changes, we perform a check-in operation. This operation:

- ° Saves the new file version in the repository
- ° *Unlocks* the resource so other users can change on it
- ° Undoes the marking of the resource as being checked out

This model has the advantage of never having to deal with merging our changes into another file version because nobody else can modify the file while we are working. However, it has the big disadvantage that the longer we take to make our changes, the more we disallow other users to make changes to the file if they need to, imposing a serial development approach as opposed to a concurrent development approach. If concurrent development is more suited to your development style then you can use the Multiple Check-Out Model.

The **Multiple Check-Out** Model uses an optimistic concurrency scheme characterized by a Copy-Modify-Merge mode of operation, allowing multiple users at a time to modify a resource. When using this model, we go through the following operations:

1. *Check out*: When we need to make changes to a resource, we begin with a check-out operation during which:

    - ° If necessary, the resource is copied from the repository into our workspace using a `Get` command to ensure we are working on the latest version, otherwise the resource is checked out using the version from our workspace.
    - ° The resource in our workspace is prepared for changing and marked as checked out.

    With this operation we have a local *working copy* on which we perform our changes. The check out is done when we begin to make changes to the resource but the SCM system *doesn't* lock the resource in the repository. Other users can perform check-out operations on it independently and work concurrently on the same resource.

2. *Modify*: We modify the contents of the resource. We must test the changes, to ensure that the changes do not break the project build.

3. *Merge*: After we are done with making changes, a merge operation is performed against the two resource versions, the one in the repository and the one in our workspace. This can be either done using an explicit get operation or during the check-in operation.

4. *Check in*: After we resolve all the possible conflicts that may appear, we perform a check-in operation during which:

    - ° The new file version is saved in the repository
    - ° The resource is unmarked as being checked out

This model has the advantage of concurrent development as it doesn't lock the resource during the check-out operation. Multiple users can modify the resource at the same time. However, the more the users change the same resource, the more conflicts can arise, making it difficult to merge the changes.

When using Check Out-Modify-Check in, use the check-out model that best suits your needs. If you want exclusive access to resources, use the exclusive check-out model to prevent other users from changing them at the same time. If, however, you are interested in a concurrent development approach, use the multiple check-out model to allow multiple users to work on the same resources at the same time.

Let's now talk about the other cooperation model, the Modify-Merge-Commit model.

Modify-Merge-Commit

This model is similar to the Multiple Check-Out Model we saw earlier, the main difference being that it doesn't use check outs in any way. As a result nobody knows for sure if somebody is modifying a resource. This model is used by some SCM tools as a disconnected working model when a connection to the repository is not available. The typical succession of operations performed when using this model is:

1.   *Modify*: We can start modifying any resource in the workspace without performing a check-out operation and without the need to have a connection to the repository. The resources in the workspace are always ready to be modified.

2.   *Merge*: After making the changes to the resources, we must merge them into the latest repository versions. This can be done using automatic merging or, if conflicts are detected, using manual merging.

3.   *Commit*: This operation is the equivalent of the check-in operation. After resolving all possible conflicts, the changes are committed by simply saving the resources in the repository. The difference from the check-in operation is somewhat semantic. Since the resource wasn't initially checked out and marked as check-out, it cannot be checked in and unmarked as checked out. The commit operation is used just to synchronize the workspace with the repository by committing the workspace changes to the repository.

This model is very simple as it doesn't require checking out and checking in resources, maximizing concurrent development. We can start modifying resources as soon as we need to, without worrying that the resource may be locked by another user as in the Exclusive Check-Out Model. This is especially useful when working offline when we don't have a network connection with the repository. The only time a network connection is required is when we need to merge and commit our changes.

However, this freedom comes at a cost. Not being required to check out our resources, even for informational purposes only, makes it likely that multiple users perform changes on the same resources. This can cause conflicts and increases the risks when merging the changes back into the repository.

History Management

We've seen that apart from the fact that the repository provides us with a place to store our resources, it provides us with resource versioning, adding another dimension to what would otherwise be just a storage area—time. Every resource version we check in into the repository creates a revision that becomes a part of history, our development history, keeping a record of our project evolution. This is an essential ability as we can always go back to a certain point in time if we need to. SCM systems provide the ability to *browse*, *search*, *sort*, and *filter* the history of a project.

The following figure shows a group of five different resources with several different revisions.

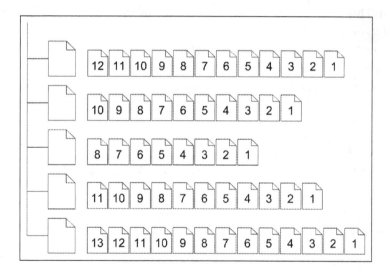

As time passes, however, this record becomes bigger and bigger. Searching for something specific could be like searching for a needle in a haystack. To identify important development events, SCM systems provide labels or tags.

Labels

Labels are an important feature for managing repository history. They provide a way to associate a friendly name with a specific version of an entire project, a folder, or a single resource, taking a repository snapshot at a certain moment in time that you can identify later when needed. We can create a label on the current repository state or, as supported by some SCM systems, on past states, based on certain information like a specific date.

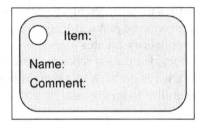

When creating a label we must provide some information consisting of:

- Item: This represents the resources we are labeling and it can be a project, a folder, or a file.
- Name: A label's name is usually a short description for the label. This can be anything from a version number to a short sentence.
- Comment: This is the place where we can enter some detailed information about the label. Not all SCM systems, however, provide this field.

Using Labels

Labels allow us to make a repository snapshot. But when and why is it worth using labels?

Usually we use labels before or after an important event. We use labels to identify important events like:

- Project changes: If we need to make some important project changes, we want to mark the project's state, to have a snapshot of the latest project structure before beginning to make them.
- Project builds: Just like project changes, we want to keep track and identify project builds. This feature can be used by automatic building tools when getting the latest version of the resources in the repository to label the specific versions used in the build.
- Project releases: Releasing a project is a big development event. We want to make really sure we know which resource versions were used to build a production project version.

The figure below shows the same group of files using labels:

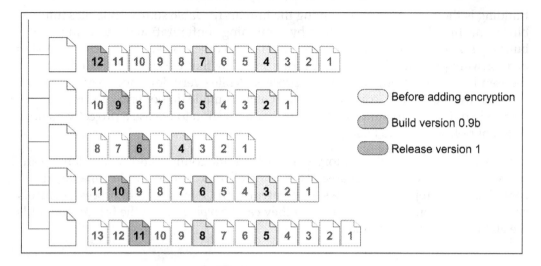

The first label was applied before, let's say, encryption was added to the project. If we later wanted to see what the project's state was before adding encryption, we could get the specific version using this label.

The second label was applied when building the 0.9b project version. This makes retrieving the project's state at that time very easy.

The third label was applied when version 1 was released. Again, retrieving the specific project version is very easy.

Best Practice
Use labels as often as you can as they are an efficient way to mark a specific project state.

We can use labels with any other events when we need to have a snapshot of the project's state. If later we want to recreate the exact snapshot generated by the label, we can simply get the specific resource versions from the repository associated with the label.

We've so far seen the advantages of Software Configuration Management. We have a centralized place to safely store our project resources — the repository, we have workspaces to do our work and keep every user separate, we have cooperation support to work concurrently on the project, we have resource versions and history, and we have history management to keep track of project versions.

Build and Release Management

Building is the process of transforming the human-readable source code files into binary machine-level executable files by combining configuration items, using building scripts, make files, compilers, linkers, and other tools, and creating a version of a software program. Building can take from a few files to several hundreds or thousands of files making it a delicate process. While every developer performs test builds in the workspace to ensure that the changes made do not break the repository state, when it comes to building the entire configuration to release a project version, different policies have to be in place.

We saw the ability of the repository to record specific configurations: how labels can be used to create repository snapshots. Having all source code files in a managed central area, the repository, allows for greater control over the build process, controls specific project configurations ensuring they can be *reproduced* in the future, and adds the ability to *automate the build* process.

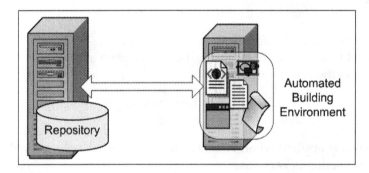

Automating the building process brings great benefits and boosts the productivity as possible problems are spotted earlier and on a regular basis. This can be achieved by using frequent integrity builds with regression testing (*sanity* builds), using automated building and testing environments.

Release management is closely related to build management as a release is in fact a production build of the project. Release management is the process of releasing a built and tested system into the production environment with the scope of making the application available to the end users. When releasing a product version, the configuration used to generate the release build must be recorded and stored to ensure that at a later time the build can be reproduced identically. This allows us to see exactly what resource versions were used in the build and be able to release future improvements and bug fixes based on that configuration.

Upon releasing the first version of a product, things aren't very complicated. The entire development team effort is focused on developing this first version. But as the product comes together and the moment for it to be released is nearing, things change.

After the first version is released the effort is divided into at least two paths, one to continue the development towards the next release and the second to maintain the released version. These efforts must be conducted in parallel and SCM must be able to cope with this situation. For these cases SCM provides support for parallel development.

Parallel Development

Let's imagine the following situation. We are working on our product and here comes the time to release our first version. Intensive testing is done by the test team to ensure there are no bugs and everything works as it should. Meanwhile, the development team can go ahead and start the development towards the next product version. While the first version is under testing we don't want to modify the repository with new changes that would make testing a never ending story. So, what can we do?

One method would be to stop or freeze development on the project until the first version is tested and released, allowing only modifications related to the release. This approach, however, causes development to come to a complete stop, affecting productivity.

Another method would be to create a new repository, copy all the resources from the first one and continue development in the new repository while testing is being done in the first. So far so good, but there's a good chance the testing process finds some bugs the developers did not catch. The bugs are fixed in the first repository used for the release, but they are still to be fixed in the second one. For every change in the first repository there has to be a change in the second one. And somebody has to do it manually.

But wait, there's more. Let's say we managed to release our version and we are happy we can continue to work towards the next one. Some time after the release, however, some more issues appear that were not caught by the testing process. We must fix these issues and create service packs to patch the already installed production release.

We can find ourselves in two situations depending on the method we used to manage the release. If we used the freeze method to stop development in the repository until the release is out, now the repository contains new changes since the release version. Fixing those issues in the current version cannot be accomplished as it contains new unfinished and untested features implemented for the next release. But fortunately we labeled the release version and now we can retrieve it and fix those issues separately. After fixing the issues in the release version and creating the service pack, we have to again fix them in the current development version manually.

The same operation applies if we used the second method by using two repositories. After fixing the issues in the first repository we have to manually apply them to the second. And we must do this every time a new issue appears.

So far we have only one released version but imagine having more, maybe having one customized for a specific customer. As you can see this is not a very elegant approach, is error prone, and time consuming.

It would be much better if we could somehow continue development on new features while still releasing our upcoming versions and doing bug fixes at the same time. Fortunately SCM deals with these issues too. For this purpose, SCM defines the concept of parallel development. Parallel development means working in parallel on more than one product version in the same repository.

This is where we need to define the concept of codelines.

Codelines

A **codeline** represents a project's development evolution across time, having a continuous history. A codeline has a point in time where it began to exist and evolve with its own history.

When we begin working on a product, we create a codeline and we develop our project on this codeline.

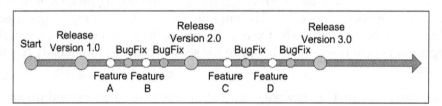

As time passes, the project evolves, reaching several milestones. Milestones are important events in the course of the development effort like version releases. Until we reach our first product version, we can work on a single development codeline. When time comes to release a new version we must stabilize the codeline by testing it and fixing the bugs found. While doing so we may want to continue working towards the next version while being able to integrate changes we made in the testing process. After releasing one version, we will have to maintain it and fix all the bugs that testing didn't discover. Using just a singe codeline makes development follow a single path and suffers from the problems we discussed earlier as project freezes when approaching a release and maintenance problems.

The solution is to have more than one codeline and be able to create new codelines as necessary. To enable this scenario SCM systems support branches.

Branches

Branches are used to split codelines from other codelines, creating several development paths. The terminology comes from the analogy with a real tree. The first codeline is the tree trunk. Then, by splitting other codelines we create branches.

The following figure shows how branching allows us to continue development on the project while maintaining different project versions:

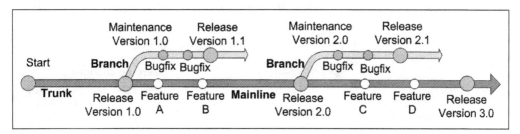

We begin development in a single codeline that forms the trunk or mainline and head towards our first release. Upon releasing the first version, instead of freezing development we create a new codeline by creating a branch from the mainline. This new codeline will support testing and maintenance on the first release, evolving in parallel with the mainline. Detected issues and bugs are fixed and service packs are built and released on this new maintenance branch. The case is the same for the next releases.

As we continue to work towards the next product releases in the mainline, we want to integrate the bug fixes performed in the maintenance line. Because the maintenance line is branched from the mainline, it has a common history until the branching occurred. What this means, is that although they were separated at a certain point in time, they still share common content. How can we integrate the fixes from the maintenance line in the mainline? The answer becomes very simple if we make a connection with the Multiple Check Out or the Modify-Merge-Commit model. If we consider that branches are concurrent modifications performed by users in their workspaces on a base resource version, then integrating those modifications back into the repository involves a merge operation.

Merging Branches

Although the concept of merging branches is similar to merging resource versions, in the context of merging branches the result of the merge operation is slightly different. While in merging resources we make a single version out of other different versions, in merging branches we are in fact integrating changes performed in one branch into another branch. After the merge operation the two branches still exist, one or both of them being updated with changes performed in the other. In our example, changes performed in the maintenance line are merged into the mainline:

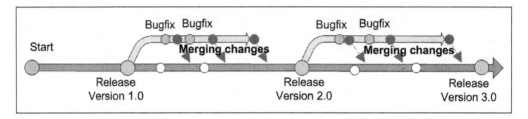

Using parallel development solves many problems. In this case we used a maintenance branch for every release. Changes to the maintenance branch are merged into the mainline. Branching is a powerful mechanism allowing development on several codelines at the same time. This allows for greater control over the software configuration and adds the ability to strictly control product releases and any other milestone.

Conclusion

Using SCM we have the ability to manage the development process and the software development lifecycle. SCM plays an important role by integrating every aspect of the software development process:

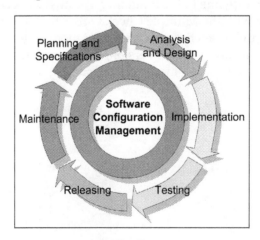

Software Configuration Management plays an active role in the entire process of developing software products, beginning with resource management, resource access control and security, resource versioning, development support, and history management and ending with parallel development, build management, and release management.

Summary

In this chapter we took an overview of the Software Configuration Management basic terminology and principles and how it provides the means to control and manage the evolution of software products. We learned about resource management using the centralized repository that stores all the resources we use to build the final product, and about the workspace that each participant uses to work independently but in sync with the other participants. We've seen that the repository is much more than a simple storage area, providing resource versioning using resource revisions, providing cooperation support using several cooperation models, and history management using labels. These features also allow us to manage the build and the release process. After releasing a new product version we must work in parallel and maintain the release while advancing towards a new release. SCM manages these situations providing parallel development on more than one codeline by creating branched codelines from the trunk or mainline. Later, when we need to integrate changes such as bug fixes between codelines, SCM provides the ability to merge the branched codelines.

2
The SourceSafe 2005 Architecture

Chapter 1 laid the theoretical foundation for the concepts that we are going to use through the rest of the book. From now, we will concentrate on the Microsoft Visual SourceSafe 2005 SCM tool.

Visual SourceSafe has a lot of history behind it. It is either loved for the fact that it is easy to use and integrates with many other Microsoft products, or hated probably because of the headaches given by using it improperly. It is designed to be used by individuals or by small and medium sized teams and not as an enterprise-level SCM tool (such as Visual Studio Team System). The SourceSafe 2005 edition addresses many of the past issues and adds new features, one the most notable being the support for internet connections when using Visual Studio .NET.

Any tool and technology is as good as the way you use it. Likewise you can drive a car better if you know how it works under the hood. In this chapter, we are going to take a look at the SourceSafe 2005 architecture, its core components, and how those components work together to do the job. We will look at the network configurations, the server components, the database, the client components, and the integration with Microsoft Visual Studio .NET 2005.

Visual SourceSafe 2005 has three main components:

- The **Server** applications and services
- The **Database** (repository)
- The **Client** applications

The following figure illustrates an overall look at these components. They will be described in more detail in the following sections.

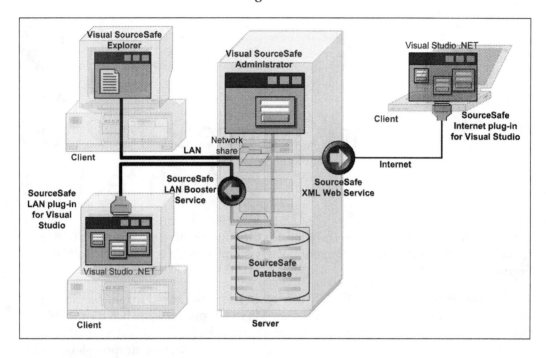

The Visual SourceSafe Server

The Visual SourceSafe server machine has the responsibility of maintaining one or more SourceSafe databases and to manage the server-side components. The server applications and services are:

- Visual SourceSafe Administrator application
- LAN booster service
- Remote access XML Web service

The Visual SourceSafe Administrator Application

The Visual SourceSafe Administrator is the main **Graphical User Interface** (GUI) administration tool.

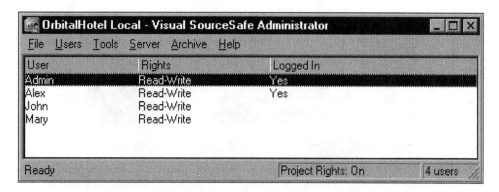

The Visual SourceSafe Administrator allows us to:

- Create databases (repositories)
- Manage database policies
- Manage users and user rights
- Configure databases
- Configure the server services
- Backup and restore databases

Detailed information about the administration tasks is provided in the administration Appendixes B and C at the end of the book.

The Visual SourceSafe Administrator application can actually be used from any client machine connected to the server through the LAN but for maximum performance it is recommended to use it directly on the server, especially when backing up and restoring databases.

The LAN Booster Service

The LAN Booster Service is a Windows service used to increase the performance of the Visual Studio SourceSafe LAN access plug-in. It is used to speed up operations like getting file names that have newer versions on the server or getting file statuses. It uses the **Remote Procedure Call (RPC)** protocol for communication. The following figure illustrates the LAN booster's Windows service properties:

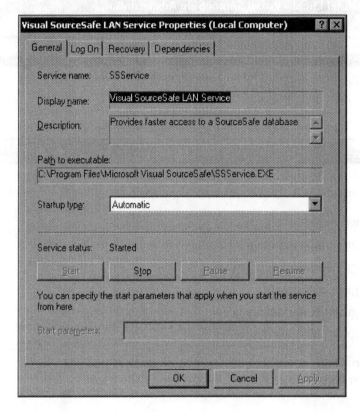

 The LAN booster service is only available using the Visual SourceSafe LAN plug-in in Visual Studio.

The XML Web Service

The XML Web service provides an internet interface for remote users who need to access the SourceSafe databases on the Visual SourceSafe Server.

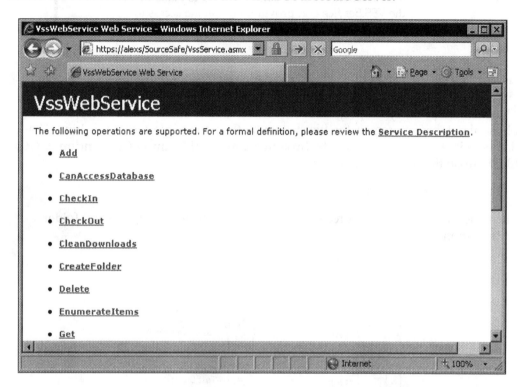

The service is installed by default on the **Internet Information Server**'s **(IIS)** default website at http(s)://[serverdomain]/SourceSafe/VssService.asmx and it is used by the Visual Studio SourceSafe internet plug-in.

 By default, attempting to browse the service as shown in the above figure will generate an ASP.NET error. The service description page is disabled for security reasons, and can be re-enabled if needed by editing the service's web.config file.

The SourceSafe internet plug-in supports operations like database open, database add, check in, check out, get, undo check out, rename, delete, share, diff, and merge, but does not provide more advanced functions like get by time or by label, history, properties, labels, or branches.

Remote access is only accessible using the Visual SourceSafe internet plug-in in Visual Studio. Third-party tools similar to SourceSafe Explorer can be written to make use of the VSS Service and provide stand-alone access to VSS databases.

The Visual SourceSafe Database

The central repository for project resources is the Visual SourceSafe database. The physical database storage is the file system on the SourceSafe server machine. The database is accessed by the clients through a **Universal Naming Convention (UNC)** file share on the server, for example:

```
\\VssServer\VssDatabase
```

The structure of a typical SourceSafe database uses the following file and folder organization:

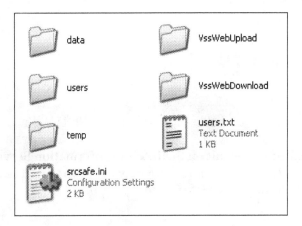

User and database options are kept in initialization (.ini) files.

Data Folder

The data folder holds the database data. It contains many physical files with obfuscated names like DCBAAAA that store the real source files added to the database and their history. The data folder is organized in a series of folders from a to z and additional labels, locks, and loggedin folders containing database metadata.

a	i	n	v	names.dat
b	j	o	w	rights.dat
c	k	p	x	status.dat
d	l	q	y	um.dat
e	labels	r	z	version.dat
f	locks	s	aaaaaaaa.cnt	
g	loggedin	t	crcs.dat	
h	m	u	ddcerr.log	

For every file in the project, Visual SourceSafe creates a pair of files in the a to z folders, one with an extension and one without an extension. The file without an extension is the log file for the stored file, containing internal information about which user added the file, the file location, and the differences between file versions (history). The file with an extension (.A or .B) represents the most recent version of the file. Each time the file is checked in, the extension alternates between .A and .B using the extension that doesn't exist at that moment. After the check in, Visual SourceSafe calculates the difference (the delta) between the two file versions and adds the difference to the log file. After adding the difference to the log file, it deletes the old file so at any given time, under normal conditions, there aren't two files with both .A and .B extensions.

The labels folder contains a label cache for the labels applied to projects and files in the database.

The locks folder contains lock files with the .LCK extension for every file locked by SourceSafe. Files are locked during update operations to prevent other users from making modifications while they are being updated.

The loggedin folder contains a file for each logged-in user and an Admin.lck file if the database is locked by an administrator. The database can be locked by an administrator during backup and restore operations or during database maintenance.

The aaaaaaaa.cnt file contains the physical name of the last file added to the database.

The crcs.dat file contains **Cyclic Redundancy Check (CRC)** information used to speed up the get and check out operations.

The ddcerr.log file contains errors generated by the DDCONV utility. The utility is used to convert different database formats.

The names.dat file contains the names of the files whose full name is longer than 34 characters.

The `rights.dat` file contains user and project security information and specifies the relationships between users and project rights.

The `status.dat` file is a cache file that contains check out status information for database files and is used to speed up the display of Visual SourceSafe Explorer.

The `um.dat` file contains user management information (names and passwords) and a unique database identifier. The database identifier is a **Globally Unique Identifier (GUID)**.

The `version.dat` file contains the Visual SourceSafe database version information.

Temp Folder

The `temp` folder is used by Visual SourceSafe 2005 for older databases to place temporary files while it is running. These files are deleted when SourceSafe closes. For databases created with SourceSafe 2005, a local temporary folder is used instead of a shared network folder. For security reasons it is recommended to use a personalized temporary local folder instead of a folder shared between all SourceSafe users.

Users Folder

The `users` folder contains a folder for each user configured to use the database. These folders are named as much as possible like the user's name (`users\`
`<username>`). If the username exceeds eight characters it is truncated. The folder holds user-specific initialization and customization files. Each folder contains an `ss.ini` file. Each time a user logs from a different computer, this file is used to save window positions and other computer-specific information:

```
; Your current SourceSafe project.
Project = $/
Checkout_LocalVer_Default  = Yes
mssccprj = *.sln, *.vbproj, *.vbp, *.csproj, *.vcproj, *.dsp, *.mdp,
*.mak, *.vfpproj, *.vdp, *.vdproj, *.dbp, *.vsmproj, *.vsmacros,
*.hwproj, *.etp, *.etpproxy, *.actproj, *.atp, *.dmp, *.mdmp, *.dsw,
*.vjsproj, *.csdproj, *.vbdproj
Columns (UI) = 150,85,135,100
Dock_Toolbar (ALEXS) = Yes
Maximized (ALEXS) = Yes
OutputHeight (ALEXS) = 150
Position_Toolbar (ALEXS) = 0, 44, 468, 71, 976, 658
PrjWidth (ALEXS) = 204
Toolbar (ALEXS) = Yes
```

```
Toolbar_DockSite (ALEXS) = 59419
Window (ALEXS) = 44, 44, 776, 499, 976, 658
```

The administrator will also have an `ssadmin.ini` file, stored in `users\admin`. This file contains the window and toolbar settings for Visual SourceSafe Administrator:

```
; ssadmin.ini
;
; This file contains all the variables that "customize" the
; SourceSafe
; Administrator program to your particular needs.

Columns_UI (UI) = 124, 259
Columns (UI) = 150,135,100
Maximized (ALEXS) = Yes
Window (ALEXS) = 223, 103, 701, 380, 984, 657
```

The users folder also contains a `template.ini` file used to store default values for new `ss.ini` files. When new users are created, this file is used to create the default settings for them. If we need to make common settings for new users, we make changes to this file once.

VssWebDownload Folder

The `VssWebDownload` folder is used as a virtual directory in Internet Information Server (IIS). This folder is used by the SourceSafe internet plug-in, which communicates with the HTTP Web service, to download files from the SourceSafe database.

VssWebUpload Folder

The `VssWebUpload` folder is used as a virtual directory in IIS. This folder is used by the SourceSafe internet plug-in, which communicates with the HTTP Web service, to upload files to the SourceSafe database.

Srcsafe.ini File

The `srcsafe.ini` file is used to store global database settings and configuration information for all users. When opening a database, this is the file we have to browse for.

The srcsafe.ini file is read by Visual SourceSafe only when the database is opened (which is generally done at start-up), therefore any configuration changes that occur after that do not affect the client operation. For reconfiguration, the clients have to be restarted.

An example of the contents of srcsafe.ini:

```
; The two important paths used by SourceSafe.
Data_Path = data
Temp_Path = temp

; This tells admin where to put personal directories for new users.
Users_Path = users

; From this, find users.txt; from that, in turn, find ss.ini for a
; user.
Users_Txt = users.txt

PrjEntryTimeout = 15
Multiple_Checkouts = Yes
Checkout_LocalVer_Disabled = Yes
UseHelperService = Yes

DownloadVDir = VssDownload_db1
UploadVDir = VssUpload_db1
Web_Service = http://win2003e/SourceSafe/VssService.asmx
```

A closer look at these configuration files is provided in the administration appendixes at the end of the book.

Users.txt File

The users.txt file contains the users configured to use the SourceSafe database and the path to their ss.ini files:

```
Admin = users\admin\ss.ini
Guest = users\guest\ss.ini
Alexandru = users\alexandr\ss.ini
```

The file maps the full username with the corresponding folder in the users folder (which is truncated if the username exceeds eight characters).

The Visual SourceSafe Clients

Visual SourceSafe has two main client applications used to access and work with databases:

- Visual SourceSafe Explorer
- Visual SourceSafe command-line utility

Visual SourceSafe Explorer

Visual SourceSafe Explorer is the main client application used to work with the SourceSafe databases.

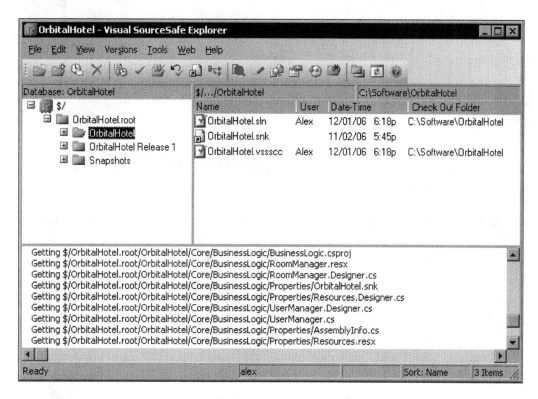

Visual SourceSafe Explorer provides a rich graphical user interface used for almost all Visual SourceSafe commands. The left pane contains the hierarchical file system-like structure that shows the projects in the database. The right pane contains the files in the selected project and their properties. The bottom pane shows the operations performed by the Visual SourceSafe Explorer.

Visual SourceSafe Command-Line Utility

The command-line `ss.exe` utility supports most commands available in the Visual SourceSafe Explorer and some that are available only in the command line. The most important usage of the command-line utility is in batch operations for repetitive tasks, where commands must be executed in succession.

Like its predecessor SourceSafe 6.0, SourceSafe 2005 stand-alone application still uses a distributed client application architecture. This means that each machine running the SourceSafe client applications accesses the repository directly.

However, when used from within an **Integrated Development Environment (IDE)** like Microsoft Visual Studio, Visual SourceSafe 2005 has a *client-server* architecture, where the development machines (the clients) can connect to the server using the server's SourceSafe services that handle their requests.

The SourceSafe Integration with Visual Studio .NET

Visual SourceSafe 2005 has a deep integration with Visual Studio .NET, allowing for easy operation with projects and files. Visual Studio integration is achieved with the help of two compatible source control plug-ins that use the source control adapter package in the IDE.

The two Visual SourceSafe plug-ins for Visual Studio are:

- **SourceSafe LAN**: This is the standard plug-in for accessing the SourceSafe database over a Local Area Network connection. This plug-in has the capability of using the **LAN booster service** on the SourceSafe server for improved performance.

- **SourceSafe Internet**: This plug-in is used by remote users to access the SourceSafe database over the Internet using the **XML Web service** on the SourceSafe server.

Plug-In Selection in Visual Studio .NET

From within Visual Studio .NET we can only work with one source control provider
at a time. Selecting the appropriate source control plug-in is done by using the
Options dialog from the **Tools** menu. Expand the **Source Control** node in the
Options tree view and select **Plug-in Selection**. Expand the **Current source control
plug-in** combo box and select **Microsoft Visual SourceSafe** for the LAN plug-in or
the **Microsoft Visual SourceSafe (Internet)** for the XML Web service plug-in.

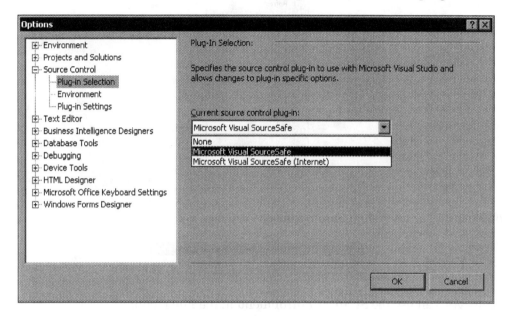

Accessing the Source Control Commands

Once a source control plug-in is selected, Visual Studio activates the source control access commands. These commands can be accessed using the context menus for items in the **Solution Explorer** window:

You can also use the Visual Studio **Source Control** toolbar:

Finally, you can use the **Source Control** menu in the **File** menu:

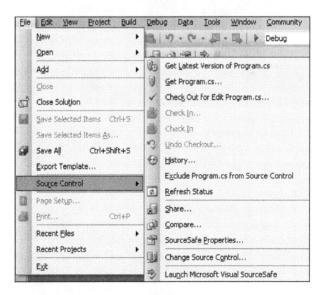

Network Configurations

Considering their location, client machines can be *local* or *remote*. Local clients are those that can access the server using a Local Area Network (LAN). This is the local development site where the server resides and from where the majority of the work is accomplished.

Sometimes, however, there are situations in which users need to connect from remote locations. Maybe they work from home or are in a different location and need to make a change to the database.

Local users can access the SourceSafe server directly through the LAN connection, while remote users can reach it through the XML Web service, or through a Virtual Private Network.

Accessing the Server using the LAN Connection

At the local development site the clients use the LAN access configuration to access the Visual SourceSafe server database. The following figure illustrates this network configuration:

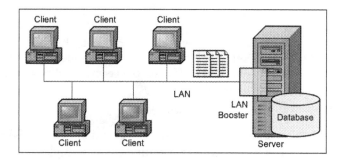

In the LAN access configuration, the LAN booster service is used to increase the file access speeds in Visual Studio. This is the fastest way to access the SourceSafe database. However, if users are required to access the database from remote locations, they can do so by using one of the following remote network access methods.

Accessing the Server through a Virtual Private Network

An old method to remotely connect to the SourceSafe server is by using a **Virtual Private Network (VPN)** connection. A VPN connection has the ability to connect the remote clients to the LAN at the local development site. This type of connection creates what is called a **virtual tunnel** between the clients and the server, making them appear to be physically connected to the LAN. The connection speed, however, is determined by the speed of the user's internet connection.

The following figure illustrates the VPN access configuration:

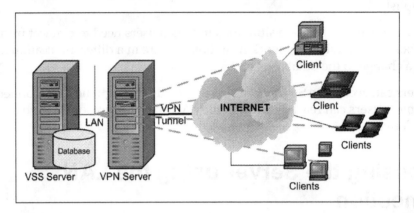

The remote clients connect via the VPN tunnel to the VPN Server and have access to the local network through this server as if they were working from the local development site. Connection security is achieved by using an encrypted VPN tunnel.

 Giving unauthorized remote users access to the Local Area Network from the local development site presents a security risk. Use special security policies for VPN connections.

Although this illustration shows two separate server machines (the SourceSafe server and the VPN server) their services can be combined into a single machine acting as both SourceSafe server and VPN server. Also, the VPN server can be replaced with a router supporting VPN connections.

Accessing SourceSafe through HTTP/HTTPS

The new native method in Visual SourceSafe 2005 that allows remote connections over the Internet uses the XML Web service. The service communicates over a simple HTTP or a **Secure Socket Layer** (**SSL**) HTTPS connection. This connection can be filtered through a network firewall for increased security.

The following figure illustrates this network access configuration:

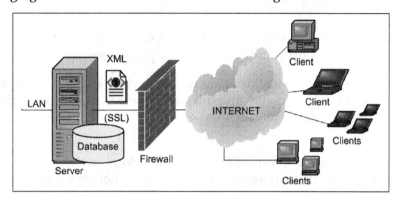

The remote clients use the public Internet to access the XML Web service to connect to the SourceSafe server. The firewall can be used to filter unauthorized connection attempts according to the local security policy.

 Remote access is only accessible using the Visual SourceSafe internet plug-in in Visual Studio. Third-party tools similar to the SourceSafe Explorer can be written to make use of the VSS service and provide stand-alone access to VSS databases.

Security can be strengthened by encrypting the client-server connections using the SSL protocol. This protocol is used for secure document transmission over the public Internet by providing authentication and data encryption. The administration appendixes describe in detail how to set up this remote configuration.

For maximum flexibility you can use a combination of these network access methods.

Summary

In this chapter we looked at the Visual SourceSafe 2005 architecture. It is composed of three main components:

- The Server applications and services
- The Database (repository)
- The Client applications

The server is responsible for storing the SourceSafe database and services such as the LAN booster service and the XML Web service for remote connections. The main server application is the Visual SourceSafe Administrator used to manage the SourceSafe databases.

The SourceSafe database is structured in a series of folders and files that store database data, user, and configuration information.

On the client side, the main stand-alone GUI application is the Visual SourceSafe Explorer. For batch scripts SourceSafe offers a separate command-line application.

For Visual Studio development there are two SourceSafe source control plug-ins: the LAN plug-in and the Internet plug-in. These plug-ins use the SourceSafe LAN and Internet server services and are used using the Visual Studio source control commands.

Depending on the location, SourceSafe users can be local or remote. To connect to the SourceSafe database they can use one of the following network configurations:

- LAN connection (available for all local users)
- VPN connection (available for all remote users)
- HTTP(S) connection (available only for remote Visual Studio users)

The remote access configurations must be secured using security policies and firewall filters.

3

Creating a Service-Oriented Application

For the purpose of this book I could have used a simple "Hello World" type application that demonstrated Software Configuration Management with Visual SourceSafe 2005 and Visual Studio .NET 2005. However, I felt the need to give you as much value as possible, given the fact that the development process of building software is rarely so trivial and easy.

So, let's take a more realistic software development scenario. What I am going to build is a room-reservation system for the newly launched Orbital Hotel. As you well know, this is the very first space building, after the International Space Station, used for tourism, allowing people to enjoy a view of our blue planet and stars from their private rooms. OK, OK, the Orbital Hotel doesn't yet exist, but when it does, it must have a room reservation system anyway. Who knows, it might be this one.

I will build a prototype for a hotel reservation system outlining the way Software Configuration Management makes the job easier. Don't worry if you are not fully familiar with the technologies used. The purpose of this application is purely for reference, so you can sit back and relax.

At this point I will use my time machine and get a screenshot for the final application so you can see how it will look like. Or, I can insert the screenshot after it finished. I think the first way seems more reasonable. This is what the public reservation site looks like:

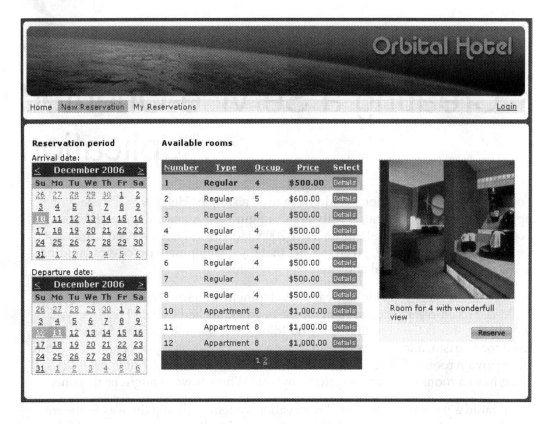

If you like it, you can download the application from the book's website: http://orbitalhotel.alexandruserban.com.

Now let's get back to our time and start the development lifecycle on the Orbital Hotel product. The first phase is the specifications phase.

Specifications—Project Architecture

In order to build a software system, we need a list of requirements. What is the purpose of the system? What are the actions performed by the system and against the system? Who will use the system and how? The answers to these questions will let us identify the main parts of the system and the way these parts work together.

System Requirements

Let's take a look at the Orbital Hotel's reservation system's requirements. The purpose of the reservation system is to allow guests to make room reservations. There are several room types each having a number, occupancy, price, availability, description, and image. The reservations can be made by using the hotel's internet website, through the websites of travel agencies (third parties), or by making phone calls to the hotel's client service. Reservations can be also made by internal client service staff who receive phone calls from guests.

When guests use the hotel's website, they will create a user with a username and password and input their personal details such as first name, last name, address, city, zip code, state, country, phone, email address, and card number. Then they will choose a room and complete the reservation details such as arrival date, the number of nights they will be staying and the number of adults, teenagers, children, and pets. They will also be able to cancel their reservation.

When making a reservation over the phone, a guest will provide the same personal information and reservation details to the hotel's client-service staff. The staff will create a reservation for the guest using an internal application. The staff members will also authenticate using a username and password.

Travel agencies and other third parties must also be able to make hotel reservations.

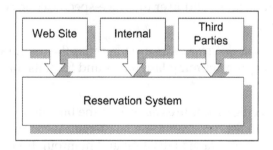

Taking a big picture about the type of system we are going to build, what we need is an application design that will be as flexible as possible. It should provide us with a variety of options like reservations through phone calls, personal or third-party websites, smart devices like PDAs or cell phones, and so on. This is where we gather the specifications and plan the system architecture. In this phase we have to consider as many aspects as we can, based on our requirements and specifications.

So, let's see what the main existing application architectures are, and see what application architecture fits our requirements.

Application Architectures

The computer and computer programming history is a very short one in comparison with that of other industries. Although it is short, it has evolved and continues to evolve very rapidly, changing the way we live. Taking into account the architectures used at the beginning of computer programming, we can see an evolution from the single, powerful, fault-tolerant, expensive super mainframe computer applications, towards multiple, distributed, less expensive smaller machine applications, the personal computers.

During this evolution, three main application architectures can be identified:

- Compact application architecture
- Component application architecture
- **Service-Oriented Architecture (SOA)**

We are going to take a brief look at these application architectures and outline their characteristics.

Compact Application Architecture

During application development for the single mainframe, there was no clear separation between application layers and no reusable components were used. All the data access, business logic, and user interface-specific code were contained in a single executable program.

This traditional *compact architecture* was used because the mainframe computers had specific *proprietary* programming languages and formats for accessing and manipulating the data.

All the data access-specific procedures as well as the business logic and business rules code are written in this programming language. At the surface, a user interface is presented to the user for data visualisation and manipulation.

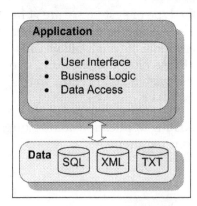

This application architecture works for applications that do not need data input from multiple sources and can be easily developed by a single programmer. However, this approach has several major disadvantages when it comes to building large-scale systems:

- Application components cannot be reused in other applications because they are *tightly coupled* and dependent on one another. Tight coupling means that in order for a piece of code to use another piece of code, it must have intimate knowledge about its implementation details.

- Being tightly coupled, a change to one component can affect the functionality of another, making debugging and maintenance a difficult task.

- The application is actually a black box; no one, except the main developer, knows what it is in there.

- Applying security is another problem because the user interface cannot be separated from the business logic components using security-specific mechanisms like authentication and authorization.

- Application integration is affected because the code is platform dependent. Integration between two such applications requires special and specific coding and can be difficult to maintain.

- Scalability issues are considered when the system grows and need to be scaled across several machines. Using this application architecture, scalability is not possible as you can't separate different application parts across different physical boundaries because of the tight coupling.

To address the issues with the compact application architecture, the *component-based application architecture* was developed.

Component Application Architecture

In the component application architecture, the application's functionality is defined using *components*. A component is like a black box, a software unit that encapsulates data and code and provides at the surface a set of well-defined interfaces used by other components. Since a component only needs to support a well-defined set of interfaces, it can change the inner implementation details without affecting other components that use its external interfaces. Components that export the same interfaces can be interchanged, allowing them to be *reused* and *tight coupling* to be eliminated. This makes them *loosely coupled* because they don't need to know internal implementation details of one another.

This separation of application functionality using components allows the distribution of development tasks across several developers and makes the overall application more maintainable and scalable. In the Windows environment, the most used component application architecture is the **Component Object Model (COM)**.

Typically, components are grouped into logical layers. For example, an application uses the data access layer to access the different data sources, the business logic layer to process the data according to the business rules, and the presentation layer also known as the user interface layer to present the data to end users.

Using well-defined application layers allows for a *modular design*, component *decoupling*, and therefore the possibility for component reuse.

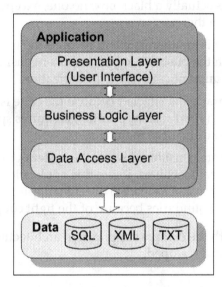

Data Access Layer

This architecture forms a chain of layers that communicate with one another. The base is the data access layer, which is responsible for querying, retrieving, and updating the data from and to different data sources while providing a uniform data view to the layers above.

Business Layer

Above the data access layer is the business logic layer. The business logic layer uses the uniform data provided by the data access layer and processes it according to the business rules it contains. The business logic layer doesn't need to know from what source and how the data was obtained. Its purpose is only data manipulation and processing.

Presentation Layer

At the top of the chain is the presentation layer or the user interface layer. Its purpose is to present the data processed by the business logic layer to end users and to receive input and commands from these end users. The presentation layer will propagate these commands down the chain to the business layer for processing.

Characteristics

The component application architecture solves many software problems and it has been used extensively in the past. But because software evolves continuously, new requirements introduce new challenges.

Let's suppose we have several applications on different platforms, each incorporating its presentation layer, business logic layer, and data access layer. We want to integrate them into a bigger distributed system, a system that spans across several heterogeneous environments. At some point, one application will need to access the data existing in another application. While components can work well in a homogenous environment on the same platform, for example COM in the Windows environment, problems appear in components working across several platforms. For example, it is very difficult for a COM component to be used from a Java application or vice-versa, mainly because they don't speak the same language.

Integration between two or more applications running on different platforms would require a middle component-dependent intercommunication layer that is expensive, difficult to build, and reintroduces *tight coupling* between systems, which is what we tried to avoid in the first place. Avoiding building this intercommunication layer would require that the data exchange between these applications be done by a person who will read the necessary data from the source application and write it into the target application.

We need to integrate these systems, and maintain the loose coupling between them. What we need to do, is make these components understand each other, making them to speak the same language. This is where the concept of *services* and **Service-Oriented Architecture (SOA)** comes into play.

Service-Oriented Architecture

SOA describes an information technology architecture that enables distributed computing environments with many different types of computing platforms and applications.

To enable distributed computing environments, SOA defines the concept of services. A **service** is a well-defined, self-contained unit of functionality, independent of the state of other services.

Let's see how services can be used to create distributed applications, integrate component-based applications, and make them communicate with each other. We keep our data access layer and business logic layer as they are, but we completely *decouple the presentation layer* so we can change it later without affecting the other layers. In order to expose the functionality of the business logic layer, we wrap it in a *service interface*. The service interface wraps the business logic layer components offering a *point of access* for any process that needs to access the business logic, whose functionality has now become a *service*.

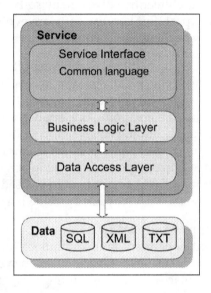

Service-oriented architecture is basically a collection of services that communicate with each other. The communication can involve either simple data passing or it can involve two or more services coordinating some activity. Whatever the required functionality may be, we have now separated the functionality of applications into specific units, the services that we use to construct flexible, distributed applications.

Typically services reside on different machines. They are exposed to the outside world by service interfaces. A service provider provides its functionality using the service interfaces that are used or consumed by the service consumers. A service consumer sends a service request to a service interface and receives a service response. The following figure represents a typical service consumer-service provider request.

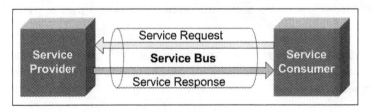

A service can be a service provider and a service consumer at the same time as it can consume other services. They communicate using a communication medium like a local area network for internal services or the Internet for external services. This communication medium is called a **service bus**.

We saw that services don't have a presentation layer as we've decoupled the presentation layer from the rest. This presents an advantage because we can now use any platform able to understand and consume the service to build a presentation layer. The service interface has to provide a standard and open way of communication, a common language that both service providers and service consumers can understand, regardless of the machine type they are deployed on, their physical location, and the language in which they are written.

XML Web Services

In today's world, the communication standard used to connect services is achieved using **web services**. Web services are small, reusable applications that help computers with many different operating system platforms work together by exchanging messages. Web services are based on industry protocols that include **XML (Extensible Markup Language)**, **SOAP (Simple Object Access Protocol)**, and **WSDL (Web Services Description Language)**.

These protocols help computers work together across platforms and programming languages enabling data exchange between otherwise unconnected sources:

- *Client-to-Client*: Devices, also called *smart clients*, can host and consume XML web services, allowing data sharing anywhere, anytime.
- *Client-to-Server*: A server application can share data with desktop or mobile devices using XML web services over the Internet.
- *Server-to-Server*: Independent server applications can use XML web services as a common interface to share and exchange data.
- *Service-to-Service*: Systems that work together to deliver complex data processing can be created using XML web services.

The following figure shows an example of services exposed using web services, which deliver their functionality to a wide variety of platforms and applications.

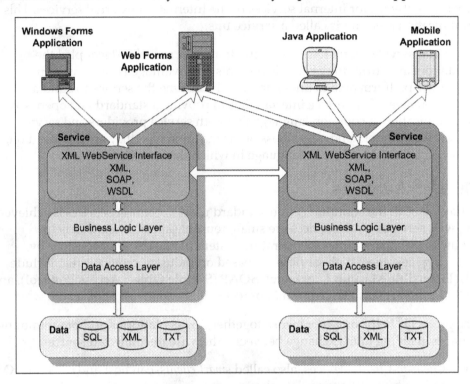

Service-oriented architecture provides us with the maximum flexibility in building applications. Individual services define specific application functions and interact with one another to provide the entire business process functionality.

Using service-oriented architecture provides many benefits such as:

- **Encapsulation**: Just as an object encapsulates its internal implementation details inside while providing public methods to external objects, services encapsulate their internal complexity and implementation from the service consumers who don't have to know the internal details.

- **Mobility**: As services are independent and encapsulated, they can be deployed in any location. Since they are using the same standard communication language, they are accessed in the same way irrespective of their physical location or implementation details.

- **Parallel development**: A service-oriented application is built using several service layers and clients. These application components can be built in parallel by developers specialized in specific layer functionality, speeding up the development process.

- **Platform independence**: Service providers and service consumers can be written in any language and deployed on any platform, as long as they can speak the standard communication language.

- **Security**: More security can be added to a service-oriented application at the service interface layer. Different application components require different security levels. The security can be enforced by using firewalls configured to allow access only to the required service providers only by the required service consumers. In addition, by using **Web Service Enhancements** (**WSE**), authentication, authorization, and encryption can be easily added.

- **Reusability**: Once a service is constructed and deployed, it can be used by any other service consumer without problems related to platform integration and interoperability.

Choosing an Application Architecture

Now that we have seen the existing application architectures, we must choose one that meets our project requirements. As you may have guessed by this point, the best application architecture we can use for our project is a Service-Oriented Architecture (SOA). The SOA allows us to build a distributed system, a system that has great flexibility and interoperability with other systems on other platforms. This will allow us to build the business logic functions and expose them as services that will be used by higher functionality layers.

Choosing an Application Platform

After choosing our application architecture, we must choose a platform capable of building and supporting it. For the purpose of our system we will choose the Microsoft .NET Framework platform and build the system using Microsoft Visual Studio.NET 2005 and Microsoft SQL Server as the back-end database for storing the data.

Microsoft .NET Framework

From a Service-Oriented Architecture point of view, the .NET Framework is the Microsoft strategy for connecting systems, information, and devices through software such as web services. .NET technology provides the capability to quickly build, deploy, manage, and use connected, security-enhanced solutions through the use of web services.

Intrinsically, the .NET Framework is an environment for development and execution that allows different programming languages and libraries to work together to create Windows-based applications that are easier to build, manage, deploy, and integrate with other networked systems.

The .NET core components are:

- **The Common Language Runtime (CLR)**: A language-neutral development and execution environment that provides a consistent model and services to manage application execution that includes:
  - ° Support for different programming languages: A variety of over 20 programming languages that target the CLR, such as C#, VB.NET, and J#, can be used to develop applications.
  - ° Support for libraries developed in different languages: Libraries developed in different languages integrate seamlessly, making application development faster and easier.
  - ° Support for different platforms: .NET applications are not tied to a single platform and can be executed on any platform that supports the CLR.
  - ° Enhanced security: The .NET Code Access Security model provides a managed environment for application execution and security.
  - ° Automatic resource management: The CLR automatically handles process, memory, and thread management, enabling developers to focus on the core business logic code.
- **The Framework Class Libraries (FCL)**: An object-oriented library of classes that extends a wide range of functionality including:
  - ° Support for basic operations: Input/output and string management, standard network protocols, and network standards such as TCP/IP, XML, SOAP, and HTTP are supported natively to allow basic operations and system connections.
  - ° Support for data access and data manipulation: The FCL includes a range of data access and data manipulation classes forming the ADO.NET technology that natively supports XML and data environments such as SQL Server and Oracle.
  - ° Support for desktop applications: Rich desktop and mobile client applications can be easily created using the Windows Forms technology.
  - ° Support for web applications: Thin web clients, websites, and web services can be created using web forms and XML web services technologies that form ASP.NET.

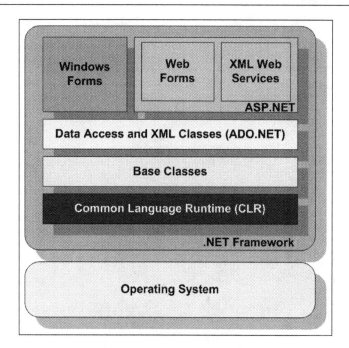

In the planning phase we've gathered the project requirements and specifications and we've also chosen an application architecture. The next phase is the design phase.

Designing the System

In the design phase, we will create an application design based on the application architecture, project requirements, and specifications. Gathering all the information needed to design the system is a difficult task, but the most important step is to start writing down the first idea.

System Structure

The system will be composed from the following main component categories:

- *Core* components (Data Access Layer, Business Logic Layer) forming the middle-tier component layers.
- *Web service* components (XML Web service) forming the Service Interface layer.
- *Website* components (ASP.NET website) forming the front-end *WebReservation* application, a web presentation layer.
- *Windows Application* components (Windows Forms Application) forming the *WinReservation* application, a Windows presentation layer.

The following figure illustrates the overall system structure, outlining each system component:

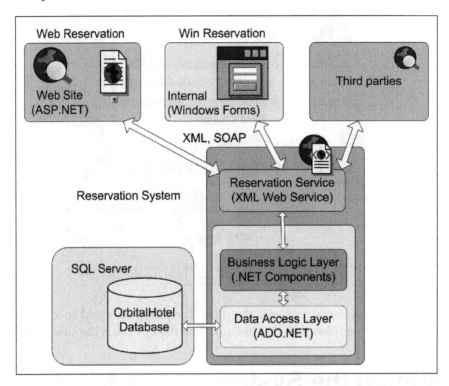

As we saw earlier, one major advantage of a service-oriented application is the decoupling of the presentation layer from the business logic layer. This allows for the business logic layer being exposed as a web service to be used by other third parties to integrate its functionality into their business process.

Database Structure

The back-end database is hosted by a Microsoft SQL Server system. According to the project specifications the internal database structure will be composed of the following database tables:

- User (Contains the user accounts)
- Guest (Contains the personal details of the guests)
- Room (Contains the details of each of the hotel's rooms)
- Reservation (Contains the details of the reservation made by each user)

The following figure illustrates these tables and the relations between them. The bold fields are mandatory (not NULL).

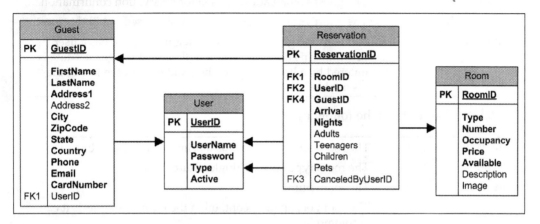

The User table contains the following rows:

UserID	The user identifier used as the primary key of the User table.
UserName	The user name.
Password	The user password.
Type	The user type, such as Guest, Internal, or ThirdParty.
Active	User accounts can be active or they can be deactivated according to business rules.

The Guest table contains the following rows:

GuestID	The guest identifier used as the primary key of the Guest table.
FirstName	The first name of the guest.
LastName	The last name of the guest.
Address1	The first line of the address of the guest.
Address2	The second line of the address of the guest. This field can have a null value.
City	The guest's city.
ZipCode	The guest's zip code.
State	The guest's state.
Country	The guest's country.

Phone	The guest's phone number.
Email	The guest's email address used for reservation confirmation.
CardNumber	The guest's credit or debit card number used to bill the guest.
UserID	Contains the guest's user identifier, if the guest has a user account. This field can have a null value if the guest's data is entered by a hotel staff member, and is a foreign key of the User table.

The Room table contains the following rows:

RoomID	The room identifier, used as a primary key of the Room table.
Type	The room type such as Single, Double, etc.
Number	The room number.
Occupancy	The room occupancy, containing the number of guests it can accommodate.
Price	The price of the room.
Available	The room availability. Some rooms may not be available due to repairs or other events.
Description	The room description. This field can have a null value.
Image	The room image. This field can have a null value.

The Reservation table contains the following columns:

ReservationID	The reservation identifier, used as a primary key of the Reservation table.
RoomID	The reserved room identifier, a foreign key of the Room table.
UserID	The identifier of the user that made the reservation, a foreign key of the User table. This is required because hotel staff can make reservations for guests too.
GuestID	The identifier of the guest for whom the reservation was made, a foreign key of the Guest table.
Arrival	The arrival date.
Nights	The number of nights for the reservation
Adults	The number of adults.
Teenagers	The number of teenagers.
Children	The number of children.
Pets	The number of pets.
CanceledByUserID	The identifier of the user that canceled the reservation, a foreign key of the User table.

After creating the back-end database structure we create the Visual Studio .NET solution structure for our project.

Visual Studio .NET Projects and Solutions

Before we start organizing the source code structure of our system, it is important to understand how Visual Studio .NET organizes and manages source code locally and by using a source control provider such as Visual SourceSafe.

Visual Studio .NET Projects

Visual Studio .NET uses projects to organize and manage the configuration, settings, and the build process that generates a .NET assembly. Assemblies are collections of types and resources that are built to work together forming a logical unit of functionality. They are the building blocks of any .NET application and form a fundamental unit of deployment, version control, reuse, and security.

Depending upon the project language, Visual Studio .NET projects have different file extensions such as `.csproj` for C# or `.vbproj` for Visual Basic .NET. Although there are many project types such as class libraries, console applications, Windows applications, websites, or web services, projects fall into two main project categories:

- Non-web projects
- Web projects

Non-Web Projects

Non-web projects, sometimes called Windows projects, are application projects that do not necessarily deliver content to web browsers and do not need a web server to run. These include projects like Windows applications, console applications, and Windows services. Non-web projects can run from any system folder without any additional configuration.

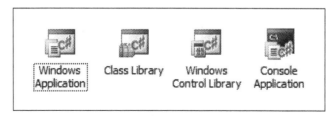

Web Projects

Web projects are application projects that deliver their content to web browsers and, in order to run, need a web server. In this category are websites and web services. Web projects usually live inside a web server's virtual folder and are usually referred to using a URL path.

Visual Studio .NET Solutions

Because larger applications are built using multiple projects, Visual Studio .NET uses *solutions* to group projects together. Solution files have a .sln extension. Apart from grouping projects together, solutions maintain *project dependencies* controlling the order-dependent projects that are built.

> A project can be part of one or more solutions but solutions can't be part of other solutions.

The following figure shows a solution including a class library project (1) , a Windows application (2), a console application (3), a web service (4), and a Windows application (5) project:

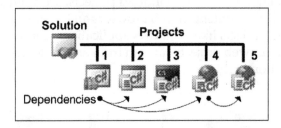

Projects will be built starting with the ones that are not dependent on other projects and continue on the dependency chain until all the projects are built.

Project 1 is not dependent on any other project. Projects 2, 3, and 4 are dependent on project 1. Project 5 is dependent on project 4. The solution maintains the dependency between projects so if we, for example, build project 5, project 1 and project 4 will be built first and project 5 will be built last. This ensures project 5 is built against the latest versions of the other referenced projects.

The solution that contains all the projects is called the *master* solution. The master solution ensures the final application is built by rebuilding the latest version of each individual project.

Partitioning Solutions and Projects

When dealing with solutions that contain a large number of projects developed by several teams, having a single master solution is not always the best option for development. In our example, the teams that work on project 1 don't need to have the other projects in their solution. Likewise, the teams that develop the Windows applications don't need to have the web applications in their solution. For this purpose, solutions and projects can be partitioned.

There are three main models for solution and project partitioning:

- Single solution
- Partitioned single solution
- Multi-solution

Single Solution

Using a single solution model is the easiest and the recommended way to contain all the projects in the application. The projects reference each other directly using project references instead of a file reference to a project assembly already built outside the system. This avoids assembly versioning because a referenced project is automatically rebuilt by Visual Studio .NET, if changes are made to it. Changing between solution configurations (release, debug) and application rebuilding is also very simple.

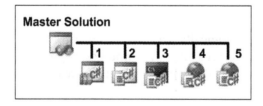

However, this model has its disadvantages when it comes to a large number of projects. For example, if we want to work on a single project in the solution we are forced to get the source code for all the projects. Minor changes to a base project trigger the rebuilding of all dependent projects. Unnecessary rebuilds for solutions containing many projects can be very time consuming.

Partitioned Solution

For larger applications where the master solution has many projects, we can eliminate the disadvantages associated with the single master solution by partitioning the projects using subsolutions and creating a partitioned solution.

Each subsolution contains the projects associated with a logical application sub-system. The following figure shows how related projects can be grouped into subsolutions:

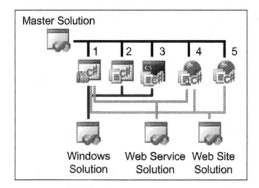

The Windows solution contains the projects 1, 2, and 3, associated with the development of the Windows sub-system. The web service solution contains projects 1 and 4, associated with the development of the web service sub-system. The website solution contains projects 1, 4, and 5, associated with the development of the website sub-system. Note that project 1 is a part of three solutions while project 4 is a part of two solutions.

The master solution is used to build the entire system, containing all the application projects.

Each subsolution contains logically grouped projects that reference each other using project references. This presents all the advantages of project references and allows development on individual subsystems without the need to have all the projects in the solution.

Note that we cannot group projects randomly. Projects must be grouped following the reference chain. In order to work on a top-level project we must include in the subsolution all the project referenced by the top-level project. For example, when working on project 5, we need to have project 4 and project 1 in the solution too, in order to use project references. But when working on project 1, which does not reference any other projects, we can create a subsolution containing only project 1.

Also, when adding new projects to the master solution, we must manually add them to the other subsolutions that reference these projects.

Multi-Solution

The multi-solution model is similar to the partitioned solution. The difference is that there is no master solution and projects outside a solution are referenced using external file references.

The following figure shows the multi-solution model:

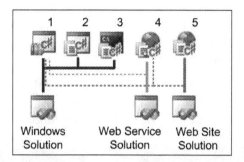

The Windows solution uses project reference between the contained projects.

However, the web service solution containing only project 4, references project 1 using an external file reference, a reference to an already built assembly for project 1.

The same case applies for the website solution that contains only project 5. Project 1 and 4 are referenced using external file references to already built assemblies for project 1 and 4.

With this model, a project is included in only one solution. Adding or removing projects is easier as we don't have to add or remove them from every solution they are part of.

Projects can be grouped in any way, unrelated to the way projects reference one another. This allows for a system subdivision according to any criteria.

This model has its disadvantages too. Solutions use file reference instead of project reference. File references do not set up build dependencies and build order. The build process must be *handled separately* and adds more complexity when building the solution.

Best Practices for the Solution Physical Structure

To ensure that the development and build processes work effectively in a team environment, it's essential to start with a correct solution folder structure that is consistent across all the development workstations and build servers.

Failure to create a well designed solution folder structure will result in problems in the later addition to a source control provider repository and the recreation on other machines.

Hierarchical Folder Structure

The best way to organize a solution in order to be consistent across source control repositories, workstations, and servers is to use a hierarchical folder structure, where the solution is the *root* and the projects are *sub-nodes*. This structure ensures there is a symmetrical correspondence between the physical solution structure in the workspaces and the structure in the source control repository.

The solution is created in a root folder and the individual projects are created in subfolders below the root folder. The **Solution** folder contains the master solution file Solution.sln. The individual project folders are under the **Solution** folder.

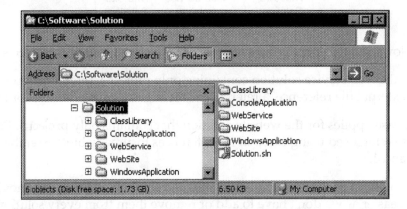

You can see that the web projects (**WebService** and **WebSite**) too are in this hierarchical structure and not under the default C:\Inetpub\wwwroot folder, which is the default root folder for Internet Information Services (IIS) web server. Let's see how this configuration is created.

Creating Web Projects

To maintain the hierarchical solution structure we must create all the projects in a specific solution under the solution's folder. For non-web projects this is achieved by default by Visual Studio .NET when creating such projects.

Web projects, however, can be created in multiple ways using different locations such as:

- File system
- Local IIS
- FTP site
- Remote site (using Front Page Server Extensions)

Visual Studio *does not* support source control integration when using FTP sites.

Source control integration for remote sites is supported, but this requires either installing Visual SourceSafe on the remote machine or using light locking mechanisms provided by FrontPage. Also additional configuration is required on the remote machine after creating the web projects.

The best way to work with source-controlled web projects is to use one of the first two options, *File System* and *Local IIS*. A new web project can be added using the **Add New Web Site** dialog window by selecting **File | Add | New Web Site**. The **Add New Web Site** dialog window requests the type of the web project and its location.

Using the File System

The file system location is selected in the dialog window's bottom **Location** area using the left combo box. The file system path is specified using the right combo box and must be under the solution's folder:

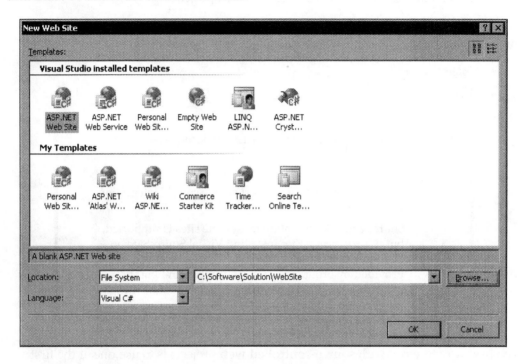

In the **Solution Explorer** window of Visual Studio .NET we can see the following solution structure:

Note that the names of the web projects represent the physical path on the local file system.

Using Local IIS

The local IIS location is selected in the dialog window's bottom **Location** area using the left combo box. The HTTP path is specified using the right combo box or clicking **Browse**:

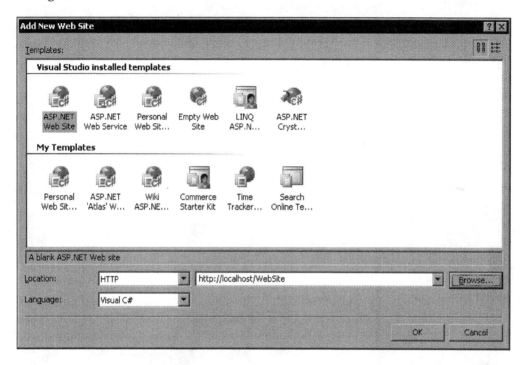

Note, however, that if we click **OK** in this state, the physical **WebSite** folder will be created under the **C:\Inteptub\wwwroot** folder, breaking the solution folder structure.

To create the folder hierarchically under the solution folder we must take additional steps and create a virtual folder that will map the physical folder in our folder structure.

After clicking on the **Browse** button another dialog window presents us the view of the local IIS **Default Web Site** structure:

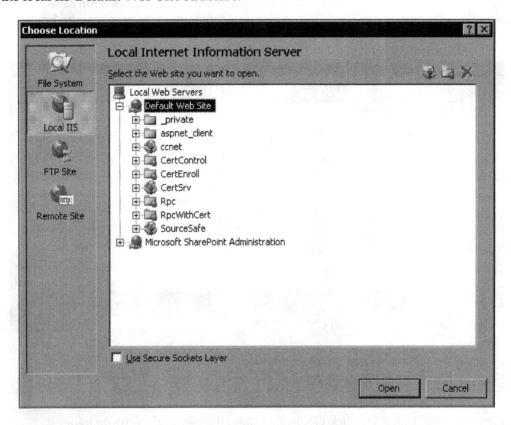

We create a virtual folder by selecting the folder node under which we want to create the virtual folder, typically the **Default Web Site** node, and clicking the second button in the top right window area. Another dialog window asks us for an **Alias name** and a **Folder** path. We must specify a folder path *under* the solution's folder.

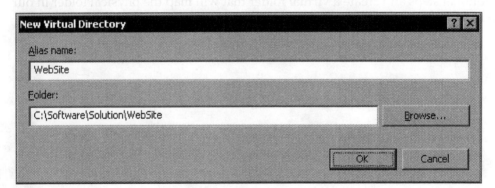

The **Alias name** and the **Folder** name must match.

We then click the **OK** button of the **New Virtual Directory** dialog and select the newly created virtual directory in the **Choose Location** dialog. To finish the operation we click the **Open** button of the **Add New Web Site** dialog window. The web project will be created in the virtual folder under the solution folder.

In the **Solution Explorer** window of Visual Studio .NET we can see this solution structure:

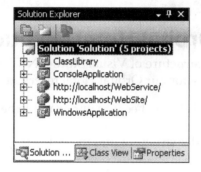

Note that the names of the web projects represent their URLs in the local IIS server.

File System versus Local IIS

The main difference between the file system location and the local IIS location is the web server used for running the web project when developing the project.

When using the file system location, the ASP.NET Development Server is used. Each web project in our solution is run by an individual ASP.NET Development Server. This web server is started automatically when we run the web project for the first time.

When using local IIS, the local Internet Information Services web server is used to run all the web projects in our solution.

While developing several web projects, using an individual web server for each one presents the advantage of being able to debug all of them at the same time. When using a single server, a debugging session affects all the web projects the server runs and only one project can be debugged at a time.

When solutions that contain local disk web projects are added to source control, Visual Studio automatically creates in the source control database a folder structure that will match the hierarchical structure on the local disk.

The best way of developing web projects is by using the file system method with the local ASP.NET Development Server.

Creating the Orbital Hotel Solution

After considering the best structure of Visual Studio .NET solutions we can now create the solution structure for our Orbital Hotel reservation system product.

I will use a single (master) solution because our example has a small number of projects,
and divide the solution folder structure into the following sections, mapping the system's design:

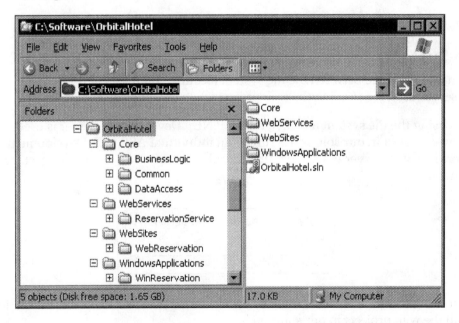

The **OrbitalHotel** folder is the root folder for the solution. Note an intermediary set of folders named **Core, WebServices, WebSites,** and **WindowsApplications** that contain the individual solution projects. These folders contain the main system components.

The following figure shows the detailed master solution structure in the Visual Studio .NET **Solution Explorer** window:

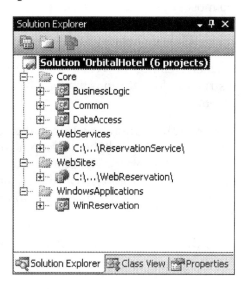

You will also notice that the web projects are created using the local file system instead of IIS. This configuration allows us to run the web projects without having to install IIS and configure virtual directories that match the physical project locations on the development machines and, as we saw earlier, we are able to debug multiple web projects at the same time. Also, using local file system web projects will help later to create a project structure in the source control database matching the structure on the local disk.

You can also see how the physical solution structure maps the logical solution structure in Visual Studio.NET.

Summary

In this chapter we started the development lifecycle for the Orbital Hotel product.

The first phase is gathering the system specifications. Once the specifications are clear we analyze them and decide which application architecture is the most appropriate for its implementation. For the Orbital Hotel application, service-oriented architecture is the most appropriate because it allows the greatest flexibility and interoperability.

We then moved on to the design phase and designed the system's structure and components. We saw that when creating the Visual Studio .NET solution, we must take into account the best structure for solutions that will be developed under source control by multiple team members.

The best structure is the hierarchical solution structure that maps directly into the source control database and is the same on all the development machines preventing binding problems especially for web projects. The best way to develop web projects is by using the local file system and the ASP.NET Development Server because they are created in the same hierarchical folder structure as the solution and because it avoids supplementary IIS configurations.

At the end, we've created the Orbital Hotel solution structure based on all the best practices we've seen in this chapter.

4

Adding Solutions to the SourceSafe Database

If you got a little bored with the theory so far, this chapter starts a series of more practical ones, as we are taking the first step in working under source control. We are going to add a new Visual Studio solution to the SourceSafe database. I will use the Orbital Hotel solution created in the previous chapter and add it to a new database. You are invited to create a solution of your own if you haven't done it already and take the same steps as me.

Ready? Let's Go!

Setting up the Database

I will create a new SourceSafe database for the Orbital Hotel solution created in the previous chapter. The database named `OrbitalHotel` is created on a network server named *alexs* using the following physical path on the server: `C:\SourceSafe\OrbitalHotel`.

 I will not cover the SourceSafe installation and the database creation steps here. For detailed information about installing, creating the initial configuration of a SourceSafe database, and enabling internet access please consult Appendix B and Appendix C.

I will choose `C:\SourceSafe\OrbitalHotel` as the shared network folder so the LAN **Universal Naming Convention (UNC)** network path to this database is `\\alexs\OrbitalHotel\`.

I will also enable remote internet access for this database using HTTP with SSL (HTTPS). The server's internet domain name is `vss.alexandruserban.com` so the URL path to the SourceSafe web service will be `https://vss.alexandruserban.com/SourceSafe/VssService.asmx`.

After setting up the database, the next step is to connect to it, and add it to the database list.

Connecting to the Database

Depending on the location, we have two options for connecting to a SourceSafe database:

- Local Area Network (LAN) access (we are at the local development site)
- Remote internet via HTTP(S) (we are at a remote location)

A LAN connection allows us to connect to the SourceSafe database using all the available SourceSafe client applications:

- Visual SourceSafe Explorer
- Visual SourceSafe Administrator
- Visual Studio with the SourceSafe LAN plug-in
- Command-line utilities

A remote internet connection via HTTP(S) on the other hand allows us to connect to the SourceSafe database using only Visual Studio with the SourceSafe internet plug-in. This plug-in uses the SourceSafe XML web service and it is optimized for best performance over remote connections.

There is actually a third option for connecting to a SourceSafe database as we've seen in Chapter 2—a Virtual Private Network (VPN) connection. A VPN connection is, logically speaking, somewhat a hybrid between a LAN and an internet connection, a remote-local connection. Because a VPN connection gives us access to the LAN where the SourceSafe server resides, from the SourceSafe point of view connecting through the VPN involves the same steps as connecting directly using the LAN. However, the speed of this type of connection affects the performance of Visual SourceSafe Explorer and other SourceSafe applications. A VPN connection should be used only in situations where we don't have a Visual Studio installation with the SourceSafe internet plug-in or we need to perform remote administration tasks that we are unable to do otherwise.

Adding the Database to the Database List

For each computer user, Visual SourceSafe maintains a list of previously accessed SourceSafe databases. This *database list* saves the specific connection settings for each database for easier access.

Adding the Database over the LAN

When using the LAN we can add a SourceSafe database to our database list using:

- Visual SourceSafe Explorer
- Visual SourceSafe Administrator
- Visual Studio with the LAN plug-in

Adding a database using the Visual SourceSafe Administrator is identical to adding it with the Visual SourceSafe Explorer so I will just cover adding the SourceSafe database using Visual SourceSafe Explorer.

Using Visual SourceSafe Explorer

To add a database using the Visual SourceSafe Explorer we use **the Add SourceSafe Database Wizard**.

If there are no databases in the database list yet, the Visual SourceSafe Explorer will open the **Add SourceSafe Database Wizard** from the start. Otherwise we can open this wizard by going to **File | Open SourceSafe Database** or by pressing *Ctrl+P* in the Visual SourceSafe Explorer.

The wizard starts by presenting its first page, the welcome page.

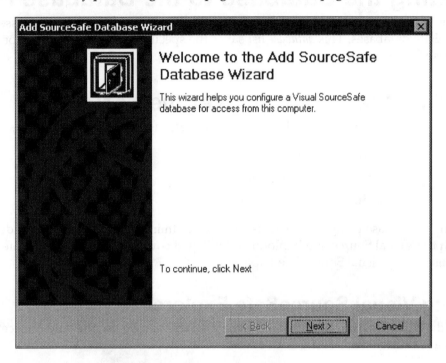

Click **Next** to advance to the second page.

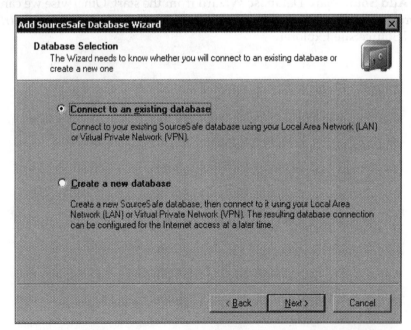

The second page has two options, **Connect to an existing database** and **Create a new database**. Since the database is already created, I will choose the first default option and click **Next**.

The wizard then shows the third page.

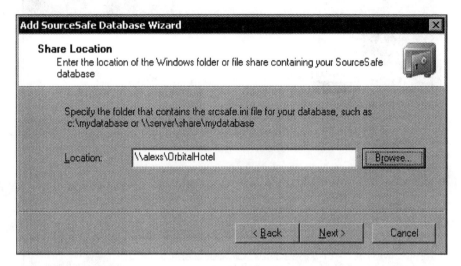

In the third page we have to specify the LAN network path to the database shared folder that contains the `srcsafe.ini` file. In my case, the path is `\\Alexs\OrbitalHotel`. The shared network folder must be configured with the specific security rights for allowing access to the database. For more information about configuring security please see Appendix B.

The path can be entered manually or by using the **Browse** button to browse the network for the specific path:

Click **Open** to select the specified path, close the browse dialog, and click **Next** in the third wizard page.

The wizard shows the fourth page.

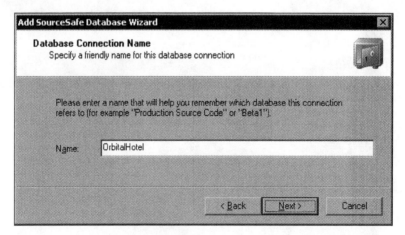

The fourth page gives us the opportunity to choose a new name for the database.

Click **Next** to advance to the fifth and last page:

The last page shows the summary of the file share settings used to add the new database to the database list. Click **Finish** to add the database.

The **Open SourceSafe Database** dialog shows all the databases we've added to the database list so far:

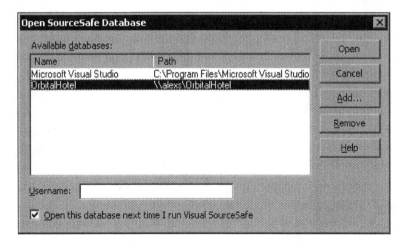

This dialog can be accessed using **File | Open SourceSafe Database** or by pressing *Ctrl+P* in Visual SourceSafe Explorer. To add more databases click the **Add** button. To remove a database from the list, select it and click the **Remove** button.

In the **Username** textbox we can specify a default username to log in to the opened database.

Using Visual Studio with the LAN Plug-In

To add a SourceSafe database to the database list over a Local Area Connection using Visual Studio, we must use the current source control plug-in in Visual Studio – the SourceSafe LAN plug-in. For more information on how to select plug-ins please see the *Plug-In Selection in Visual Studio .NET* section in Chapter 2.

After making sure the LAN plug-in is selected, open the **Open Project** dialog in Visual Studio using the **File | Open | Project/Solution** menu command and click on the **SourceSafe (LAN)** button on the left:

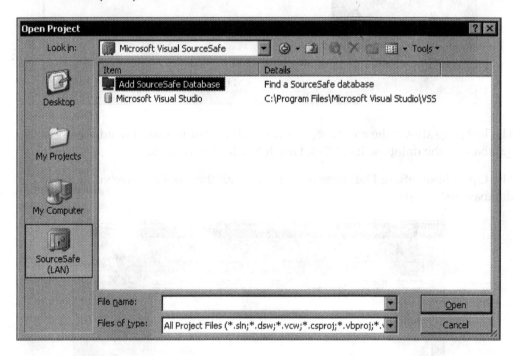

Select the **Add SourceSafe Database** list item and click **Open**.

The **Add SourceSafe Database Wizard** starts and shows the first welcome page, which is identical with the one we saw earlier while adding the database using Visual SourceSafe Explorer.

Click **Next** to advance to the second page:

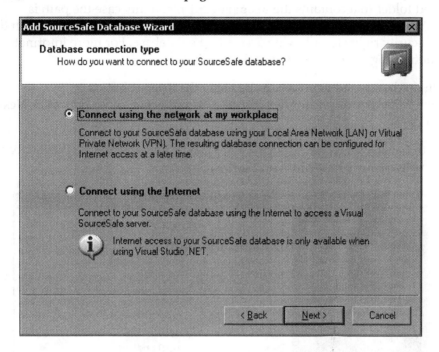

The second page shows two options, **Connect using the network at my workplace** and **Connect using the Internet**. We will see a bit later how to connect using the Internet, so for now we are going to use the first option and click **Next** to advance to the third page:

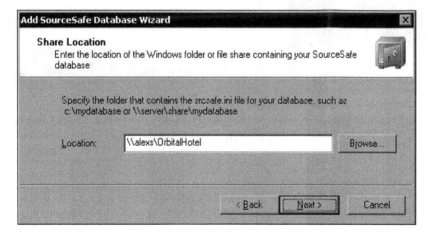

In the third page we have to specify the LAN network path to the database in the shared folder that contains the `srcsafe.ini` file. In my case the path is `\\Alexs\OrbitalHotel`. The shared network folder must be configured with the specific security rights for allowing access to the database. For more information about configuring security please see Appendix B.

The path can be entered manually or by using the **Browse** button to browse the network for the specific path. After entering the correct network path click **Next** on the third page.

The fourth page gives us the opportunity to choose a new name for the database. Click **Next** to advance to the fifth and last wizard page:

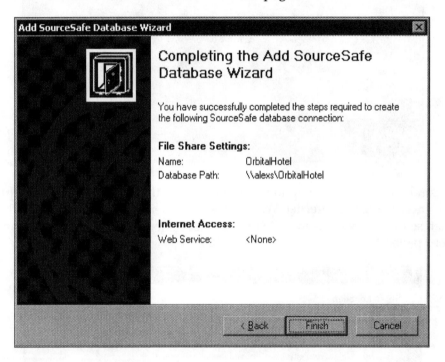

The last page shows the summary of the file share settings used to add the new database to the database list. Click **Finish** to add the database.

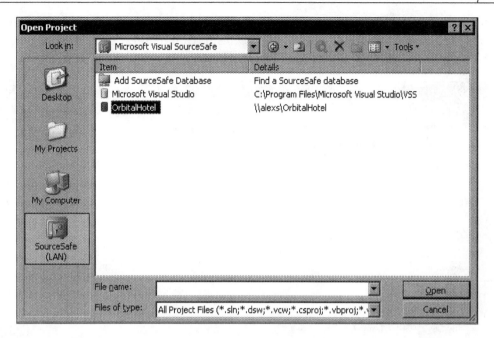

The database list now contains the newly added database. To add more databases repeat the above steps.

Adding the Database over the Internet

To add a SourceSafe database to the database list over the Internet using Visual Studio, we must use the SourceSafe internet plug-in in Visual Studio as the source control plug-in. For more information on how to select plug-ins please see the *Plug-In Selection in Visual Studio .NET* section in Chapter 2.

After making sure the internet plug-in is selected, open the **Open Project** dialog in Visual Studio using the **File | Open | Project/Solution** menu command and click the **SourceSafe (Internet)** button on the left.

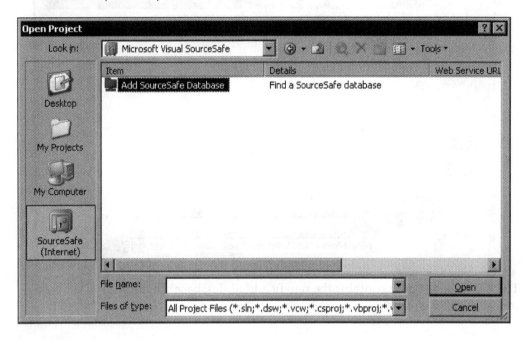

Select the **Add SourceSafe Database** list item and click **Open**.

The **Add SourceSafe Database Wizard** starts and shows the first welcome page, which is identical to the one we saw earlier while adding the database using Visual SourceSafe Explorer.

Click **Next** to advance to the second page:

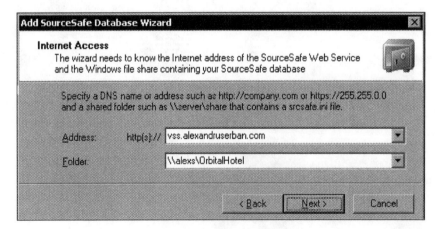

In this page, we have to configure the access settings to connect to the database.

The **Address** combo box is used to specify the **Domain Name System (DNS)** or IP address of the server that hosts the SourceSafe web service. In my case this is the vss.alexandruserban.com.

The **Folder** combo box is used to specify the shared network folder on the remote SourceSafe server where the database resides. In my case the path is \\alexs\OrbitalHotel.

After entering the required information click **Next**. The wizard will try to connect to the SourceSafe web service.

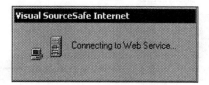

If everything is configured correctly, the wizard will connect to the web service and ask for credentials to access the SourceSafe server and database.

To continue, enter your *Windows* user name and password in the **User name** and **Password** fields to authenticate to the server.

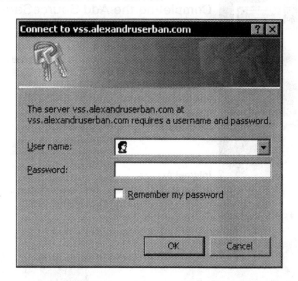

The shared database network folder on the remote SourceSafe server must be configured with the specific security rights for allowing access to the database. For more information about configuring security please consult Appendix B.

If the credentials are valid and the security on the server is set correctly, the wizard will connect successfully and advance to the third page.

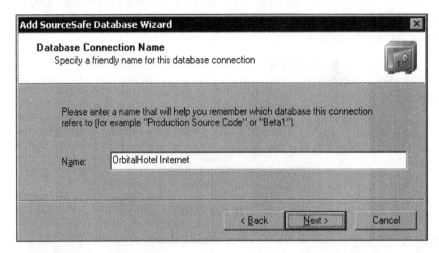

The third page gives us the opportunity to choose a new name for the database. Click **Next** to advance to the last summary page.

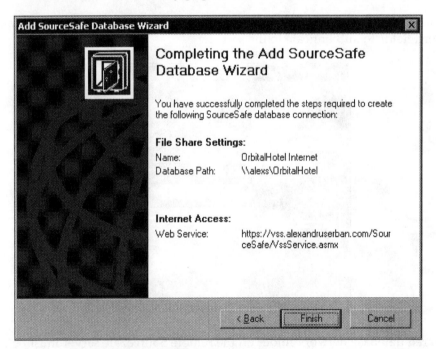

Click **Finish** to add the new database.

In the **Open Project** dialog we can see the newly added database and the connection settings:

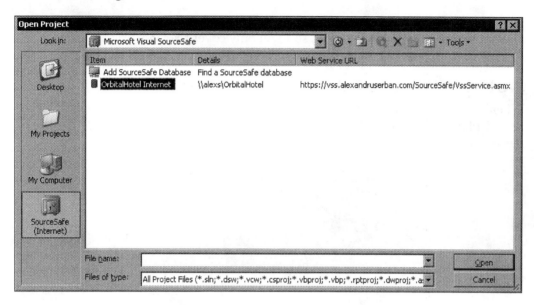

To add more databases repeat the above steps.

The default setting for the SourceSafe internet plug-in is to try to connect to the SourceSafe web service using **Secure Sockets Layer** (**SSL**). If your server doesn't use SSL for the SourceSafe web service (not recommended), clear this option to connect via a standard (unsecured) HTTP connection using the **Tools | Options | Source Control | Plug-in Settings | Advanced** button.

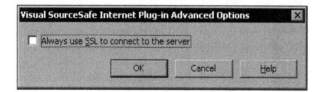

Opening the Database

After adding a database to the database list, opening it is a straightforward operation. Using a LAN connection the database can be opened using:

- Visual SourceSafe Explorer
- Visual SourceSafe Administrator
- Visual Studio with SourceSafe LAN plug-in

Using an internet connection the database is opened using Visual Studio with the SourceSafe internet plug-in.

Opening the database using Visual SourceSafe Administrator is identical to opening it using Visual SourceSafe Explorer, so I will only cover the later.

Using Visual SourceSafe Explorer

When starting, Visual SourceSafe Explorer will try to open the last accessed database and display the **Log On to Visual SourceSafe Database** dialog, asking for the **User name** and **SourceSafe password** for the database.

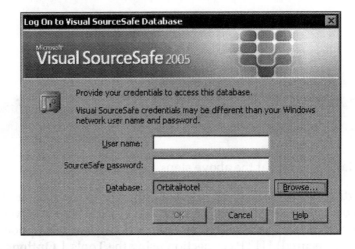

If you want to open the last accessed database highlighted in the **Database** field, you must enter your SourceSafe user name and password for the database and click **OK**.

To open another database, click **Browse** to activate the **Open SourceSafe Database** dialog.

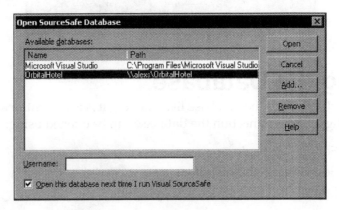

To open another database we must select it in the list and click the **Open** button. The **Log On to Visual SourceSafe Database** dialog will ask for the credentials (user name and password) for the selected database. At any time, we can also open this dialog by selecting **File | Open SourceSafe Database** or by hitting *Ctrl+P* in Visual SourceSafe Explorer.

I'm going to open the OrbitalHotel database I set up earlier. Visual SourceSafe Explorer displays the empty database as shown in the following figure:

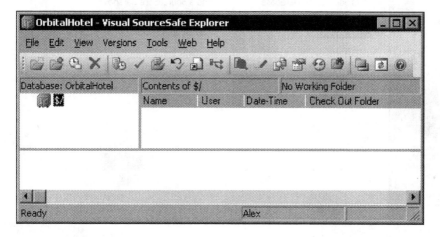

Notice the **$/** database absolute root folder. All the other projects will be added under this root.

Using Visual Studio with the LAN Plug-In

To open a SourceSafe database using a LAN connection we must first select the SourceSafe LAN plug-in for Visual Studio. For more information on how to select this plug-in please see the *Plug-In Selection in Visual Studio .NET* section in Chapter 2.

After making sure the LAN plug-in is selected, open the **Open Project** dialog in Visual Studio using the **File | Open | Project/Solution** menu command and click on the **SourceSafe (LAN)** button on the left.

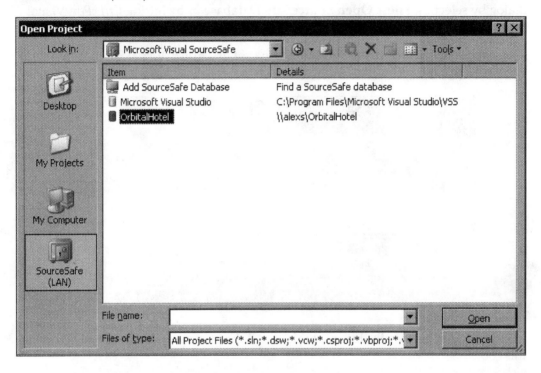

In the database list you can see all the SourceSafe databases you've added so far. To open a database, select its name from the list and click the **Open** button.

The **Log On to Visual SourceSafe Database** dialog appears asking for the SourceSafe user name and password for the database.

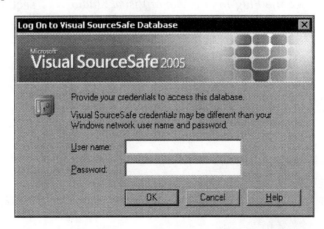

I am going to open the OrbitalHotel database I've set up earlier. The **Open Project** dialog displays the empty database.

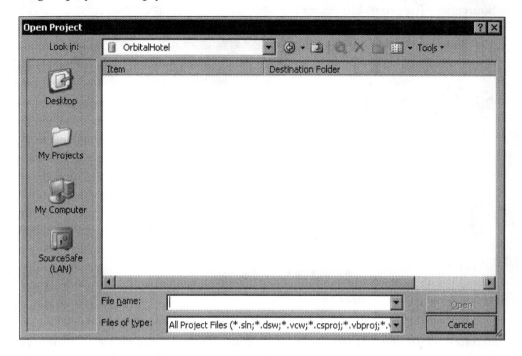

Using Visual Studio with the Internet Plug-In

To open a SourceSafe database using a LAN connection we must first select the SourceSafe internet plug-in for Visual Studio. For more information on how to select this plug-in please see the *Plug-In Selection in Visual Studio .NET* section in Chapter 2.

After making sure the LAN plug-in is selected, open the **Open Project** dialog in Visual Studio using the **File | Open | Project/Solution** menu command and click on the **SourceSafe (Internet)** button on the left:

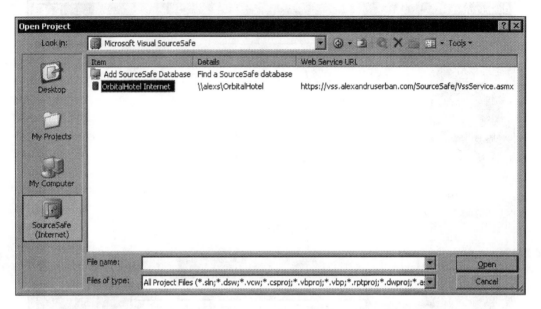

In the database list you can see all the SourceSafe databases you've added so far. To open a database, select its name from the list and click the **Open** button.

The **Log On to Visual SourceSafe Database** dialog appears asking for the SourceSafe user name and password for the database:

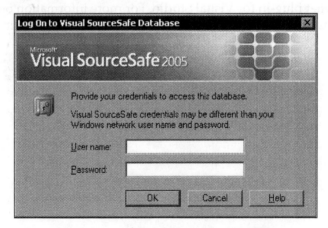

I am going to open the OrbitalHotel database I've set up earlier. After entering the user name and the password for the SourceSafe database you will be asked for the *Windows* user name and password to authenticate to the SourceSafe web service server.

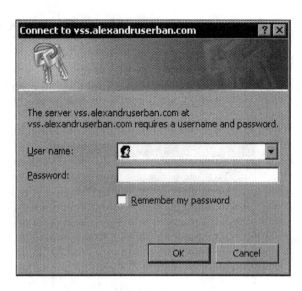

After entering these credentials, the **Open Project** dialog displays the empty database.

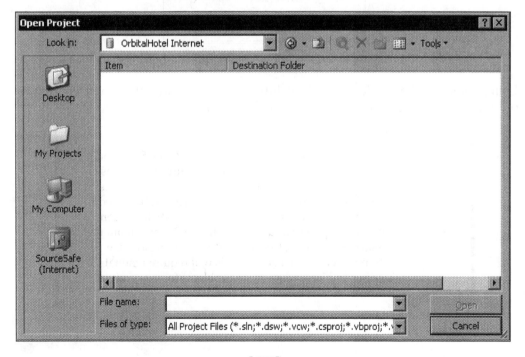

So, we've seen how to connect to and open a SourceSafe database. We have everything set up to begin working with it. What we have to do next is to add the initial solution to the new database.

Adding the Solution to the Database using Visual Studio

I'm going to add to the SourceSafe database the initial Orbital Hotel solution created in Chapter 3. If you remember, the master solution structure has the following layout in the Visual Studio Solution Explorer:

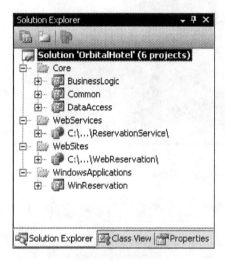

Using Visual Studio to add the initial solution structure under the source control provided by SourceSafe is the *only supported* method.

Tools like Visual SourceSafe Explorer or Visual SourceSafe command line can be used to perform source control tasks but mixing source control actions from Visual Studio and external tools is discouraged. Solution files can be added in the SourceSafe database using Visual SourceSafe Explorer. However, the project and solution files will not contain the necessary information for Visual Studio to consider the solution under source control. This will require manual rebinding and later cause more problems for you and the other team members!

This is because Visual Studio already knows a great deal about the solution, the projects, the project files, the relations between them, and last but not the least, it knows about the non-version-controlled files in the solution so it will not add them to the database (such as built binary files). Also, Visual Studio knows which files to modify to enable source control integration for the solution and project files.

Files Subjected to Source Control

The solution contains all the initial projects, source code files, and settings. When it comes to the settings, these are divided into:

- Global settings
- User-specific settings

Global settings affect the entire solution and all the projects across all users. These settings are stored in files like:

- *Solution* files (`*.sln`): These files contain information such as the list of projects, dependency information, and build configuration.
- *Project* files (`*.csproj`, `*.vbproj`, etc.): These types of files contain information such as assembly build settings, referenced assemblies, and the list of files in the project.

User-specific settings affect only a specific user and are stored in files like:

- *Solution user option* files (`*.suo`): These files contain personalized customizations made to Visual Studio by an individual developer.
- *Project user option* files (`*.csproj.user`, `*.vbproj.user`, etc.): These files contain developer-specific project options and an optional reference path that is used by Visual Studio to locate referenced assemblies.
- *WebInfo* files (`*.csproj.webinfo`, `*.vbproj.webinfo`, etc.). These files keep track of a web project's virtual root location (when using IIS).

Global and user-specific settings are stored in *different* files for a good reason. The reason is that user-specific files *aren't* subjected to source control because they differ from one user to another, reflecting the configuration of an individual user.

The following figure shows a list of some version-controlled and non-version-controlled files in the OrbitalHotel solution:

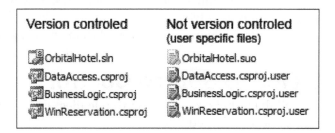

The first step to add the solution to source control is to open the solution in Visual Studio.

Then we have to select the appropriate SourceSafe plug-in for the operation. For more information on how to select SourceSafe plug-ins please see the *Plug-In Selection in Visual Studio .NET* section in Chapter 2.

After making sure the correct plug-in is selected, right-click on the solution in the **Solution Explorer** window and select the **Add Solution to Source Control** menu item.

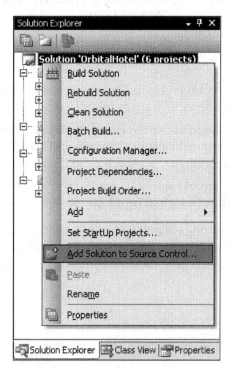

Another way to access the same command is to use the **File | Source Control | Add Solution to Source Control** menu item as shown in the following figure:

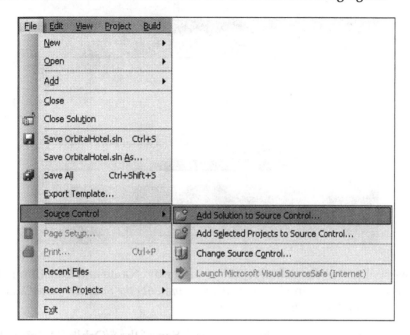

Visual Studio with the LAN Plug-In

When using the SourceSafe LAN plug-in, after using the **Add Solution to Source Control** command, the **Log On to Visual SourceSafe Database** dialog opens asking for the username and password for the current database. If required, choose another database by clicking the **Browse** button.

After entering the username and password, the **Add to SourceSafe** dialog opens showing the empty database.

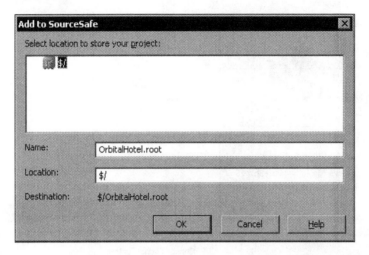

For now we will accept the default settings under the **Name** and **Location** fields. We will discuss these settings in *How SourceSafe Represents the Solution – the Data Model* later in this chapter. Click **OK** to continue.

SourceSafe prompts a dialog asking for the creation of the **$/OrbitalHotel.root** project.

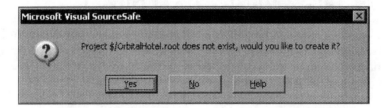

We will talk about what this project represents later in this chapter in the *Projects, Subprojects, and Files* section.

After clicking **Yes**, SourceSafe will start adding the entire solution to the database.

Once the add operation completes, the solution is successfully added to the database.

Visual Studio with the Internet Plug-In

When using the SourceSafe internet plug-in, after using the **Add Solution to Source Control** command, the **Open SourceSafe Database** dialog opens showing the current database list. The database list contains all the databases added using the internet plug-in:

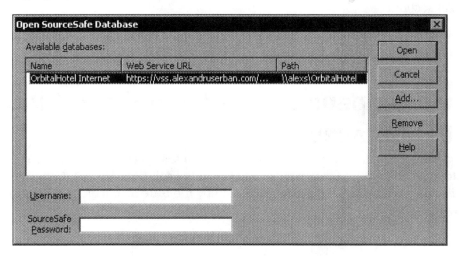

When using the HTTPS protocol to access the web service, the dialog also shows a username and password field for the selected database. We can enter them here or, later by clicking the **Open** button to reach the **Log On to Visual SourceSafe Database** dialog, which asks us for the username and password for the selected database.

After entering the credentials, the **Add to SourceSafe Internet** dialog opens showing the empty database.

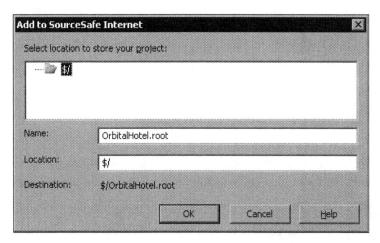

For now we will accept the default settings under the **Name** and **Location** fields. We will discus these settings under the *How SourceSafe Represents the Solution – the Data Model* section later in this chapter. Click **OK** to continue.

SourceSafe prompts a dialog asking for the creation of the **$/OrbitalHotel.root project**. We will talk about this project later in this chapter in the *Projects, Subprojects, and Files* section.

Click **OK**, to start adding the entire solution to the database. Once the add operation completes, the solution is successfully added to the database.

What Happens after Adding the Solution to the Database

After adding the solution to the database, you will see specific source-control icons next to the solution and every project and file in the solution. The solution, projects, and files all have checked-in status, indicated by the **blue lock** icon as shown in the following figure:

The project and solution files have been modified (prior to adding them to the database) to indicate that solution is now controlled.

In addition, Visual Studio creates additional files containing metadata that provide source control integration for the solution and projects. For the solution there will be a `<SolutionName>.vssscc` file, and for the projects there will be a `<ProjectName>.csproj.vspscc` file that will also be added to the source control database. Depending on your solution's configuration on the local disk, another file `<SolutionName>.vsscc` may be added to the source control database (do not confuse this with `vssscc`). These files contain Visual Studio metadata for source control.

Visual SourceSafe will also create on your local disk an `mssccprj.scc` file for each controlled solution and project file. This file contains source control bindings and is used by Visual Studio to complement the binding metadata stored in the solution and project files.

In each folder having source controlled files, Visual SourceSafe will also create a hidden file `vssver2.scc`, which will be used to correctly track the identity and versions of the database files you have in your enlistment.

You shouldn't edit any of these files directly as they are used internally by Visual Studio and modifying them could break the source control integration with the SourceSafe database. *Do not* delete any of these files as you will either break source control integration or break features like synchronization of deleted and renamed files, correct merge of files in multi-checkout scenarios, check out of a local version, etc.

At this point we have successfully added the solution to the SourceSafe database. We are now ready to begin the development process with the benefits of source code management.

But before that, it is very important to familiarize ourselves with what happens behind the scenes in the SourceSafe database and see how the database is organized.

How SourceSafe Represents the Solution—the Data Model

When the solution is organized in a hierarchical structure, Visual Studio will add it to the SourceSafe database without any issues and match the folder structure.

To see how the solution looks in the database, open the database using Visual SourceSafe Explorer. For details on opening a database see the *Using Visual SourceSafe Explorer* section under *Opening the Database* earlier in this chapter.

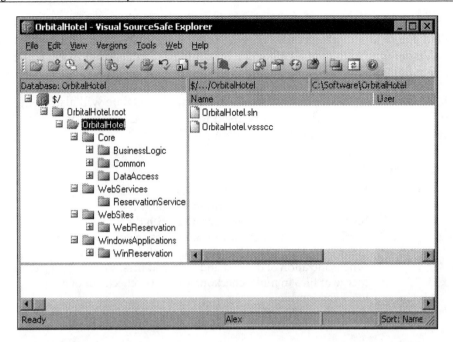

In this image you can see that above the **OrbitalHotel** solution folder there are two additional folders **$/** and **OrbitalHotel.root**. If you remember, we've accepted these default settings when we added the solution to the database. It's now time to explain them.

The **$/** folder is the **absolute root** folder in every SourceSafe database. We can make an analogy with a physical file system drive name, for example C: \. This folder is specified in the **Location** field of the **Add to SourceSafe** dialog. All other folders are created under this folder.

Under the **$/** folder there is the **OrbitalHotel.root** folder. This folder is specified in the **Name** filed of the **Add to SourceSafe** dialog. This is called a **unified root** folder and will contain all the files and folders in the solution. This will be very useful later when we will branch our solution. It also allows us to keep the hierarchical folder structure when we later need to add additional solutions and projects without breaking the tree.

Under the unified root folder, Visual Studio will create subfolders for each connection to the source control database. In the above example, a `$/OrbitalHotel.root/OrbitalHotel` folder was created and used for the solution connection's root. Because of the hierarchical structure of the solution on the local disk at the time of adding the solution to source control, all other projects in the solution have reused the solution's connection to the database. In other words, in the hierarchical structure, Visual Studio maintains the connection only to the solution root folder, the other ones being determined relatively to the solution's root folder; yet another benefit of having a hierarchical solution structure.

There is a symmetrical correspondence between the solution file system structure and the solution database structure:

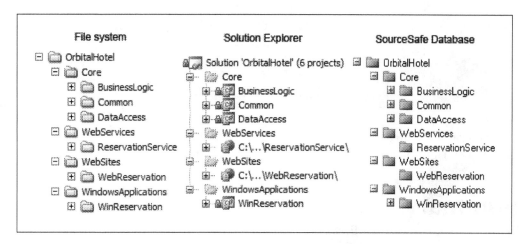

This structure will prove its effectiveness when getting the solution on other development machines.

Projects, Subprojects, and Files

Until now I've referred to the nodes in the SourceSafe database structure with the term *folder*. Although these actually represent physical file system folders, SourceSafe has another term to describe them. In the SourceSafe terminology they are referred to as **projects**.

We can see this if we right-click on an existing project.

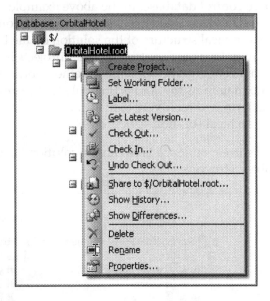

In the hierarchical structure, a SourceSafe project contains additional projects (subprojects) and files, mapping the physical folder structure.

Summary

In this chapter we took the first step towards working under source control — adding a new solution to the SourceSafe database.

After setting up a new database, we must add it to our database list by connecting to it either using the LAN or the Internet. When using the LAN we use SourceSafe Explorer or Visual Studio with the LAN plug-in. When using the Internet, the only option is Visual Studio with the internet plug-in. Then, we open the database and check whether everything is in order.

When adding the solution to the database, however, the only option is to use Visual Studio because, since we are going to do all the development using it, Visual Studio knows what is best on how to handle the solution. It only adds the necessary solution files to the database, avoiding problems related to local user files that should not be subjected to source control such as user settings and binary output files that are large and can be built at any time.

The solution structure is matched in the database, so a correct hierarchical structure produces the best results. This will make it very easy for other developers to get the new solution from the database and start the team development.

5

Developing Solutions under Source Control

In this chapter we are going to learn about the source control operations we use daily in our development activities. We will start by setting up a new workspace and get the solution from the SourceSafe database. Then, we will add new files to the solution, check them in, examine their history, and get the latest versions.

We will also explore the team cooperation models and see what are the differences between them, their advantages and disadvantages, and operations such as item comparison, undoing changes, file merging and pinning, and conflict resolution.

Towards the end, we will see how to search for files in the database, how to share files across multiple projects, how to move files and projects, how to rebind projects, and how to move and delete projects and files.

Setting up the Workspace

If you remember, we've talked about *workspaces* back in Chapter 1. While the main solution is contained in a central SourceSafe database on a server machine, users (developers and testers) work individually on their machines.

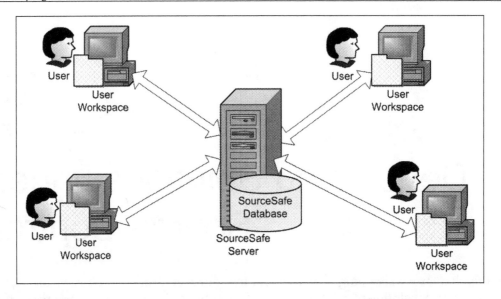

The purpose of the individual workspace is to provide users with an area where they can work separately from the main solution stored in the SourceSafe database and to separate users in order to prevent their changes from affecting one another while they are working. Users make changes to the workspace content, adding, modifying, and deleting files without the worry that they will affect the main solution in the database or anybody else for that matter, until their changes are ready to be integrated into the main solution in the SourceSafe database.

Workspace Mappings

To maintain a link between the SourceSafe database and the local workspaces, SourceSafe clients use two types of workspace mappings:

- SourceSafe working folders
- Visual Studio source control bindings

A SourceSafe **working folder** represents a mapping between a logical SourceSafe folder (also called a project) and a physical system folder on the user's machine.

After adding the solution to the SourceSafe database, the Visual Studio SourceSafe plug-in automatically configures the working folder. In my case, the working folder for the user that I used to perform the adding operation (named Alex) is set to C:\Software\OrbitalHotel, the directory that contains the solution .sln file.

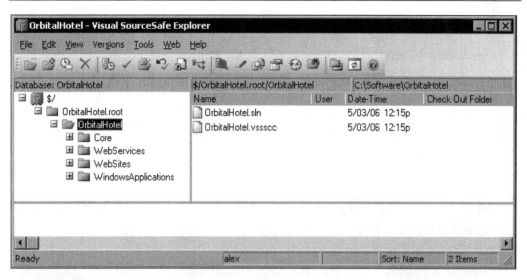

The physical location for subfolders is calculated based on the working folder's absolute path and the subfolder's relative path in the database. We can see this if we open **Visual SourceSafe Explorer** after adding the solution to the SourceSafe database. Selecting the working folder reveals its physical workspace location. Selecting subfolders shows their calculated location. This is another advantage of the hierarchical solution structure because only one working folder needs to be defined — the solution folder. The other folders are automatically determined based on the hierarchical structure:

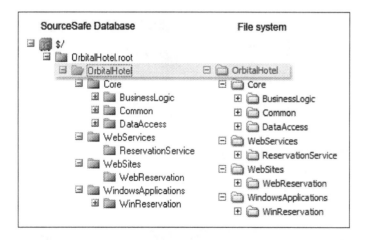

SourceSafe working folders are saved in the `ss.ini` file that is specific to every SourceSafe user. However, SourceSafe working folders are only used by SourceSafe stand-alone clients. They are not used by the Visual Studio plug-ins. Although it has automatically set the SourceSafe working folder, Visual Studio uses another type of mapping between the SourceSafe database and local workspace folders. These are the **source control bindings** and are stored in the solution file and in some types of project files (such as web projects).

We can view the source control bindings by opening the **Change Source Control** dialog in Visual Studio using the **File | Source Control | Change Source Control** command. We can see the mappings between the SourceSafe database and the physical file system folders. I've rearranged the default column order to show the following information:

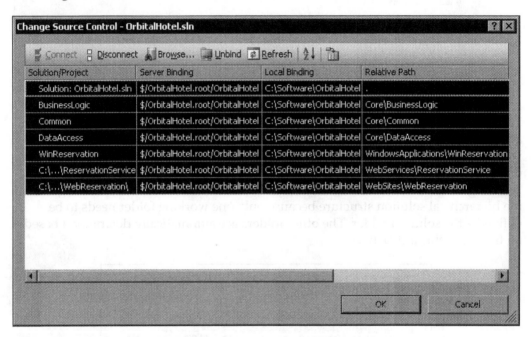

You can see there is an entry for the solution as well as for each project in the solution in the **Solution/Project** column. In this case, source control bindings also use relative paths for the locations of subprojects. The **Server Binding** and **Local Binding** columns show the mappings between the SourceSafe database folders and the local file-system folders. The physical folders for the projects are resolved using the local binding folder and the relative paths displayed in the **Relative Path** column.

Getting Solutions from the Database

Centralizing the initial solution in a new SourceSafe database is the first step in developing it further in a distributed environment. The next step is to propagate the solution to the team members that will participate in the development.

The team members need to have access to the SourceSafe database and need to have usernames and passwords set up initially by the SourceSafe database administrator. For more information about configuring security, usernames, and passwords please consult Appendix B.

Team members can get the solution from the SourceSafe database using either Visual Studio with the SourceSafe LAN or the internet plug-in.

When the solution contains web projects that use the local file system instead of IIS, it is recommended to get the solution on the partition having the same drive letter. This is because this type of project is named using the partition's name. Having the solution on the same partition will ensure that the project names remain the same across all users and there will be no need for unnecessary synchronization checkouts.

Using Visual Studio with the LAN Plug-In

Before we can get the solution from the SourceSafe database, we must add the SourceSafe database to our database list and then open the database using our credentials (username and password).

For more information about these tasks please see the *Using Visual Studio with the LAN Plug-In* section under the *Adding the Database over the LAN* section and *Using Visual Studio with the LAN Plug-In* section under the *Opening the Database* section in Chapter 4.

Opening the SourceSafe database will show the database folder structure for the solution. We must navigate to the folder that contains the solution .sln file.

I'm going to open the OrbitalHotel SourceSafe database that I set up in Chapter 4. The solution file is in the `OrbitalHotel.root/OrbitalHotel` folder.

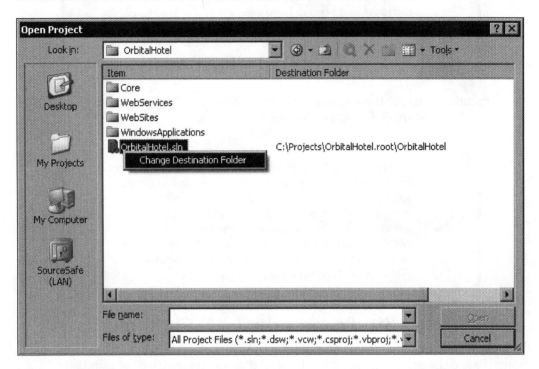

When a user opens a SourceSafe database for the first time on a new machine, he or she has no working folder defined. As you can see, in this case Visual Studio automatically constructs a new working folder using the Visual Studio project's location path set in the Visual Studio **Options** dialog and the path in the SourceSafe database.

You can accept this default working folder or you can choose another folder by right-clicking on the solution file and choosing the **Change Destination Folder** command.

To get the solution from the SourceSafe database click the **Open** button.

The Visual Studio SourceSafe LAN plug-in performs the get operation asynchronously.

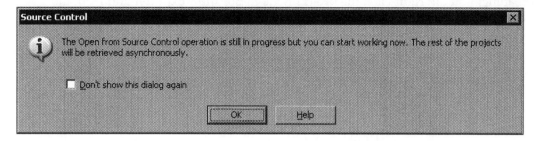

The projects will be loaded one by one but you can start working on the ones already loaded.

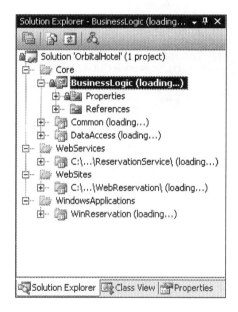

If you need to work on a project sooner than Visual Studio has it scheduled for loading, you can right-click the project node in **Solution Explorer** and from the context menu use the **Load Project** command to force it to reschedule that project with a higher priority for loading.

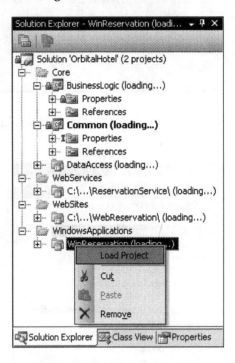

Similarly, if you need to work on a file, you don't have to wait until Visual Studio gets all the project files from Source Control. Once the project node has been loaded and can be expanded, you can right-click any file node and select **Open** to force Source Control to retrieve immediately that file and open it in the editor.

 Whether a project is retrieved synchronously or asynchronously from Source Control depends on the project type. For instance Visual C++ projects are synchronously opened from Source Control, while Visual Basic, C#, and Web projects are asynchronous.

After all the projects are loaded, the entire solution is ready. A message will be displayed in the **Output** window when the solution is completely retrieved from the Source Control database.

Using Visual Studio with the Internet Plug-In

Before we can get the solution from the SourceSafe database, we must add the SourceSafe database to our database list and then open the database using our credentials (username and password).

 For more information about these tasks please see the *Using Visual Studio with the Internet Plug-In* section under the *Adding the Database* section and the *Using Visual Studio with the Internet Plug-In* section under the *Opening the database* section in Chapter 4.

After opening the SourceSafe database we will see the database folder structure for the solution. We must navigate to the folder that contains the solution `.sln` file.

I'm going to open the OrbitalHotel SourceSafe database that I up in Chapter 4. The solution file is in the `OrbitalHotel.root/OrbitalHotel` folder.

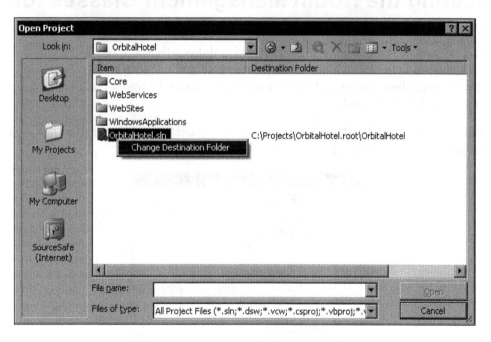

When a SourceSafe user opens a SourceSafe database for the first time on a new machine, he or she has no working folder defined. As you can see, in this case Visual Studio automatically constructs a new working folder using the Visual Studio project's location path set in the Visual Studio **Options** dialog and the path in the SourceSafe database.

You can accept this default working folder or you can choose another folder by right-clicking on the solution file and choosing the **Change Destination Folder** command.

To get the solution from the SourceSafe database click the **Open** button.

Unlike the Visual Studio SourceSafe LAN plug-in, the SourceSafe internet plug-in doesn't perform the **Get** operation asynchronously so we must wait until the operation completes. After all the projects are loaded, the solution is ready.

Adding New Project Files

In the following examples, I am going to start development on the Orbital Hotel solution by adding new files, building the data access layer, common classes, and business logic objects for the hotel's room management. You can sit back and read these sections or you can join me and take similar steps on one of your own solutions.

Creating the Room Management Classes for Orbital Hotel

First, I will create the common class *RoomDS*, a dataset that will be used to read and update room information. The class is created by right-clicking on the **Common** class library project, then choosing **Add | New Item...** and selecting a **DataSet**. The name for the file is **RoomDS.xsd**.

After clicking the **Add** button, Visual Studio will create new files for this class and add them to the **Common** class library project:

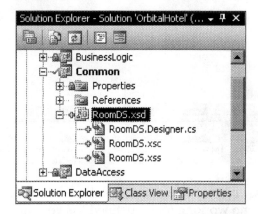

As the list of files that form the project is kept in the project file, (in this case the Common.csproj file) to be able to add the new file to the project, the project file must be edited. By default, Visual Studio automatically checks out the project file and adds the new `RoomDS.xsd` file. This information can be seen by looking at the **Output** window and viewing the output generated by **Source Control**.

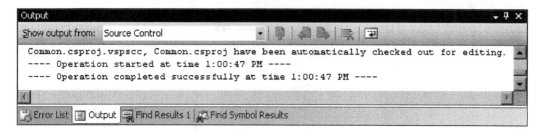

When a project or file is checked out by the current user, its Source Control status icon in **Solution Explorer** will change from the **blue lock** to the **red check mark** icon.

Newly added files are represented using a **yellow plus** sign, which shows the current Source Control status as a newly added solution file.

After creating the *RoomDS* dataset, I will add a new *DataTable* to it by using the **Server Explorer** connection to the OrbitalHotel SQL Server database. To create the new table, I will drag and drop the Room database table from **Server Explorer** to the **DataSet Designer** I've opened by double-clicking on the new `RoomDS.xsd` project file.

Dragging the Room table from the database creates additional files used to store database connection information.

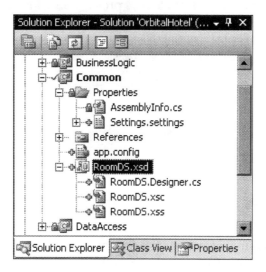

In the *RoomDS* dataset, a *Room DataTable* and a *RoomTableAdapter* class are created. The **RoomTableAdapter** class has by default two methods for reading the table's data: **Fill** and **GetData**, which use text SQL commands.

I will modify the SQL commands used by these methods to use stored procedures to select, insert, delete, and update the *Room* table having the following structure:

Visual Studio automatically creates the underlying dataset and adapter classes when saving dataset design. The dataset and adapter classes are created in the same file, the `RoomDS.Designer.cs`. Because of this, Visual Studio keeps the data access layer and the business objects layer in the same assembly.

To be able to keep my designed layers separate, I will keep the common objects (like datasets) used by all other projects in the common assembly and the data access layer in a separate data access assembly. For this I will have to make some manual changes.

I will add a new code file in the **DataAccess** project named **RoomTableAdapters.cs** as shown in the following figure:

The same behavior occurs here too. The project file is automatically checked out and the new file is added to the project.

To separate the common objects from the data access objects, I will cut the code generated by the *RoomTableAdapter* class from the `RoomDS.Designer.cs` file and paste it into the `RoomTableAdapters.cs` file, being careful to change the class namespaces accordingly.

I will also copy and include in the **DataAccess** project the `config` and the `settings` files from the **Common** project, used to store and access database connection information. I will also add a reference to the **Common** project so that I can access the dataset from the data assembly.

Finally, to create the business objects, I will add a new component class file and a new class diagram file in the **BusinessLogic** project along with references to the **Common** and **DataAccess** projects.

A class diagram file allows us to visually design classes.

Designing the Classes using the Class Diagram

To be able to design the necessary classes, we have to open the diagram file by double-clicking on the `ClassDiagram.cs` file. I'm going to use the class diagram to visually design the **RoomManager** component class by dragging the `RoomManager.cs` file from the **Solution Explorer** and dropping it in the class diagram designer. The designer shows the current default component class structure:

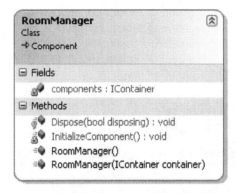

I will add two new methods:

- GetAllRooms, which returns a *RoomDataTable* object filed with all the rooms in the database.
- UpdateRooms, which updates the database with the information contained in the rooms parameter.

The designer updates and shows these new methods:

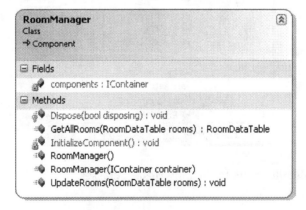

Designing the RoomManager class using the class diagram automatically generates the underlying code:

```
/// <summary>
/// Gets all the rooms in the database
/// </summary>
/// <remarks>If the rooms parameter is not null, this method
/// will fill this object
/// with room information and return it, otherwise a new
/// RoomDataTable object
/// will be created and returned</remarks>
/// <param name="rooms">A RoomDataTable object to be filed
/// with room information.
/// If this is null, a new RoomDataTable will be created and
/// returned</param>
/// <returns>A RoomDataTable containing all rooms in the
/// database</returns>
public RoomDS.RoomDataTable
 GetAllRooms(RoomDS.RoomDataTable rooms)
{
    throw new System.NotImplementedException();
}

/// <summary>
/// Updates the room database with the information in the
/// room parameter
/// </summary>
/// <param name="rooms">The RoomDataTable object containing
/// the information to be updated</param>
public void UpdateRooms(RoomDS.RoomDataTable rooms)
{
    throw new System.NotImplementedException();
}
```

The method bodies will be implemented by other team members, so I need to save (check in) all the changes made to the solution so far to the SourceSafe database before other developers can do their parts.

Best Practice

Do not let the workspace become too valuable. Check in the changes to the database as often as possible after testing the solution and making sure the database contents can be successfully built.

Checking In to the Database

After successfully building the solution, I will check in the changes I've made so far. All pending changes to the database are referred to as **pending checkins**. At any time, we can view the pending checkins by looking in the **Pending Checkins** window in Visual Studio. The **Pending Checkins** window can be activated using the **View | Pending Checkins** command or by right-clicking on the solution in the **Solution Explorer** window and using the **View Pending Checkins** command.

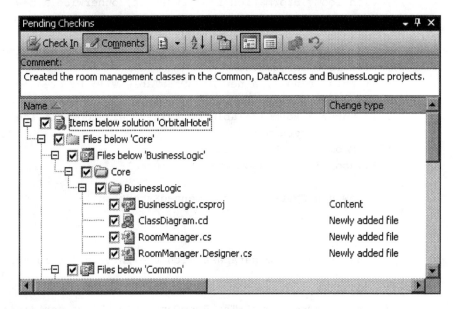

The window shows all the changed files along with the change type. We can see all the newly added files and the edited files. The figure above contains only a subset.

The **Comments** button in the **Pending Checkins** window shows and hides the **Comment** text box.

>
> **Best Practice**
>
> Every check in can and should be associated with a comment that explains what was modified. Give a detailed explanation about what was changed and why, as it will help in easily identifying bugs and other issues.

After entering the check-in comment, we are ready to perform the check in and synchronize the changes with the database. The check in is performed by clicking on the **Check In** button. After the operation completes, all the files will be checked in to the SourceSafe database:

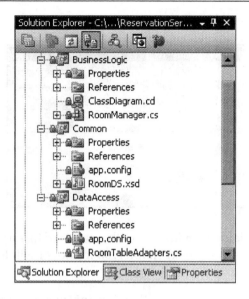

Versions and History

As we've seen in Chapter 1, a fundamental characteristic of SCM tools is file versioning and history management. During the development process, files in the database change and evolve as the project evolves. Files are modified, renamed, and moved from one folder to another, new files are added, and others are deleted. All these operations are part of the day-to-day work. The SourceSafe database keeps a track of these operations and provides the option to see the state at any time in the past since the solution was first added to Source Control.

Each time a file is added or changed and checked in to the database, a **revision** is created. Thus, a file evolves as a succession of revisions, referred to by successive numbers such as 1, 2, 3, and so on.

File Versions and History

Let's see, for example, the history of the **BusinessLogic** project file in the OrbitalHotel solution. To view the history of a solution resource we have to right-click on it and then use the **View History** command.

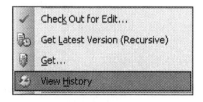

SourceSafe displays the **History Options** dialog:

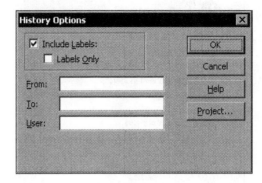

The **History Options** dialog provides us with a series of history options we can set. We will talk about labels in the next chapter, so for now I will leave the label options as they are set by default.

The **From** and **To** options can be set with a date interval to narrow the search. Dates can be entered in MM.DD.YY, MM-DD-YY, or MM/DD/YY format, but not in the traditional text format, such as March 10, 2006. Dates must be prefixed by the **D** letter such as *D03.10.2006*.

The **User** option specifies a user name, to show only the changes made by a specific user.

For now we are interested in the entire history so I will leave these options blank and click the **OK** button. This shows the history for the `BusinessLogic.csproj` project file.

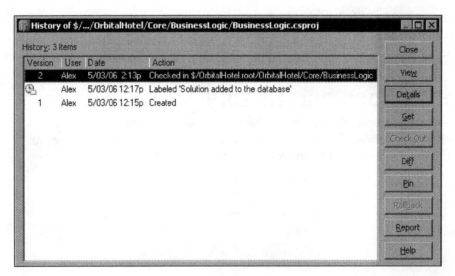

In the list we can see how the file has changed over time. We can see the file's versions, the user who changed the file, the date and the action that caused the file to change. On the right we can see a series of commands we can perform based on the file's history. For now we are interested in the default **Details** command.

Selecting the latest version and clicking the **Details** button displays the **History Details** dialog that provides more details on the specific version.

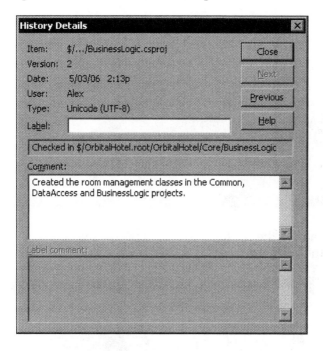

Here we can see the comments entered when this specific version was checked in. This is very useful when going through the history of a specific resource as you can see what was changed. Clicking on the **Previous** and **Next** buttons, we can go back and forth through the file's history.

Viewing the history for, let's say, the `RoomManager.cs` file will show the following:

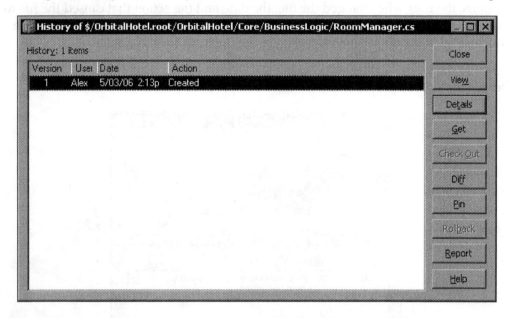

Because I've just added the file to Source Control, the history for the file begins from this point on with a **Created** action. Clicking **Details** shows the following:

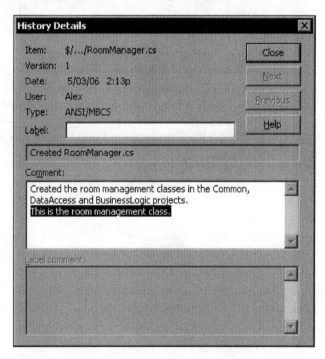

You can see the same check-in comment here as well. The comment is associated with every changed file in a specific check-in operation. Comments are editable even after the check-in operation is done. I've added an extra comment line here.

On clicking the **Close** button we are asked to save the changes made to the comment.

Click **Yes** to save the comment changes and return to the **History** dialog.

Project Versions and History

Projects (SourceSafe folders) have history too. The project history records the operations that occur on the files they contain. To view the history for a project, instead of clicking **OK** in the **History Options** dialog, click the **Project...** button to show the history for the project that contains the file.

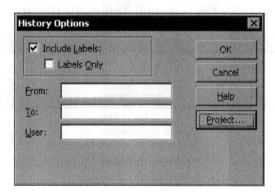

This displays the **Project History Option** dialog:

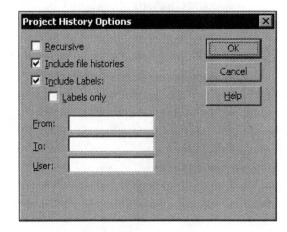

This dialog contains two extra options:

- **Recursive**: Used to recursively display the history for subprojects
- **Include file histories**: Used to display the history for the contained files

I will choose to include the file histories for the solution folder but not recursively. To show the project history click **OK**. This will display the **History of Project** dialog.

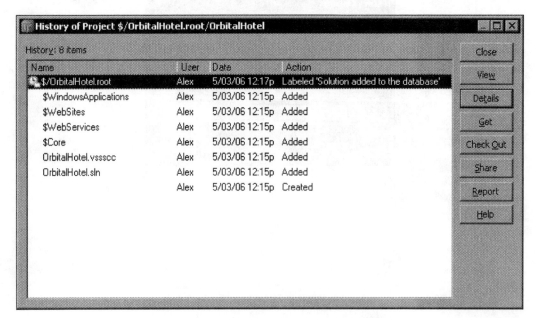

We can see the history for all the file operations in the solution folder so far.

To see the histories recursively for all the items under the solution folder I will select the recursive option also.

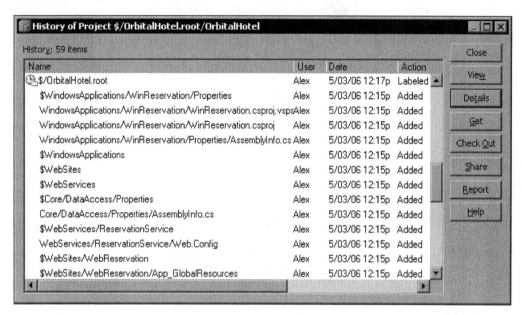

After I've added the room management classes to the SourceSafe database, the other developers need to obtain them so that they can use them and implement their specific functionality, in other words they will need to *get the latest version* of the solution.

Getting the Latest Versions

To keep the local workspace up to date with the contents of the database, we must get the latest versions for the files in the database. This operation can be applied to a single file, multiple files, projects, or solution files.

Let's see how, in my example, other developers can get the latest solution version that includes the files I've added earlier.

Before I've checked in the changes to the solution, their workspaces have the solution contents prior to my check in.

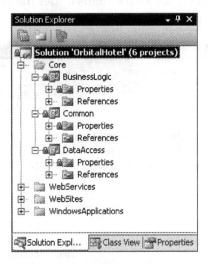

To get the latest version for all the projects in the solutions, we have to right-click the solution in **Solution Explorer** and click on the **Get Latest Version (Recursive)** command.

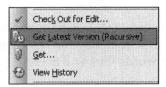

Visual Studio will retrieve recursively the latest versions for all the files in the solution including projects and files. When applied to any file container (solution, project, or folder), the **Get Latest Version (Recursive)** command gets all the items under the selected item. Looking at the **Output** window for Source Control we can see how the newer files are replaced in the workspace and how the new files are retrieved:

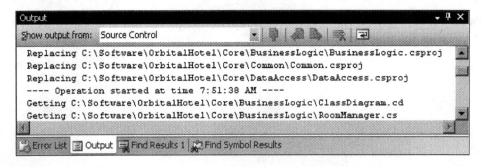

After the operation completes, Visual Studio will automatically reload all the changed projects now having the latest versions from the SourceSafe database:

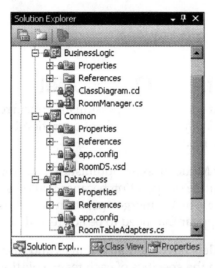

Every team member who needs to work with the latest solution version will perform the same operation. We get the latest version of a resource from the database each time we need to refresh our workspace with the latest version of a specific file, project, or even the entire solution.

Now that different team members will need to start working on the solution, it's time to address the team cooperation principles and models.

Team Cooperation

When developing the solution in a team environment, team cooperation is an essential requirement. This is where, although it can be changed later, a cooperation model must be chosen.

If you remember from Chapter 1, there are two main approaches in SCM when it comes to cooperation models:

- Check out-Modify-Check in
- Modify-Merge-Commit

Visual SourceSafe is built around the *Check out-Modify-Check in* model. This model has two sub-models of operation:

- Exclusive Check-Out Model
- Multiple Check-Out Model

Choosing a Check-Out Model

The **Exclusive Check-Out** Model uses a pessimistic concurrency scheme characterized by a *Lock-Modify-Unlock* mode of operation because it allows *only one* user at a time to modify a resource.

The **Multiple Check-Out** Model uses an optimistic concurrency scheme characterized by a *Copy-Modify-Merge* mode of operation because it allows *multiple users* at a time to modify a resource, after which a merge operation is performed. During the merge operation conflicts may appear that need to be addressed and resolved.

Both these check-out models have their advantages and disadvantages. Choosing the best model depends upon the specifics of each team, solution structure, and content.

In Visual SourceSafe 2005 the check-out model is set per database. The check-out model is set using the Visual SourceSafe Administrator application. For more information about setting the check-out model please see Appendix C.

Because the Visual SourceSafe plug-ins for Visual Studio read the configuration information when opening the solution, changes made to the database configuration afterwards do not take effect until the solution is reopened.

When making changes to the SourceSafe database configuration, close and reopen any solutions for the changes to take effect.

We are going to explore both the check-out models in the following sections while we continue to develop the room management classes.

For this example we will need two developers, Mary and John, who will implement the two empty methods I've defined earlier in the *RoomManager* class. They will get the latest solution version to obtain the files I've added earlier, each one having the task to implement one of them.

The Exclusive Check-Out Model

The Exclusive Check-Out Model lets only one user at a time to modify a specific resource. Let's suppose Mary will be the first developer to begin her work. When she opens the `RoomManager.cs` file and begins to modify it to implement the **GetAllRooms** method, by default, Visual Studio will silently try to check it out for editing. If the file isn't already checked out to another user, the operation will succeed and the file can be successfully edited.

Looking at the **Output** window for Source Control reveals the automatic check-out operation:

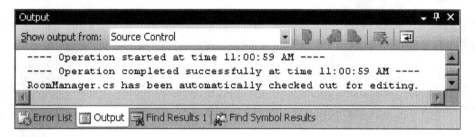

In the **Solution Explorer** window, the Source Control icon changes as we expect to a **red check mark**, showing the file is checked out to the current user, in this case to Mary:

Now, Mary can implement the method without further issues.

While she does her work, John comes in and wants to implement the **UpdateRooms** method. He opens the `RoomManager.cs` file and begins typing to implement the method's body. As in Mary's case, Visual Studio will try to perform an automatic file check out. Only this time, the check out cannot be performed successfully because the file is *exclusively* checked out by Mary.

A message box informs John about this:

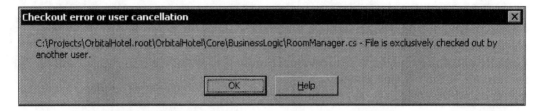

Looking at the **Output** window for Source Control, he can see the user that has the file currently checked out, and sure enough, it is Mary.

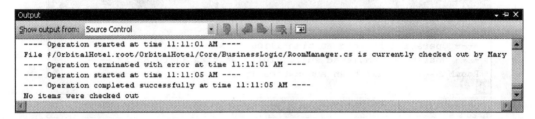

Being unable to check out the file for John, Visual Studio will refresh the Source Control status for him and show an icon representing a user, beside the RoomManager.cs file in the **Solution Explorer** window:

This is the status representation of a file being checked out by another user.

In this case, when using the Exclusive Check-Out Model, John will have to wait for Mary to finish her changes before he can make his. He can work on other files that are not checked out.

Because I talked about the file's Source Control status, let's see how we can manually refresh the status of a file, when we are interested to see what is going on with it at any given moment.

Refreshing a File's Source Control Status

When waiting for a checked out file that we need to change, we are interested to see when the file becomes available for modifications, that is, when the resource's status changes back to checked in. Or, before checking out a resource, we want to be sure it's not already checked out by another user.

To refresh the Source Control status for a file, project, or even the entire solution, we use the **Refresh** button in the **Source Control** toolbar.

 To show the **Source Control** toolbar, you can navigate to **View | Toolbars** and click the **Source Control** command button.

The **Refresh Status** command is also available under the **File | Source Control** menu. Clicking the **Refresh** button will cause a Source Control status refresh for all the files under the currently selected item. That is, if the current item is the solution, all the projects and files will be refreshed, if it's a project, all the files in the project will be refreshed, if it is a file, just the file will be refreshed.

Checking In the Changes

To see when Mary finishes her work, John will have to refresh the status for the `RoomManager.cs` file and see when the file becomes checked in again.

Meanwhile Mary implements her method:

```
/// <summary>
/// Gets all the rooms in the database
/// </summary>
/// <remarks>If the rooms parameter is not null, this method will
            fill this object
/// with room information and return it, otherwise a new
    RoomDataTable object
/// will be created and returned</remarks>
/// <param name="rooms">A RoomDataTable object to be filed with room
                        information.
/// If this is null, a new RoomDataTable will be created and
    returned</param>
```

```
///  <returns>A RoomDataTable containing all rooms in the
                database</returns>
public RoomDS.RoomDataTable GetAllRooms(RoomDS.RoomDataTable rooms)
{
    RoomDS.RoomDataTable rdt = (rooms != null ? rooms : new
                RoomDS.RoomDataTable());
    DataAccess.RoomTableAdapters.RoomTableAdapter rta =
    new OrbitalHotel.DataAccess.RoomTableAdapters.RoomTableAdapter();
    rta.Fill(rdt);
    return rdt;
}
```

Before checking in the changes, she ensures the solution can be successfully built. Then she writes a comment in the **Pending Checkins** window about what she has changed.

After that, she checks in the changes clicking on the **Check In** button, finishing her work.

Now, John can proceed to do his part, implementing the **UpdateRooms** method. He opens the RoomManager.cs file and starts making his changes. As we know by now, Visual Studio will try to automatically check out the file.

If the database is configured to only allow checkouts of the latest version, then while checking out a file the Visual Studio plug-in verifies the file's version. This is done to check if the version John currently has in his workspace and wants to edit is the latest version. In this case, because Mary modified the file and created a new version, Visual Studio will automatically get the latest version for him.

This behavior can be changed to allow checkouts of the local version (recommended). For more information please consult the *Changing the Team Version Control Model* section in Appendix C.

Now John can do his work too, and implement the **UpdateRooms** method.

```
/// <summary>
/// Updates the room database with the information in the
    room parameter
/// </summary>
/// <param name="rooms">The RoomDataTable object containing
/// the information to be updated</param>
public void UpdateRooms(RoomDS.RoomDataTable rooms)
{
    DataAccess.RoomTableAdapters.RoomTableAdapter rta =
        new OrbitalHotel.DataAccess.RoomTableAdapters.
        RoomTableAdapter();
    rta.Update(rooms);
}
```

He will also ensure the solution can be successfully built, write a comment in the **Pending Checkins** window about the modifications, and check in the changes.

Looking at the history for the `RoomManager.cs` file we can see how this file has changed over time:

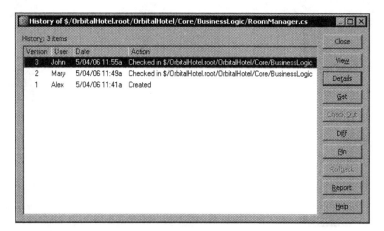

We can see when Alex created the file and then, when Mary and John modified it. This provides useful information regarding the file's history.

But what if we want to see what was modified between the file versions? It will be very helpful when we want to see how a file has changed across one or more versions.

Comparing Versions

Because history applies to both files and projects, we can compare files and projects as well.

Comparing File Versions

Viewing changes between two file versions is a simple operation. If you remember from Chapter 1, the difference between two file versions is called a **delta**. When reconstructing one specific version, SourceSafe combines all the deltas up to the desired version.

We've earlier seen the history for the RoomManager.cs file and how it has evolved over the course of three versions. Let's take a look now at the differences between these versions.

To see the differences between file versions, we are going to open the same **History** dialog. Only now, we will use the **Diff** command.

To see the differences between the last version in our workspace and the first version in the database, I will open the **History** dialog using the **View History** command and select the first version in the list, version 1 as shown in the following figure:

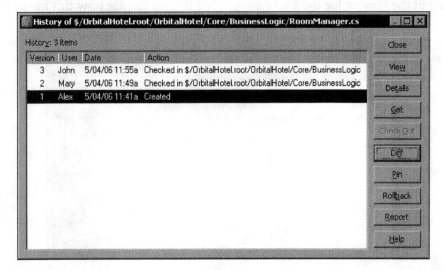

Then I will click the **Diff** button on the right side of the dialog. The **Difference Options** dialog is shown in the following figure:

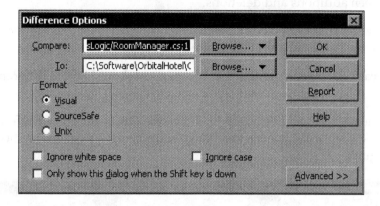

By default, the **Difference Options** dialog is set to show the difference between the file version in the local workspace and the selected version in the **History** dialog. The **Compare** text box contains the selected version in the **History** dialog and the **To** text box contains the local file path version from our workspace.

The two **Browse** buttons allow us to select other file versions either from the **SourceSafe projects** or from the **Windows folders**.

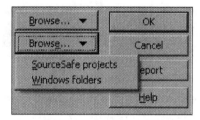

To see the differences between the two versions in history we can select the lines of the two versions to be compared before clicking the **Diff** button.

Right now we are interested in seeing the difference between the default selected versions.

The **Format** group box contains three different format options:

- The **Visual** format option will open the **Difference Viewer**, a tool used for file comparisons that uses color coding to identify added, deleted, and changed lines.

- The **SourceSafe** format option uses an old-style SourceSafe format. This format consists of a text display of lines added, deleted, and changed.

- • Finally, the **Unix** format option shows differences in the Unix format. This format consists only of the changed lines and uses text arrows to distinguish between additions and deletions.

The **Ignore white space** checkbox specifies that comparison should ignore lines that differ only in the space, tab, or other white-space characters.

The **Ignore case** checkbox specifies that comparison should ignore differences in letter case.

I'm going to leave the default options and click the **OK** button. The **Difference Viewer** tool will show the differences between the two file versions as shown in the following figure:

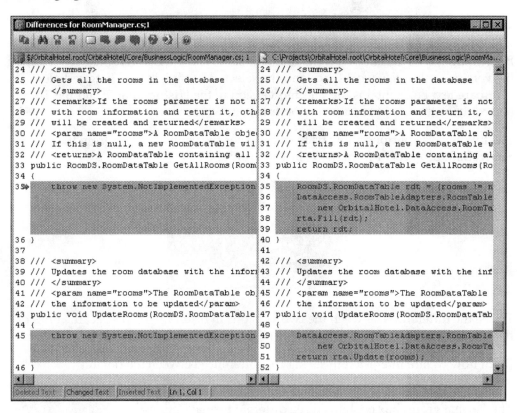

In the left window we see the **$/OrbitalHotel.root/OrbitalHotel/Core/BusinessLogic/ RoomManager.cs;1** file version and on the right we see the **C:\Software\ OrbitalHotel\Core\BusinessLogic\RoomManager.cs** file version. Sure enough, it is what we would expect. The differences between the first checked in version and the last version are represented by the changes Mary and John made to the file by implementing the two functions I did not implement in the first file version.

Note the **1** at the end of **$/OrbitalHotel.root/OrbitalHotel/Core/BusinessLogic/ RoomManager.cs;1** .This tells SourceSafe to use version 1 for the file.

The difference tool shows by default deleted text in red, changed text in blue, and inserted text in green. In the figure we can see the differences in blue, as changed text. To navigate among file differences, use the **Previous Difference** and the **Next Difference** commands in the toolbar. You can also set bookmarks in files and navigate among bookmarks, using the **Bookmarks** command and you can search for specific text in the files using the toolbar's **Search** commands.

Comparing Project Versions

Another way to compare file versions is to use the **Compare** command in the Visual Studio file context menu. We can activate the compare command by right-clicking a file in the **Solution Explorer** window and clicking on **Compare**:

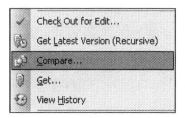

Clicking **Compare** will directly show the **Difference Options** dialog.

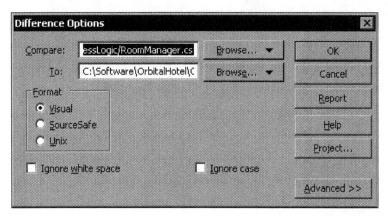

Just like the **History** dialog for files, this dialog also has a **Project...** button. Clicking this button shows the **Project Difference** dialog:

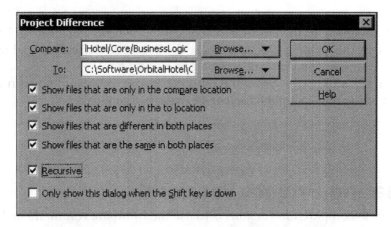

The options are self explanatory. I will also choose to display the differences recursively:

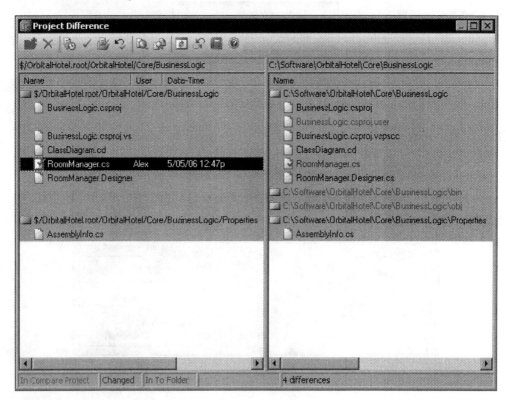

Here we can see the differences between the SourceSafe project and the local workspace folder. We can see the non-version controlled files that the Visual Studio plug-in didn't add to the database.

The toolbar has additional commands for adding, deleting, checking out, checking in, viewing a file, and project history. It also has a command to reconcile the differences between the projects. Using this command displays the **Reconcile all differences** dialog:

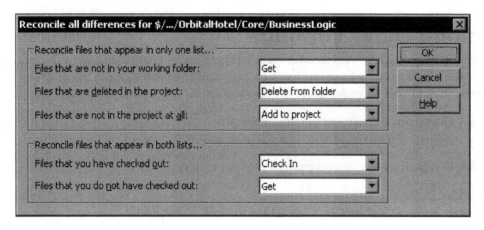

In this dialog we can set the operations that will be performed when reconciling differences between projects.

In this case, however, reconciling changes has no sense as it will add the non-version controlled files to the database, which is what we don't want.

We've seen how the Exclusive Check-Out Model operates. Before we take a look at the Multiple Check-Out Model, we will need to undo the changes made by Mary and John using the Exclusive Check-Out Model to see how the same changes are made using the Multiple Check-Out Model.

Undoing Version Changes

This is useful when we want to use a past version as a starting point for new changes.

To see how the Multiple Check-Out Model behaves compared to the exclusive check-out model, we will go through the same set of changes and observe the differences between the two models. In order to do that we need to start from the same file version we started with when using the Exclusive Check-Out Model. Hence, we need to undo the changes and revert back to the starting version.

We could, of course, manually change the file to be the same as the starting version, but we can use the built-in functionality in SourceSafe to do just that.

There are two approaches to undo version changes depending on the history we need to keep:

- Getting older versions
- Rolling back changes

Getting Older Versions

When we need to undo version changes, while keeping those changes in the history, we will need to retrieve the older version we want to revert to and start the new changes from there. In order to do that we must:

1. Check out the current version manually
2. Get the older version we want to revert to
3. Check in the older version as a newer version

To check out the current version manually, we can right-click the file in the **Solution Explorer** window and use the **Check Out for Edit** command.

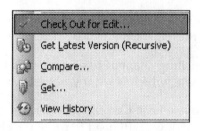

After checking out the file we use the **View History** command to show the **History** dialog and select the version we want to get.

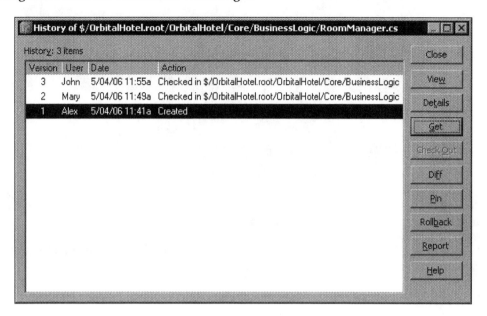

I will select version **1** and click on the **Get** button. Visual Source Safe will display the **Get** dialog.

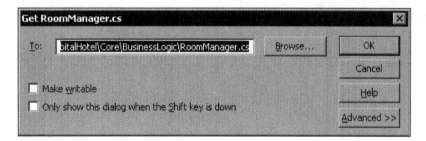

The **Get** dialog shows where the specific file version will be placed along with several options. By default the path in the **To** text box points to the file in our workspace, which is what we want.

The **Make writable** option gets the file and then marks it as writable, which is not recommended in this scenario when the file is already under Source Control. This option is useful when we are getting the file version in places other than our workspace for reasons like reference purposes and we want the file to be writable.

I will leave the settings as default and click the **OK** button. SourceSafe will detect that the file is previously checked out and ask what to do with the version we are getting.

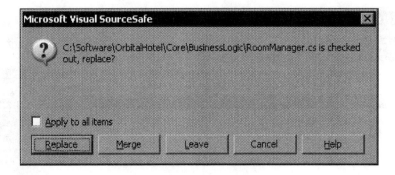

Since I want to retrieve the old version into my workspace, I will choose **Replace**. SourceSafe gets the older version and *overwrites* the one in the workspace.

Now that I have the older base version, all I have to do is check in this version and obtain a new version that is identical to the old one.

We can see this in the **History** dialog:

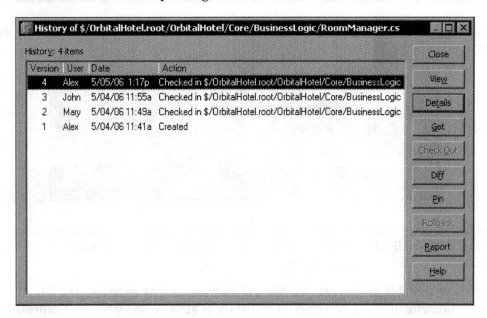

Just to make sure I have an identical version, I can select the older version I got earlier (in this case *version 1*) and click the **Diff** button, so that it will show the **Difference Options** dialog we saw earlier in the *Comparing File Versions* section. This will compare the selected version (*version 1*) and the workspace version (*version 4*).

After clicking **OK** in the **Difference Options** dialog, we can see, sure enough, that the two file versions are identical.

In this case, I've reverted to a previous file version while keeping the other versions in the file's history. If this is not a requirement, we can undo the changes to the base version by **rolling back** the changes.

Rolling Back Changes

Rolling back the changes made to a file means returning the file to a previous version and irretrievably undoing all the changes made after that.

I will use the **View History** command again, to show the **History** dialog and select version **1** as the starting point.

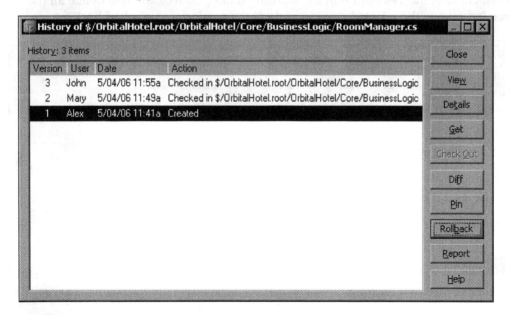

I will then click on the **Rollback** button on the right side of the dialog:

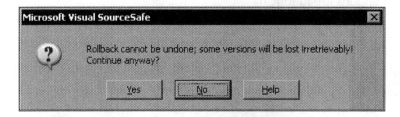

Visual SourceSafe warns about the fact that the rolling back operation will cause the versions after the selected version to be lost.

Rolling back the changes to a file will permanently remove all the versions above the selected rolled back version, causing all the changes made after that to be lost. This operation cannot be undone after it completes and is permanent. Use the rolling back operation with caution when you are sure you can safely remove all the versions after the rolled back version.

After clicking the **Yes** button in the warning dialog, SourceSafe will delete all the versions above the selected version and get the version we've rolled back to.

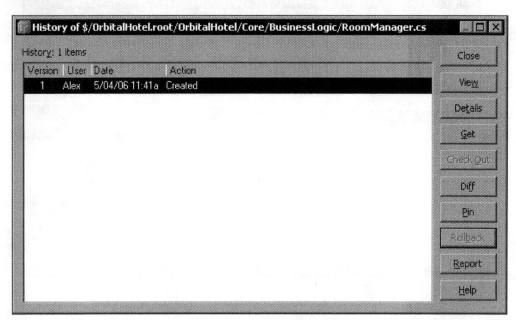

Now that we've undone the changes made while using the Exclusive Check-Out Model, we are ready to re-implement them, this time using the Multiple Check-Out model.

The Multiple Check-Out Model

Before digging deeper into the Multiple Check-Out Model, it's very important to state the following note:

Multiple checkouts are available by default only for files that contain plain text—text files. Binary files cannot be checked out by multiple users and they will always behave as in the exclusive mode. This is because binary files cannot be *merged* using default text file tools. However, custom merge tools can be configured for text and binary files as well. For more information please refer to the additional material provided online at http://www.packtpub.com/visual-sourcesafe-2005/book.

To begin using the Multiple Check-Out Model, it must first be activated.

In Visual SourceSafe 2005 the check-out model is set per database. The check-out model is set using the Visual SourceSafe Administrator application. For more information about setting the check-out model please see the Changing the Team Version Control Model section in Appendix C.

Because the Visual SourceSafe plug-ins for Visual Studio read the configuration information when opening the solution, changes made to the database configuration afterwards do not take effect until the solution is reopened.

When making changes to the SourceSafe database configuration, close and reopen any solution for the changes to take effect.

This is necessary because if the model is changed while the developers are using the old one, subsequent check out by these developers will still use the old model.

So, after Mary and John reopen their solutions they will begin to re-implement their methods. Let's say that Mary is again the first to start working. She will open the `RoomManager.cs` file and start typing to implement the **GetAllRooms** method. As in the case of the Exclusive Check-Out Model, Visual Studio will automatically check out the file for editing.

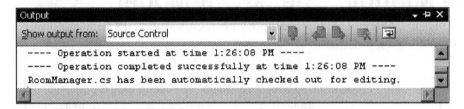

While Mary does her work, John wants to do his too. He will open the `RoomManager.cs` file and start typing to implement the **UpdateRooms** method. As in Mary's case, Visual Studio will try to perform an automatic file check out. It will detect the file is checked out to another user but, because now the Multiple Check-Out Model is activated, it knows it can successfully perform the check-out operation. However, by default, it leaves the decision to continue with the check-out operation to the user:

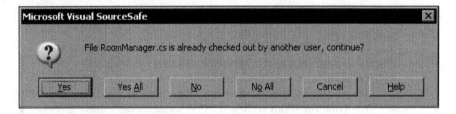

If John decides not to check out the file, and clicks the **No** button, the check-out operation will be canceled.

If John decides to check out the file anyway and clicks the **Yes** button, the check-out operation will succeed. Now he can start implementing his method too, without having to wait for Mary to finish her changes to the file.

While John implements his changes, Mary finishes implementing hers. Her file version will look like the following:

```
/// <summary>
/// Gets all the rooms in the database
/// </summary>
/// <remarks>If the rooms parameter is not null, this method will
/// fill this object
/// with room information and return it, otherwise a new
/// RoomDataTable object
```

```
/// will be created and returned</remarks>
/// <param name="rooms">A RoomDataTable object to be filed with room
/// information.
/// If this is null, a new RoomDataTable will be created and
/// returned</param>
/// <returns>A RoomDataTable containing all rooms in the
/// database</returns>
public RoomDS.RoomDataTable GetAllRooms(RoomDS.RoomDataTable rooms)
{
    RoomDS.RoomDataTable rdt = (rooms != null ? rooms : new
                                RoomDS.RoomDataTable());
    DataAccess.RoomTableAdapters.RoomTableAdapter rta =
        new OrbitalHotel.DataAccess.RoomTableAdapters.
                                            RoomTableAdapter();
    rta.Fill(rdt);
    return rdt;
}

/// <summary>
/// Updates the room database with the information in the room
/// parameter
/// </summary>
/// <param name="rooms">The RoomDataTable object containing
/// the information to be updated</param>
public void UpdateRooms(RoomDS.RoomDataTable rooms)
{
    throw new System.NotImplementedException();
}
```

She makes sure the solution, builds successfully, and checks in the file.

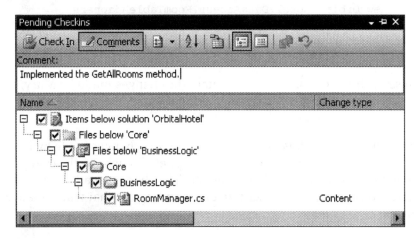

Meanwhile John finishes his changes too. His file version will look like the following:

```
/// <summary>
/// Gets all the rooms in the database
/// </summary>
/// <remarks>If the rooms parameter is not null, this method will
/// fill this object
/// with room information and return it, otherwise a new
/// RoomDataTable object
/// will be created and returned</remarks>
/// <param name="rooms">A RoomDataTable object to be filed with room
/// information.
/// If this is null, a new RoomDataTable will be created and
/// returned</param>
/// <returns>A RoomDataTable containing all rooms in the
/// database</returns>
public RoomDS.RoomDataTable GetAllRooms(RoomDS.RoomDataTable rooms)
{
    throw new System.NotImplementedException();
}


/// <summary>
/// Updates the room database with the information in the room
/// parameter
/// </summary>
/// <param name="rooms">The RoomDataTable object containing
/// the information to be updated</param>
public void UpdateRooms(RoomDS.RoomDataTable rooms)
{
    DataAccess.RoomTableAdapters.RoomTableAdapter rta =
        new OrbitalHotel.DataAccess.RoomTableAdapters.
                                        RoomTableAdapter();
    rta.Update(rooms);
}
```

As we can see, John's version does not contain the changes made by Mary, because he started working while Mary was still making them. Although she already has them checked in, they are not yet present in John's file version.

If John checks in the file as it is, this will overwrite the changes made by Mary. Fortunately, SourceSafe doesn't allow this to happen. Somehow, the changes made by Mary will have to be made in John's file too. The changes made in both the files will have to be **merged** together into one resulting file that will contain all these changes.

Merging Changes

When using the Multiple Check-Out Model, a text file can be checked out by more than one user at a time. When this happens, changes made by each user must be *merged* before a user can perform a check in on that file, to ensure that no changes are lost and the solution can still be built successfully.

By default, SourceSafe takes care of these merges automatically when it can, without any special operations from our end. However, automatically doesn't mean that it will always be the best solution. SourceSafe doesn't know C# or VB or whatever language we are using to develop our solutions. It will merge the changes strictly as text, leaving the responsibility for making sure the code in the file will still function properly after the merge on us.

Without any more details for now, let's see how John can check in his file version. He has several options:

- **Merge on check in**: Check in the file and leave SourceSafe to do the automatic merging without verifying the resulting file version.
- **Merge then check in**: Let SourceSafe to do the automatic merging, then verify that the resulting file version compiles successfully, and then check in the file.
- **Merge by getting the latest version**: Initiate the automatic merge manually, verify the resulting file version compiles successfully, and then perform the check in.

Merge on Check In

After finishing his changes, John makes sure the solution builds successfully, writes his check-in comment, and clicks the **Check in** command button; nothing out of the ordinary so far. Behind the scenes, however, SourceSafe detects that meanwhile Mary has checked in a new version for the file, which contains new changes not present in John's file. By default, it will attempt to automatically merge the two file versions. In this case it will succeed without *conflicts* (we will talk about merging conflicts later in this chapter).

After finishing the automatic merge, SourceSafe displays a dialog informing John about this.

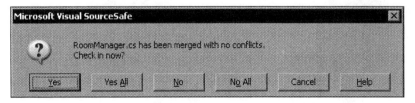

John acknowledges the automatic merge and clicks the **Yes** button. SourceSafe checks in the file that now contains both the changes made by both John and Mary.

```csharp
/// <summary>
/// Gets all the rooms in the database
/// </summary>
/// <remarks>If the rooms parameter is not null, this method will
/// fill this object
/// with room information and return it, otherwise a new
/// RoomDataTable object
/// will be created and returned</remarks>
/// <param name="rooms">A RoomDataTable object to be filed with room
/// information.
/// If this is null, a new RoomDataTable will be created and
/// returned</param>
/// <returns>A RoomDataTable containing all rooms in the
/// database</returns>
public RoomDS.RoomDataTable GetAllRooms(RoomDS.RoomDataTable rooms)
{
    RoomDS.RoomDataTable rdt = (rooms != null ? rooms : new
                                RoomDS.RoomDataTable());
    DataAccess.RoomTableAdapters.RoomTableAdapter rta =
        new OrbitalHotel.DataAccess.RoomTableAdapters.
                                                RoomTableAdapter();
    rta.Fill(rdt);
    return rdt;
}


/// <summary>
/// Updates the room database with the information in the room
/// parameter
/// </summary>
/// <param name="rooms">The RoomDataTable object containing
/// the information to be updated</param>
public void UpdateRooms(RoomDS.RoomDataTable rooms)
{
    DataAccess.RoomTableAdapters.RoomTableAdapter rta =
        new OrbitalHotel.DataAccess.RoomTableAdapters.
                                                RoomTableAdapter();
    rta.Update(rooms);
}
```

At this stage he cannot tell if the code in the resulting merged file can be built without errors. And on top of that, it is already checked in to the SourceSafe database. If the code cannot be successfully compiled, now, the SourceSafe database contains a broken solution. Anyone getting the latest solution version will get a non-working solution that stops them from making further builds.

This is not a good practice. In fact it's a bad practice.

Best Practice

Always verify the contents of the merged file before checking it in to the SourceSafe database. This will ensure that you don't break the solution from building successfully and affect other developers.

To follow the best practice, John will have to first verify if the solution can be successfully built.

This brings us to the second option for doing the file merge.

Merge then Check In

The second option begins like the first one. After finishing his changes, John makes sure the solution builds successfully, writes his check-in comment, and clicks the **Check in** command button. SourceSafe detects that meanwhile Mary has checked in a new version for the file, which contains new changes not present in John's file. SourceSafe automatically merges the two file versions. After finishing the automatic merge, SourceSafe displays the same dialog informing John about this.

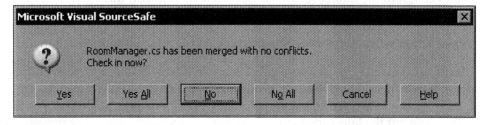

Only this time, John will click the **No** button, *preventing* the resulting merged file from being checked in. In this way, he will have the flexibility to first test the resulting version. If required, he will make the necessary changes to ensure the solution builds successfully. After that, he can safely check in the merged version.

The second option follows the best practice not to check in an automatically merged file without verifying it first and is highly recommended.

Merge by Getting the Latest Version

The third option is to manually initiate the file merge without clicking on the **Check in** command button first. To do that, instead of checking in the file, John will perform a **Get Latest Version** command on it. Because the file is currently checked out, when getting the latest version, SourceSafe will prompt a dialog for the action to be taken:

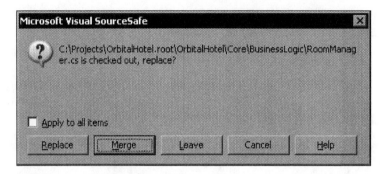

He can choose from the following three actions:

- **Replace**
- **Merge**
- **Leave**

The **Replace** action will overwrite the changes made to the local workspace file with the latest version in the database. This is not what he wants in this case as all his work will be overwritten without the possibility of undoing it.

The **Leave** action will leave the local workspace file as it is, without any changes.

The **Merge** action is the one of interest. Clicking on **Merge** will perform an automatic file merge between the latest version in the database and the local version in our workspace. This way we are able to see if other developers have made changes to the file since we've got the latest file version. We can resolve any issues that prevent the code in the merged file from compiling successfully before checking it in.

Best Practice

When possible, avoid keeping a file checked out for longer periods of time than necessary.

Sometimes, however, for one reason or another we cannot follow the best practice and we must keep one or more files checked out for long periods of time. The longer a file is checked out while using the Multiple Check-Out Model, the more the probability that it will be changed by other developers.

Best Practice:

By periodically getting the latest versions and merging the new changes in our local workspace file, we can gradually incorporate new changes and avoid one big merge at the end, which can be more difficult.

As more and more changes are made to the file in the database while we keep it checked out for long periods of time, the possibility of **merge conflicts** increases.

Merge Conflicts

Merge conflicts appear when changes made by other developers overlap the changes in the workspace file.

To show an example, let's consider the following scenario. While John is writing the code to implement the **UpdateRooms** method, I choose to modify it to return instead of void, the number of rooms successfully updated in the database. So I will check out the file and make changes as shown below:

```
/// <summary>
/// Updates the room database with the information in the room
/// parameter
/// </summary>
/// <param name="rooms">The RoomDataTable object containing
/// the information to be updated</param>
public void UpdateRooms(RoomDS.RoomDataTable rooms)
{
    throw new System.NotImplementedException();
}
```

The modified file lines are as follows:

```
/// <summary>
/// Updates the room database with the information in the room
/// parameter
/// </summary>
/// <param name="rooms">The RoomDataTable object containing
/// the information to be updated</param>
public int UpdateRooms(RoomDS.RoomDataTable rooms)
{
    throw new System.NotImplementedException();
    return -1;
}
```

After these changes, I will check in the file.

John finishes his changes and wants to check in his file too. His changes look like this:

```
/// <summary>
/// Updates the room database with the information in the room
/// parameter
/// </summary>
/// <param name="rooms">The RoomDataTable object containing
/// the information to be updated</param>
public void UpdateRooms(RoomDS.RoomDataTable rooms)
{
    DataAccess.RoomTableAdapters.RoomTableAdapter rta =
        new OrbitalHotel.DataAccess.RoomTableAdapters.
                                            RoomTableAdapter();
    rta.Update(rooms);
}
```

As I've checked in the previous changes before him, SourceSafe will try to make an automatic merge between the latest database version checked in by me and John's local workspace version. This time, however, it is unable to do so, because both of us have made changes to the same file lines—the **UpdateRooms** function. This results in a **merge conflict**.

Being unable to automatically merge the file, SourceSafe will ask John to select how he wants to continue by displaying the *three-way merge tool*:

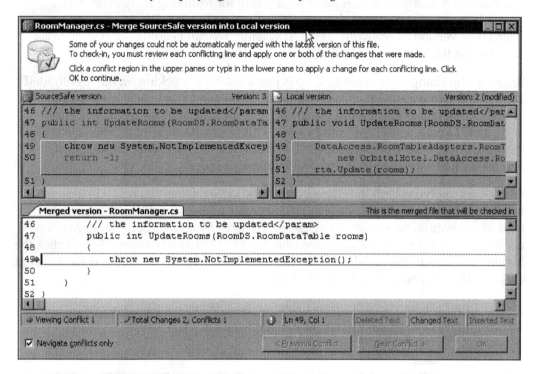

This tool helps to visually merge the SourceSafe database version into the local version by providing three windows:

- **SourceSafe version**
- **Local version**
- **Merged version**

The **SourceSafe version** window shows the last file version in the database — the file I've checked in previously is now at version 3.

The **Local version** window shows the local file version in John's workspace, the file that contains his changes. This file started from version 2.

The **Merged version** window shows the base file version, the common ancestor for both **SourceSafe version** and the **Local version**. This is the resulting file from the merge.

As we can see the conflict zone is highlighted in both the **SourceSafe version** and **Local version** windows.

Let's see how merge conflicts are resolved.

Resolving Merge Conflicts

The three-way merge tool provides an easy way for resolving merge conflicts. To resolve a conflict we must choose which changes to keep. We can keep the SourceSafe version overwriting the local version, we can keep the local version overwriting the SourceSafe version, or we can keep both changes.

Selecting the changes we want to keep is just a matter of clicking on the highlighted areas in the two windows. To keep the SourceSafe version we must click the area in the **SourceSafe version** window, to keep the local version we must click the area in the **Local version** window, and to keep both, we must click on the areas in both the windows. To deselect an area we must click it again. The selected areas will automatically be inserted in the **Merged version** window.

Sometimes applying both the changes from the upper panes can result in a merged text that cannot be compiled directly. In that case, manually editing the conflict zone in the bottom pane after applying the changes from the upper panes may be necessary. In John's case, he will keep only his local version changes. He will click the highlighted area in the **Local version** window. The merge tool will insert the selected changes into the **Merged version** window.

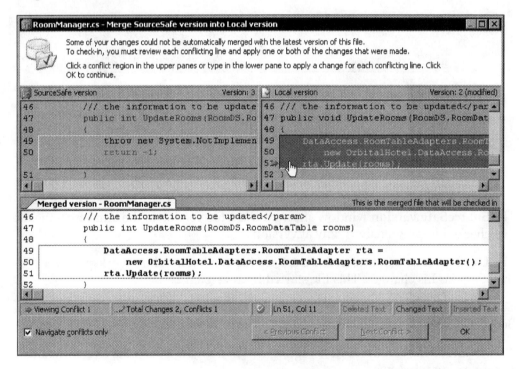

After selecting the changes, clicking on the **OK** button will close the merge tool and display the following dialog to confirm that all the conflicts have been resolved and to ask if the resulting merged file can be saved:

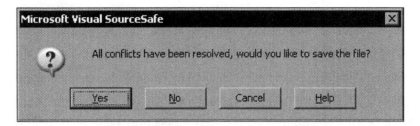

Clicking the **Yes** button will save the merged file locally in the workspace.

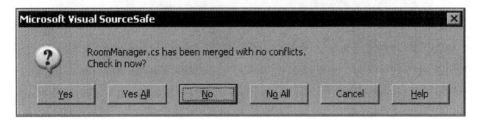

John will have to make sure that the code compiles successfully. Because I've changed the `UpdateRooms` function to return an integer result and John's code doesn't return any value, he will get a compile error.

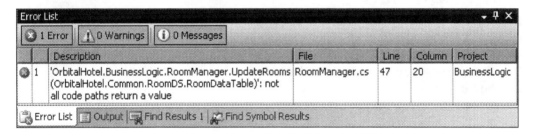

He will have to change his code accordingly for the changes to be complete and functional. (By the way, I told John verbally what the method should return so he would know what value to return, because I was too lazy to put it in the method's comments. Don't follow my example on this one.)

```
/// <summary>
/// Updates the room database with the information in the room
/// parameter
/// </summary>
```

```
/// <param name="rooms">The RoomDataTable object containing
/// the information to be updated</param>
public int UpdateRooms(RoomDS.RoomDataTable rooms)
{
    DataAccess.RoomTableAdapters.RoomTableAdapter rta =
        new OrbitalHotel.DataAccess.RoomTableAdapters.
                                                RoomTableAdapter();
    return rta.Update(rooms);
}
```

After resolving the conflict and reintegrating his changes, he can safely check in the new file to the SourceSafe database. SourceSafe asks him again if the conflicts have been properly resolved.

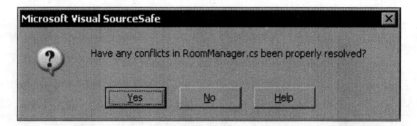

Sure enough, this time John can safely check in the file by clicking **Yes**.

Pinning Files

In certain situations we may need to use a previous file version to build or test our projects. We could get that specific version but this would not stop unaware team members from checking out the file and making additional changes to it. For this or for other purposes SourceSafe provides file **pins**. To pin a file to a specific version we use the **Pin** button in the file's history.

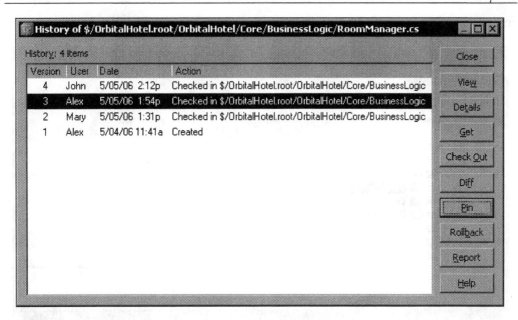

We select the specific version we want to pin the file to and click the **Pin** button. The file is pinned to that specific version and the **Pin** button turns into **Unpin**. We will use this button to later unpin the file.

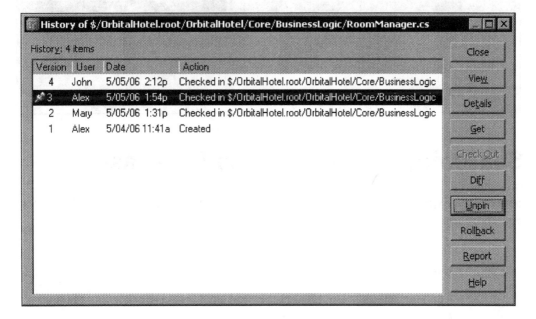

In the **Visual SourceSafe Explorer** we can see pinned files, which have a **pin** icon.

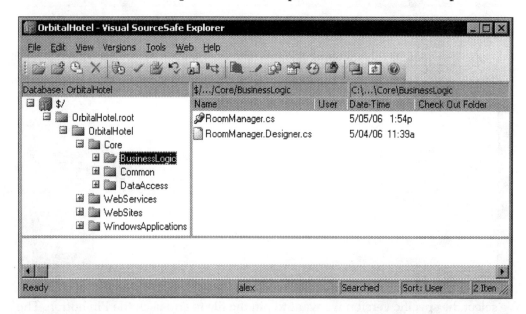

Pinned files cannot be further checked out until they are unpinned.

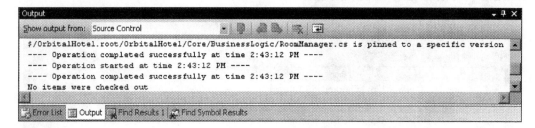

Searching for Files in the Database

If we need to search for certain files in the database, we can use the **Visual SourceSafe Explorer**'s search functions. We can find these functions in the **View | Search** menu.

Visual SourceSafe Explorer offers two search functions:

- **Wildcard Search**
- **Status Search**

Wildcard Search

The **Wildcard Search** function allows us to search for files using wildcards. Using the **Wildcard Search** command displays the **Search for Wildcard** dialog.

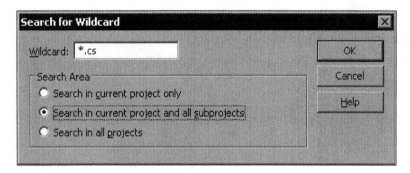

We specify the wildcard in the **Wildcard** text box and we can also specify a search area. We can search the currently selected project, the currently selected project and subprojects, or search the entire database.

This activates the *search mode*. In the search mode we can select different projects to filter their files and view the ones matching the specified wildcard. In this example, I chose to view the *.cs files recursively.

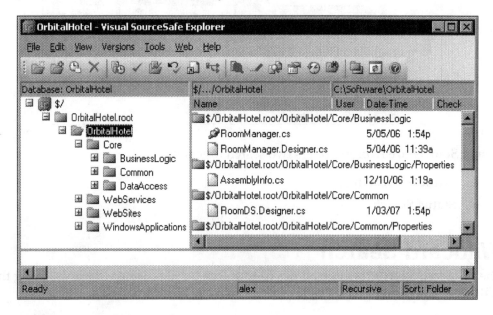

Status Search

The **Wildcard Search** function allows us to search for files that are checked out. Using the **Status Search** command displays the **Search for Status** dialog.

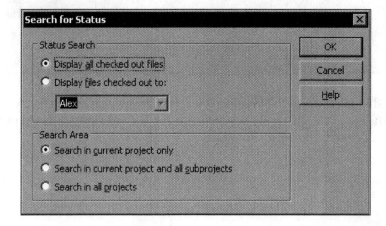

We can choose to the view all the checked out files or filter them by a specific user. The same search areas can be specified here also.

Canceling the Search Mode

After finishing the search, we must cancel the search mode and return to the default file view using the **Cancel Search** command.

Sharing Files

Sometimes we have one or more files that we need to keep in different projects but we want them to remain the same in all of them. The solution to such cases is to share a file between multiple projects. Changing one file will cause it to change in all the places it is shared.

One such case can be the strong name file we use to sign our assemblies. In this example I need the same file to sign all the assemblies.

I've added the `OrbitalHotel.snk` file at solution level but I want to keep it in the projects also.

SourceSafe provides the **Share** function for such cases. Depending on the client application we can share files using the Visual Studio LAN or internet plug-in or the Visual SourceSafe Explorer.

Using Visual Studio with the LAN Plug-In

To share a file using the LAN plug-in, we have to select first the **destination** folder. After selecting the destination folder we can use the **Share** command in the **Source Control** toolbar.

Using the **Share** command displays the **Share to** dialog:

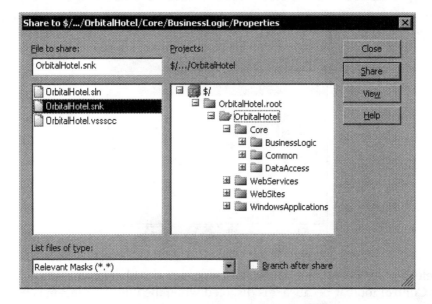

In the **Share to** dialog we select the project that contains the file we want to share from (on the right side) and select the file to share (on the left side). To share the file, click the **Share** button. This will share the selected file in the destination folder.

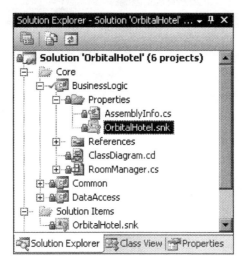

Using Visual Studio with the Internet Plug-In

To share a file using the internet plug-in, we have to first select the **destination** folder or project.

After selecting the destination folder we cannot use the **Share** command from the **Source Control** toolbar because it is disabled when the internet plug-in is being used. However, we can still use the share functionality by using the **Add | Existing Item** command.

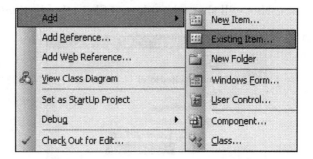

This will display the **Add Existing Item** dialog. Use the **SourceSafe (Internet)** button and browse the SourceSafe database for the file you want to share.

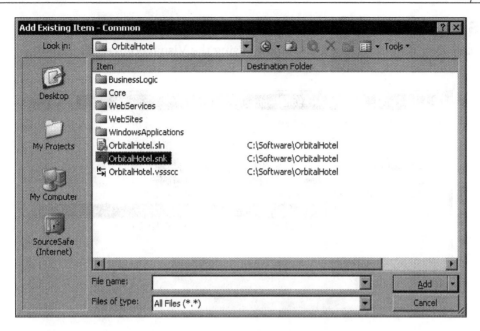

Select the file you want to share and click the **Add** button. This will display the following message dialog:

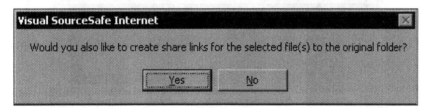

Click **Yes** to add the selected file to the destination project so as to share it.

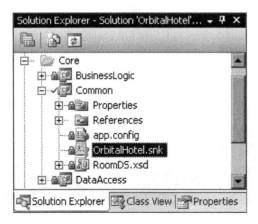

Using Visual SourceSafe Explorer

We can view files that are already shared using the Visual SourceSafe Explorer.
Shared files have an icon with a shortcut.

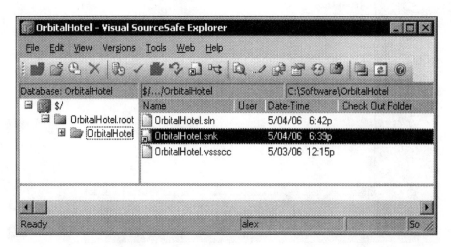

We can also view all the projects that share this file by looking at the file's **Properties**
and selecting the **Links** tab.

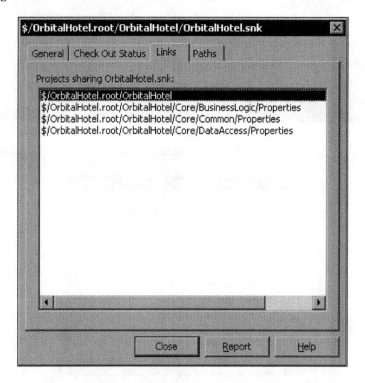

There are two ways of sharing files using Visual SourceSafe Explorer although this is not recommended because Visual Studio will be unaware of these changes. However, we can include these files in their project manually in Visual Studio later.

The first method is to select the **destination** project:

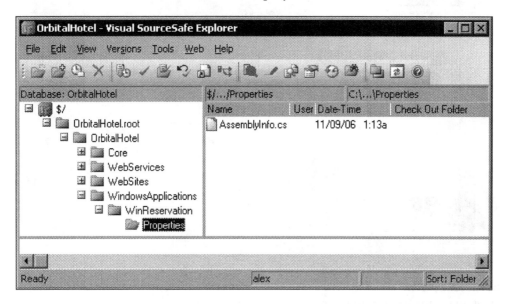

After selecting the destination project we use the **Share to** command in the **Versions** menu.

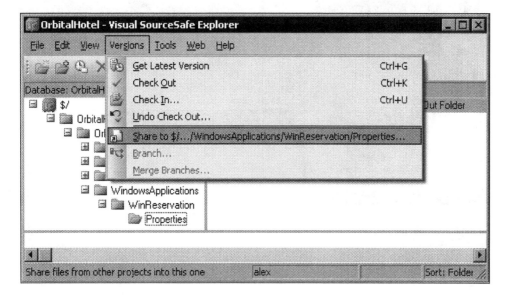

Then we select the file we want to share in the **Share to** dialog and click **Share**.

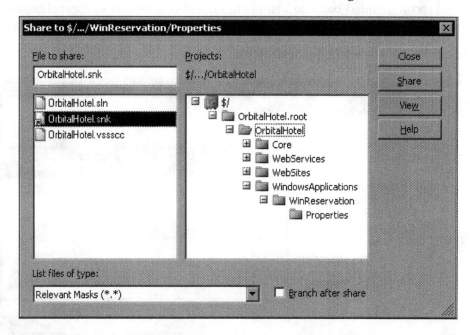

The second method is simpler as it involves a drag and drop operation. We drag the file we want to share from the *source* project and drop it onto the *destination* project.

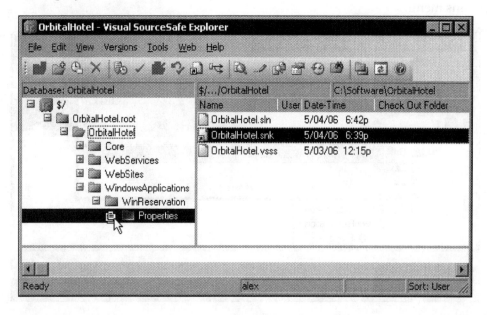

To integrate the changes with Visual Studio we have to get the latest file version using Visual SourceSafe Explorer, then display all the project files in Visual Studio by selecting the project and using the **Show All Files** command.

Then, we must select the shared file and use the **Include In Project** command from its context menu.

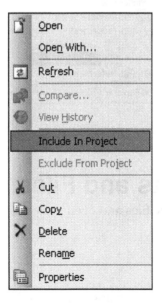

Visual Studio will try to add it to Source Control and it will detect that the file already exists (because we added it manually in SourceSafe Explorer).

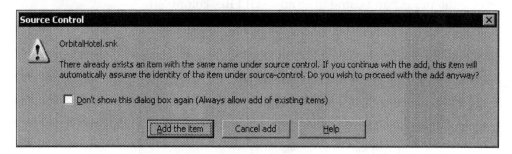

Click **Add the item** to add the item to the project.

Now we can verify the solution builds successfully and check in the changes.

Moving Projects and Files

When necessary, we can move files and even projects, although moving entire projects in not recommended.

Moving Files

The best way for moving files is by using Visual Studio. To move a file we use a drag and drop operation. We drag the file from its source project folder and drop it onto the destination project or folder. In this example I will move the `OrbitalHotel.snk` file from the **Properties** folder into the project's folder:

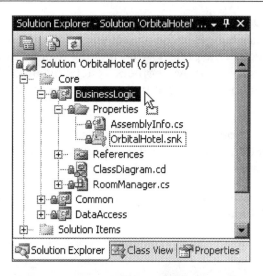

Visual Studio detects the operation and displays the following dialog:

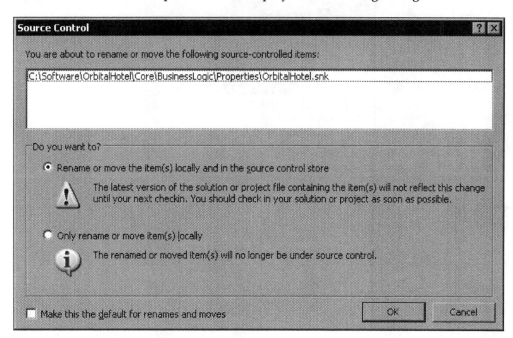

This dialog presents us with two options:

- **Rename or move the item(s) locally and in the source control store**
- **Only rename or move item(s) locally**

Choosing the first option will move the file both locally and in the SourceSafe database. However, the changes to the project will not be available to other team members until we check in the project. After moving files we have to check in the changes as soon as possible to prevent others from being affected by the fact that the file(s) no longer exist in the database at their previous locations breaking the solution in the database.

Choosing the second option will only move the file locally. This, however, will remove the file from Source Control until we check in the changes. We will also have to manually delete the file from the old location in the SourceSafe database.

In this case I'm going to use the first option. The file will be moved both locally and in the SourceSafe database.

After I check in the changes, when other team members get the new project version, they will see the following dialog:

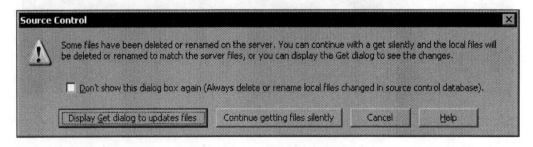

This dialog informs them that files were moved in the database and their local workspaces will have to be updated with these changes. Clicking **Continue getting files silently** will perform these changes without other notifications.

Clicking the default **Display Get dialog to updates files** displays the **Get** dialog.

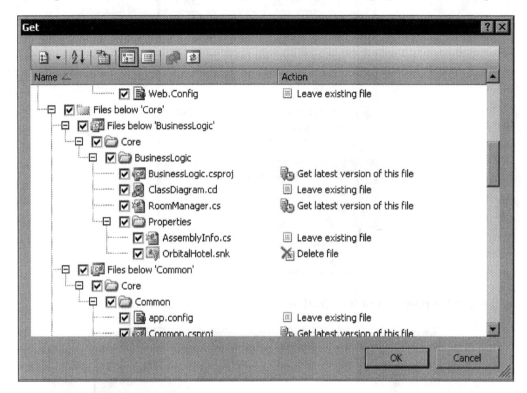

In this dialog we can see the changes about to be performed to the workspace. We can cancel the changes using the **Cancel** button or we can go ahead with the changes by using the **OK** button.

Moving Projects

To move projects in the SourceSafe database we use the Visual SourceSafe Explorer. To move the currently selected project we use the **File | Move** command.

Best Practice

Before moving projects, archive the current database configuration. Database archives are covered in Appendix C.

I will choose to move the **BusinessLogic** project from under the **Core** project to directly under the **OrbitalHotel** project.

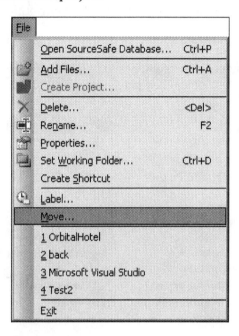

I will select the new parent (**OrbitalHotel** project) in the **Move** dialog.

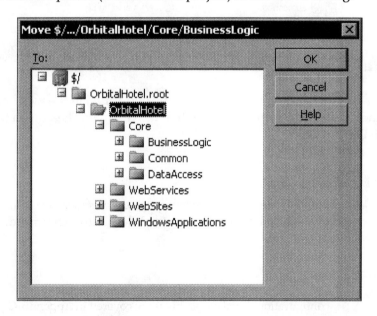

To move the project click **OK**. SourceSafe Explorer displays the new project location.

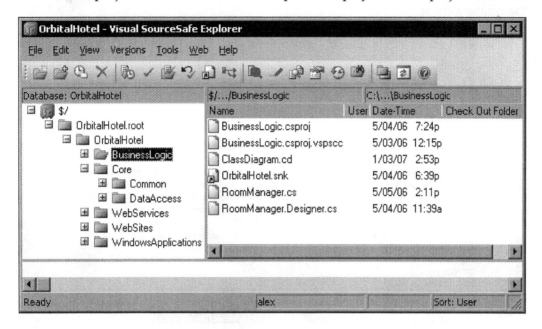

After moving the project in the SourceSafe database, when getting the latest version in Visual Studio, we are presented with the following dialog informing us about the moved files:

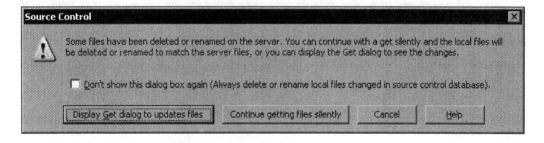

Using the **Display Get dialog to updates files** button displays the **Get** dialog with the pending changes:

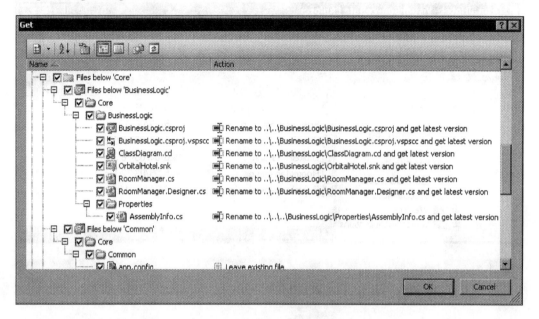

However, Visual Studio is not able to synchronize the changes because it doesn't know where the new location for the moved project is.

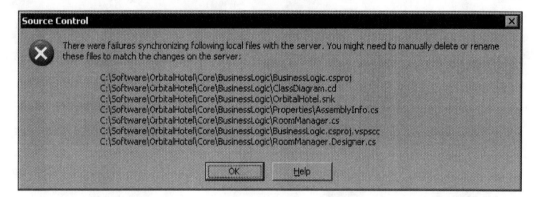

We have to synchronise the changes manually by rebinding the project to the database.

Rebinding to the Database

To rebind projects to the database we can use the **Change Source Control** command
from the **Source Control** toolbar in Visual Studio.

This will display the **Change Source Control** dialog.

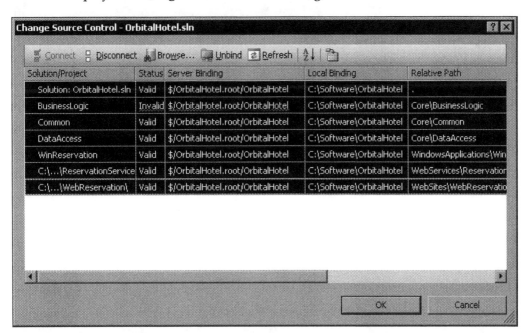

In this dialog we can see the projects that are not correctly bound to the database. In my case the **BusinessLogic** project is invalid because it was moved in the database and it no longer corresponds to the **Core\BusinessLogic** relative path.

To correct invalid bindings, we have to first unbind all the projects that use the same binding root as the invalid project and then rebind them using the correct paths. Projects using the same binding root are selected together in the list.

In my case all the projects use the same binding root so I will have to unbind all of them using the **Unbind** command.

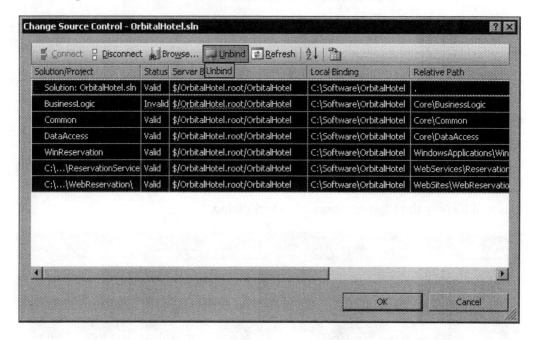

Then I will rebind the **BusinessLogic** project individually using the **Bind** command.

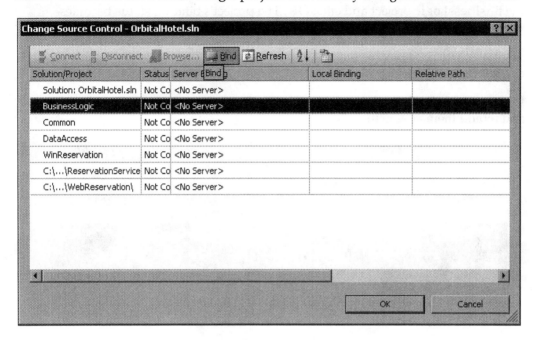

This will display the **Choose project from SourceSafe** dialog.

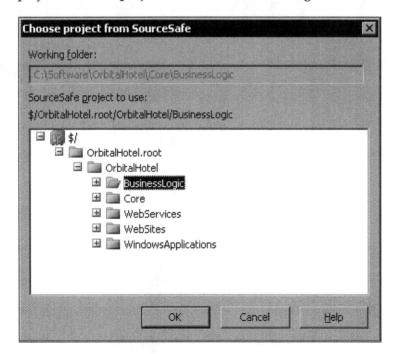

In this dialog we select the new project locations. I will select the new location for the **BusinessLogic** project and click **OK**. The project's binding status becomes valid again.

We have to do the same for the rest of the projects. To rebind multiple projects we can select all of them.

In my case I will select all the remaining projects (because they remained unchanged) and rebind them all together

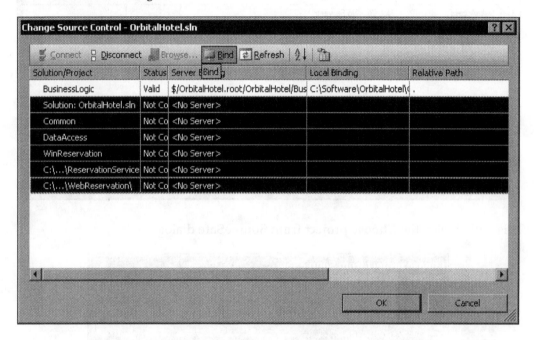

In the **Choose project from SourceSafe** dialog, I will select the original solution project (**OrbitalHotel**) in the database.

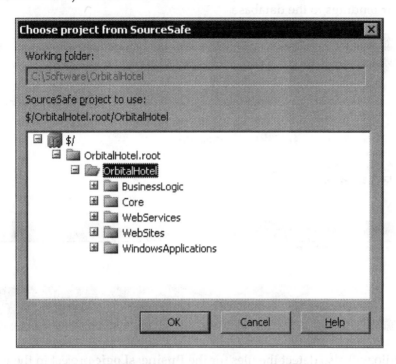

After clicking **OK**, the binding statuses for the projects become valid again.

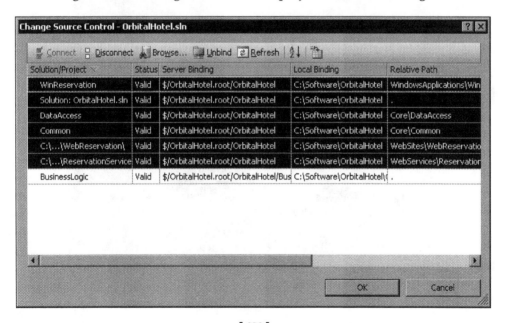

To apply the new bindings to the solution click **OK**, which closes the **Change Source Control** dialog. Visual Studio will check out the solution and the rebound project to change their bindings to the database.

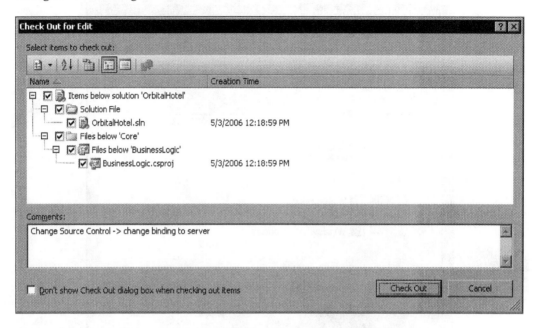

Visual Studio will also detect the files for the **BusinessLogic** project in the local workspace and ask what to do with them.

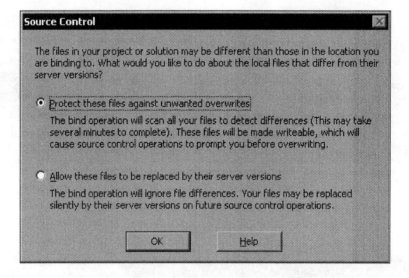

To keep the local files use the first option. To get the latest versions from the database use the second option.

Deleting, Recovering, and Purging Files

When we (think) no longer need a file, we can delete it.

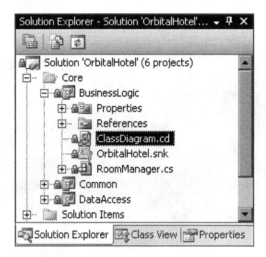

To delete a file use the *delete* key on the keyboard. Visual Studio displays a warning message telling us the file will be deleted permanently.

It will also display the following dialog asking whether to delete the file both locally and in the SourceSafe database or only locally:

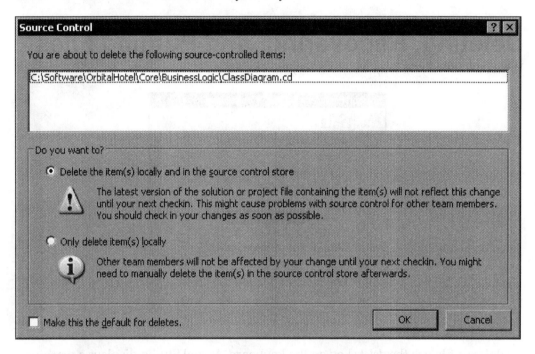

To delete the file in both locations select the first option. We will have to make sure we check in the changes as soon as possible so as to not affect the other users that will not find the file in the database anymore, preventing the previous solution version in the database from building.

To delete the file only locally, we use the second option. When using this option we will have to delete the file manually in the database later.

The file will be deleted permanently from the local workspace (actually put in the Recycle Bin) but it will *not* be permanently deleted from the SourceSafe database, although it will not be visible anymore. The file will be kept in the database and it can be recovered at a later time if our initial thought wasn't that inspired and it turned out we still need the file.

To view the deleted files for a certain project, we can display its properties in the Visual SourceSafe Explorer. We can see the deleted items in the **Deleted Items** tab:

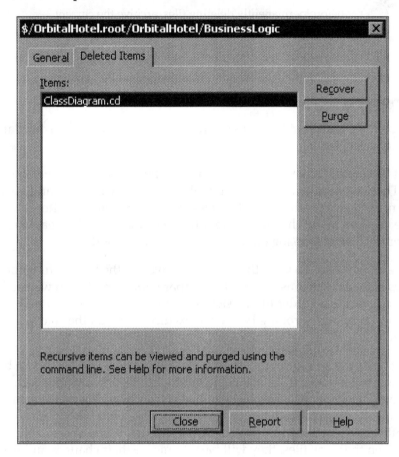

From here, we can recover deleted files by selecting them and using the **Recover** button.

We can also purge deleted files to free database space when we are *really* sure we don't need them anymore by using the **Purge** button.

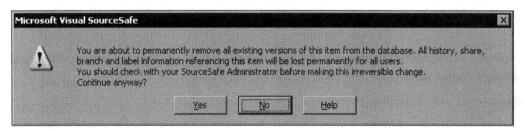

Best Practice

Before permanently deleting files, archive the current database configuration in case you ever need them. Database archives are covered in Appendix C.

Summary

In this chapter, we looked at the source control operations we use in our daily development activities.

We started by creating a new workspace and got the solution from the SourceSafe database. Then we started development on the solution by creating and visually designing new classes for the Orbital Hotel's room management. After finishing the design, we checked in the changes to the solution so that the other team members can see them and start working on implementing the methods.

Files evolve across time. To view their evolution we use the history functions. To see the changes between versions we use the compare functions. When we need to undo changes and revert to an older file version, we can to so by creating a new version containing old contents or rolling back changes discarding all the changes in between.

Depending on our team requirements and our coding style we can choose between the two check-out models. If we need a more strict development approach, we use the Exclusive Check-Out Model to prevent users from working on the same file at the same time. If we can afford a more relaxed approach but with more chances for merge conflicts, we use the Multiple Check-Out Model. When users using this model work on the same files, they will have to merge their changes and verify them before checking them in. When merge conflicts appear they need to resolve them accordingly.

Towards the end we've seen how to search for files in the database and how to share files across multiple projects. Shared files are useful when we need the same file in multiple places. Changing one file will change it in all the projects it is a part of.

We've also examined the more "destructive" commands such as moving, deleting, and purging projects and files. Before using such commands it is always a good practice to back up the database, in case something goes wrong and we need the data back at a later time.

6
Working from Remote Locations

While most of the time the development process is conducted from the local development site, sometimes situations where we need to work from remote locations arise.

To be able to work *online* from other locations, we need a way to access the SourceSafe server through the intranet or the Internet, in order to perform our source control tasks.

If we don't have an internet connection at the remote location, or if the local SourceSafe server is temporarily down, we can work *offline*, provided we already have the solution files on our remote machine. When a connection to the database becomes available again, we reconnect to the SourceSafe database and synchronize the changes. Depending on the database configuration and the Visual Studio plug-ins we use while reconnecting, there are some scenarios to consider for avoiding data loss. We will examine the possible scenarios that can lead to data loss and see how to avoid such situations.

Working Online

If we have an internet connection at the remote location, we have several ways to remotely connect to a SourceSafe database as follows:

- **Native HTTP(S) access**
- **Virtual Private Network (VPN)** connection
- **Third-party** solutions

Using the Native HTTP(S) Access

Visual SourceSafe 2005 has native HTTP(S) access by using the built-in XML web service.

> The native HTTP(S) access is available only when using the Visual SourceSafe internet plug-in with Visual Studio or any other Integrated Development Environment that supports the source control (MSSCCI) plug-ins for SourceSafe.

For more information about installing and configuring this web service please refer to Appendixes A and B.

By default, clients using the Visual Studio SourceSafe internet plug-in connect through the Internet using an encrypted SSL connection to the XML web service interface. The internet plug-in is optimized for low speed connections.

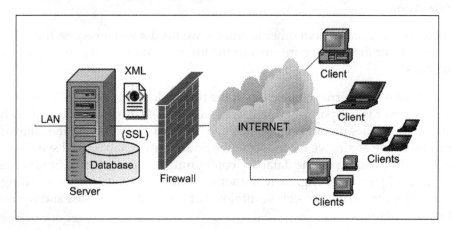

Connecting to the Database

To connect to the SourceSafe database over the Internet please see the *Adding the Database over the Internet* section under *Adding the Database to the Database List* and the *Using Visual Studio with the Internet plug-in* section under *Opening the Database* in Chapter 4.

If you already have the solution on the local machine, it is advisable to open the solution directly from the local disk using **File | Open | Project/Solution | My Computer** and using the local path to the solution.

If you choose to open the solution directly from the database again, Visual Studio will ask which version to open:

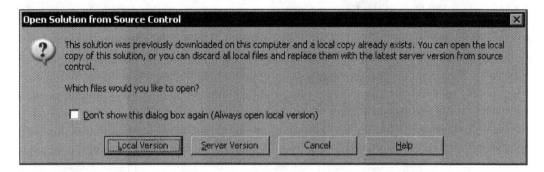

Click **Local Version** to open the version located on the local machine or **Server Version** to replace the solution with the server version.

 Opening the server version will replace the local files. If you have changes that are not checked in (pending changes), then you will lose them.

Visual Studio will open the selected solution and we are ready to work.

Differences from the LAN Plug-In

The SourceSafe internet plug-in doesn't support all the commands in the SourceSafe LAN version. Looking at the **Source Control** menu we can see the disabled commands.

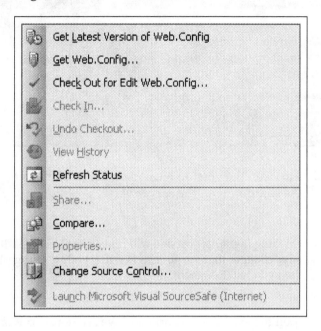

The commands not supported are:

- **View History**
- **Properties**

We cannot see previous versions of a file, or view the SourceSafe file's properties.

The **Share** command, although not enabled in this menu is still available. To share items from other locations in the SourceSafe database, we must use the **Add Existing Item** command. We must then choose the **SourceSafe (Internet)** tab at the bottom left of the dialog, navigate in the SourceSafe database, and select the item we want to share in the current project or solution. For more information on sharing files please see the *Sharing Files* section in Chapter 5.

Using Virtual Private Network (VPN) Access

The Virtual Private Network (VPN) is a connection method over the Internet that allows direct connection to the local network where the SourceSafe server is. The connection establishes a VPN tunnel that connects the clients directly to the local site.

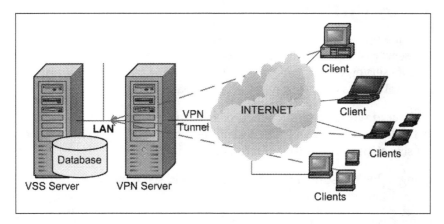

Using a VPN connection allows you to work just like when you are at the local site, using the SourceSafe LAN plug-in and all the SourceSafe tools.

 The VPN connection is affected by the internet connection speed. Low connection speeds affect the source control operations as the LAN clients are not designed to work over slow connections.

Setting up VPN is beyond the scope of this book. For more information contact your local network administrator.

Third-Party Solutions

There are several third-party solutions that allow an alternative to the native remote support such as:

- SourceAnyWhere from DynamSoft (http://www.dynamsoft.com)
- SourceOffSite from SourceGear (http://www.sourcegear.com)
- VSS Remoting from Source Remoting (http://www.sourceremoting.com)
- SourceXT from Accorden (http://www.acorden.com)
- VssConnect from VoxCode (http://www.vssconnect.com)

For a detailed description, you can visit their websites. You can also find more applications providing remote access to SourceSafe databases (including freeware or open source) by searching the Internet.

Working Offline

Working offline is a scenario that can appear at the local development site if the SourceSafe server is temporarily down, at a remote location if we lose connection to the SourceSafe server, or if we use a mobile computer at several locations where we may or may not have a connection to the SourceSafe server.

You should avoid working offline when possible as it can lead to data loss if one is not careful. If, however, you find yourself in this situation, you must consider a number of scenarios in order to avoid the loss of data.

We are going to look at some possible scenarios and see what to do and what no to do in certain situations.

Loosing the LAN Connection to the Database

In this scenario we are working using the SourceSafe LAN plug-in from the local development site. While working, for some reason, the connection to the SourceSafe database becomes unavailable. We need to perform a source control operation, for example, check out a file in order to make some changes. When trying to connect to the database, the SourceSafe LAN plug-in encounters an access error and Visual Studio asks to switch to working offline in **disconnected mode**.

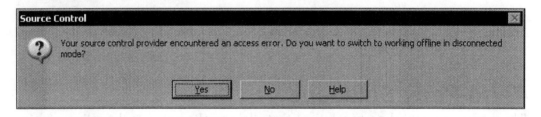

Clicking **No** will cancel the disconnected mode and abort the source control operation with the following error message:

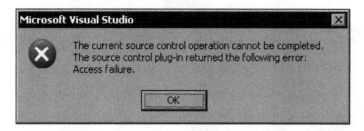

In this situation we can choose to stop any source control commands until the connection is re-established. This is the safest option but keeps us from further changing other files.

If we can't afford to wait until the connection is re-established we can choose to go into the disconnected mode.

We will first cover the scenarios that lead to the disconnected mode and then discuss it in detail.

Starting Work Offline with the LAN Plug-In

This scenario is most likely to occur if we use a mobile computer at several locations. For example, we use it to work online at the local development site and work offline at home or other locations where we cannot connect to the SourceSafe server.

When opening the solution, SourceSafe will be unable to establish a connection to the database. It will ask to open another one.

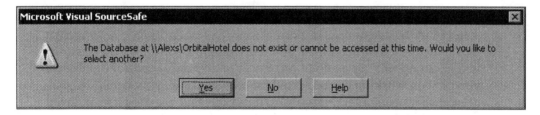

Since we don't have other available databases, we will click **No**. After that, SourceSafe will ask to switch to the internet plug-in and attempt to reconnect using HTTP.

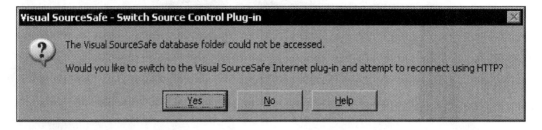

If we have internet access and we can access the SourceSafe server using the SourceSafe web service, we can connect to it by clicking **Yes**. If we don't have this type of access we click **No**. Running out of options, Visual Studio will present the **Unable to Access Database** dialog:

This dialog presents us with the following options:

- **Temporarily work offline in disconnected mode**: This option will open the solution in the disconnected mode. This disconnected mode is temporary, which means that after closing and reopening the solution Visual Studio will automatically try again to reconnect to the source control database. If you plan on working disconnected for a longer time, you should choose to manually change bindings and connections and use the **Disconnected** command in the **Change Source Control** dialog (see below).

- **Permanently remove source control association bindings**: This option will remove all the associations with the SourceSafe database and we will not be able to reconnect to the database until we perform a rebinding.

- **Manually change bindings and connections**: This option will display the **Change Source Control** dialog as shown in the following figure:

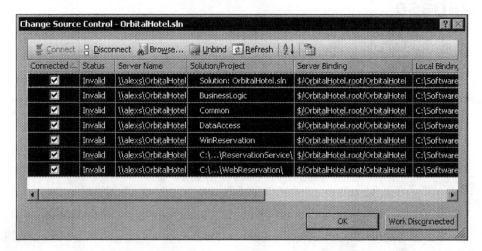

The **Disconnect** command will permanently disconnect the solution from the database, until we manually use the **Connect** command and reconnect to the database.

The **Browse** command allows us to choose another database to open and is equivalent to clicking **Yes** in the first dialog of this scenario. This makes sense only if the connection settings to the database have changed or the database has been moved to another location. Otherwise connecting to a different database makes no sense.

The **Unbind** command will perform the same source control association removal as the second option in the previous dialog. The solution will not be under source control anymore.

Since another database connection is not available in this scenario, we are left with the **Work Disconnected** command, which activates the disconnected mode.

Loosing the Internet Connection to the Database

In this scenario we are working using the SourceSafe internet plug-in from a remote site. While working, for some reason, the connection to the SourceSafe database becomes unavailable. We need to perform a source control operation, for example, to check out a file in order to make some changes. When trying to connect to the database, the SourceSafe internet plug-in encounters an access error and displays the following warning dialog:

Click **OK** to dismiss the warning dialog. Visual Studio asks to switch to working offline in disconnected mode:

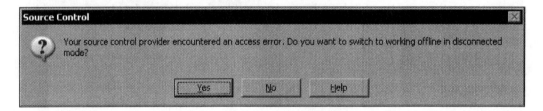

Clicking **Yes** will activate the disconnected mode. After the internet connection is re-established, we can reconnect to the database. Clicking **No** will abort the source control operation.

Starting Work Offline with the Internet Plug-In

This scenario is most likely to occur if we use an internet connection to work from a remote site.

If the internet connection is unavailable at the time we open the solution, the SourceSafe Internet plug-in will be unable to establish a connection to the SourceSafe web service and display the following dialog:

After that, it will ask to switch to the LAN plug-in and attempt to connect to the SourceSafe database directly.

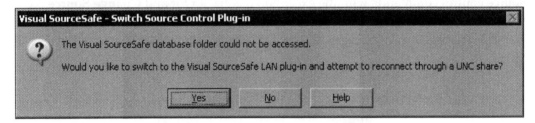

If we are able to connect to the database through a LAN or a VPN connection, we can click **Yes** and switch to the SourceSafe LAN plug-in.

If not, we click **No**. Visual Studio will display the **Unable to Access Database** dialog.

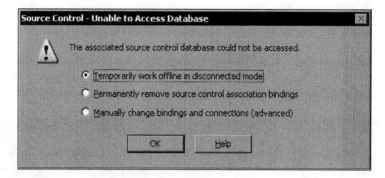

Choose **Temporarily work offline in disconnected mode**, to activate the disconnected mode. After the internet connection is re-established, we can reconnect to the database.

The Disconnected Mode

The previous scenarios led to working in disconnected mode. In this mode, all the source control commands with the exception of **Check Out** and **Change Source Control** are disabled.

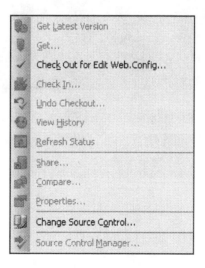

Clicking on the **Change Source Control** command lets us see the disconnected solution with the current SourceSafe **invalid** database status and current server bindings.

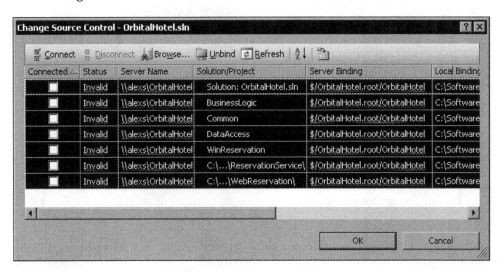

We are going to use this dialog later, to reconnect to the database when the connection becomes available again.

In the disconnected mode the **Check Out** command is available and we can further check out the files we need to work on. When trying to check out a file, Visual Studio displays the following dialog:

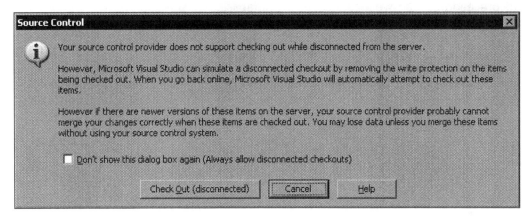

Visual Studio displays this dialog because the SourceSafe plug-in doesn't support checking out when disconnected. However, it can simulate a disconnected checkout by making the file writable so we can modify it. When reconnecting to the database Visual Studio will attempt to automatically perform a check-out on the file in the database.

This is where data loss is possible. If the SourceSafe database is configured to *only allow checkouts of the latest version* and in the mean time the file has already been modified by someone else, we will have to merge the changes manually as the SourceSafe **Merge** command will not work. We will have to compare the two versions and integrate the changes we've made into the latest version manually, in order to avoid overwriting the latest versions on the server.

If the database is configured not to allow only checkouts of the latest version (*allow checkouts of local versions*), or we are sure the database version will not be modified by someone else, we click the **Check Out (disconnected)** button and check out the file. In the disconnected mode, the check-out operation just marks the local file as writable, so we can modify it.

The check out operation is aborted using the **Cancel** button.

In the next section we will discuss how these different database configurations affect the proceedings after we reconnect to the database.

Reconnecting to the Database

The SourceSafe behavior when reconnecting to the database is influenced by two database options configured in the Visual SourceSafe Administrator application:

- **Allow multiple checkouts**
- **Only allow checkouts of the latest version**

These are available in the **Options** dialog:

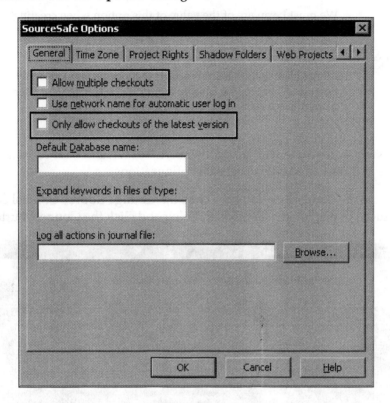

The **Allow multiple checkouts** option controls the check-out model (exclusive or multiple checkouts). This option determines whether Visual Studio can successfully check out files automatically when reconnecting to the database, if they are also checked out by others.

The **Only allow checkouts of the latest version** option is new in Visual SourceSafe 2005 and is designed especially for disconnected scenarios. It controls the file version that will be checked out as a result of a check out operation.

If it is enabled, only the latest database file version can be checked out. This is for compatibility with older SourceSafe versions.

If it is disabled, local file versions can also be checked out. The ability to check out local file versions is critical when reconnecting to the database after checking out files in disconnected mode because it avoids manual file merges and possible data loss.

> We must be aware of the value of this option when creating new databases. For databases created using Lock-Modify-Unlock (exclusive checkout model) this option is enabled by default. For databases created using Copy-Modify-Merge (multiple checkout model) this option is disabled by default. Whatever the case, this option can be changed later using the Visual SourceSafe Administrator application.

In the following sections we will see another series of scenarios for reconnecting to the database and how to handle different configurations.

To reconnect to the SourceSafe database click the **Change Source Control** command in Visual Studio to display the associated dialog and click the **Connect** button:

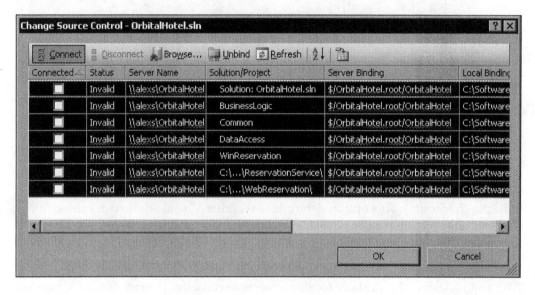

If the connection is successfully established, the dialog changes as we can see in the following figure:

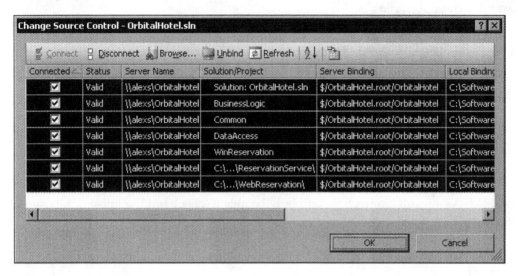

The solution is reconnected to the database and it returns to the **valid** status. Click **OK** to close the **Change Source Control** dialog.

 The solution will automatically reconnect to the database if we close it and reopen it in Visual Studio after the SourceSafe server connection becomes available, with the condition that the **Disconnect** command should not be used manually.

Visual Studio will attempt to automatically check out the files that were checked out while working in the disconnected mode.

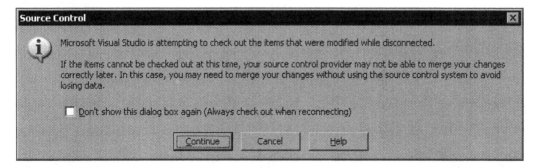

Click **Continue** to allow Visual Studio to check out the files.

Depending on the SourceSafe plug-in used and the database configuration, we can encounter a number of different scenarios after this step. The following sections examine these scenarios.

Using the LAN Plug-In

In the following scenarios we will use the SourceSafe LAN plug-in to reconnect to the SourceSafe database.

Only Allow Checkouts of the Latest Version Option Enabled

This configuration has the **Only allow checkouts of the latest version** option enabled. As a result, SourceSafe will only be able to check out the latest database version.

 This configuration has a potential for data loss if not handled correctly.

No New Revision

In this scenario, for the current file that Visual Studio is trying to check out automatically there is no new revision in the database when reconnecting.

File is not Checked Out

Also, the file is not checked out by anyone.

In this case Visual Studio will successfully check out the file in the database. When checking out, SourceSafe displays the following dialog because the file was marked as writable by Visual Studio while in the disconnected mode:

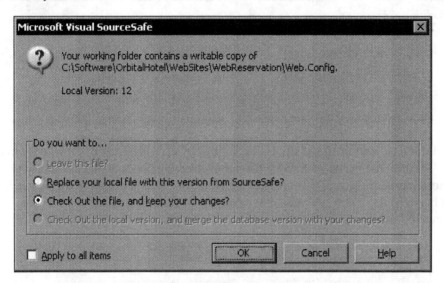

We know that there is no new revision in the database by looking at the **Local Version** label in this dialog. If there was a new revision, another label named **Database Version** would also be present.

We must choose **Check Out the file, and keep your changes** in order to keep the changes made to the file in disconnected mode or **Replace your local file with this version from SourceSafe** to *discard* the offline changes and replace the file with the original server version, *overwriting* them.

After checking out the file and testing our changes, we can safely save the changes by checking in the file.

File is Checked Out

If, however, the file is checked out in the database by someone else, Visual Studio's attempt to check out the file can encounter the following two situations:

- Allow multiple checkouts option disabled
- Allow multiple checkouts option enabled

Allow Multiple Checkouts Option Disabled

This situation is characteristic to the exclusive checkout model. In this case, Visual Studio is not able to check out the file automatically and displays the following error dialog:

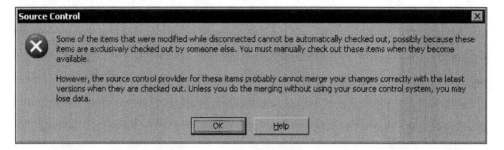

We will have to wait until the file is checked in by the other user before we can check it out. After the file is checked in by the other user we check it out manually using the **Check Out** command. When checking out, SourceSafe displays the following dialog because the file was marked as writable by Visual Studio while in the disconnected mode:

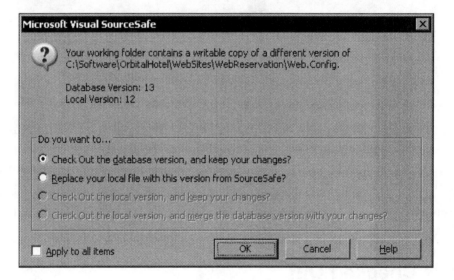

The file has a new revision because we can see the **Database Version** label. In this case the new revision number is greater by one than our file version. We must choose **Check Out the file, and keep your changes** in order to keep the changes made to the file in the disconnected mode or **Replace your local file with this version from SourceSafe** to *discard* the disconnected changes and replace the file with the original server version, *overwriting* them.

After checking out the file, the latest version is our version—version 12, because the database is configured to only allow checkouts of the latest version. If we were to check in the file as it is, we would practically overwrite revision 13 and cause data loss. We will see how to handle this situation correctly at the end of this series of scenarios, (that deal with the **Only allow checkouts of the latest version** option) in the *Handling Data Loss Situations* section.

Allow Multiple Checkouts Option Enabled

This situation is characteristic to the multiple checkout model. In this case, Visual Studio doesn't automatically check out the file and displays the following error dialog to make us aware of the potential data loss situation:

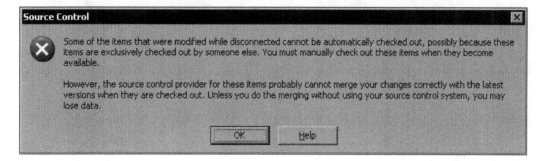

However, we are able to check out the file manually using the **Check Out** command.

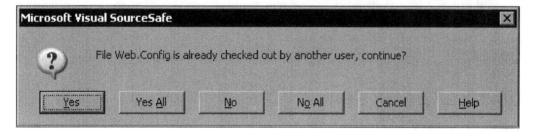

Click **Yes** to check out the file. When checking out, SourceSafe displays the following dialog because the file was marked as writable by Visual Studio while in the disconnected mode:

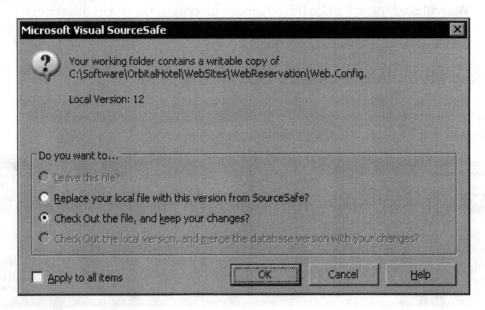

Because there isn't a new revision available yet, (as we didn't wait for the other user to check in the file) the dialog only shows the **Local Version** label. After the file is checked out, we are safe from data loss and the multiple checkout model's principles are in place. We can safely check in the file after testing that it works correctly. The other user(s) that have the file checked out will have to merge our changes into their file versions.

New Revisions

In this scenario, for the current file that Visual Studio is trying to check out automatically new revisions were created in the database while we were working in the disconnected mode. At the time of reconnecting to the database we can encounter two situations; the file may or may not be already checked out.

File is Not Checked Out

If the file is not already checked out, when checking out, SourceSafe displays the following dialog because the file was marked as writable by Visual Studio while in the disconnected mode:

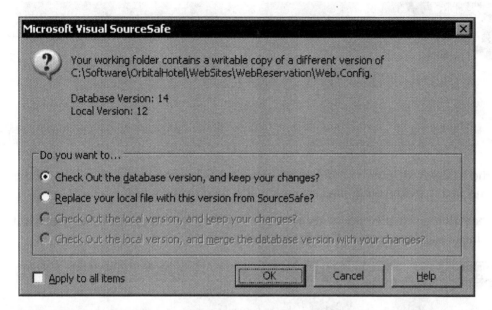

The file has new revisions because we can see the **Database Version** label also. In this case the latest revision number is greater by two than our file version. We must choose **Check Out the file, and keep your changes** in order to keep the changes made to the file in the disconnected mode or **Replace your local file with this version from SourceSafe** to *discard* the disconnected changes and replace the file with the original server version, *overwriting* them.

After checking out the file, the latest version is our version—version 12, because the database is configured to *only allow checkouts of the latest version*. If we were to check in the file as it is, we would practically overwrite revision 13 and 14, and cause data loss. We will see how to handle this situation correctly at the end of this series of scenarios, (that deal with the **Only allow checkouts of the latest version** option) in the *Handling Data Loss Situations* section.

File is Checked Out

If, however, the file is checked out in the database by someone else, Visual Studio doesn't automatically check out the file and displays the following error dialog:

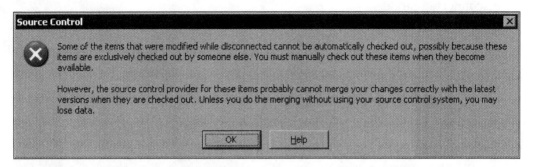

If the **Allow multiple checkouts option** is disabled, we will have to wait until the file is checked in by the other user and manually check out the file.

If the **Allow multiple checkouts option** is enabled, we can proceed and check out the file manually using the **Check Out** command:

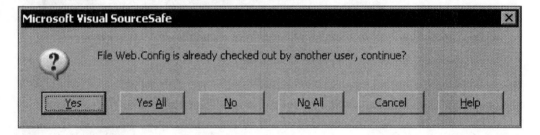

After checking out the file, we are in the same course of actions as in the above case where we found the file was not checked out. We will have to be careful and handle the check-in situation correctly to avoid overwriting the previous file revisions, which will cause data loss.

Handling Data Loss Situations

In the previous scenarios we've seen what the cases for potential data loss are. When the **Only allow checkouts of the latest version** option is enabled, data loss can occur in situations where new revisions were created by other users while we were working disconnected. Because this option causes SourceSafe to check out only the latest version, when checking out our version *SourceSafe will treat it as the latest version*. Checking in this version would cause the changes in the latest revisions to be overwritten.

To avoid this situation we must take the following steps:

1. When checking out the file, note the *Local Version* number for the file.
2. After checking out our file make a *backup* for it separately so that we can use it later.
3. *Undo* the checkout for the file and *replace* it with the latest database version.
4. Use the **History** dialog and *get* the revision we started working on, the revision number we noted in the first step. In the previous scenarios this is version 12.
5. *Replace* the file with the *backup* from step 2.
6. Use the **Get Latest Version** command to get the latest database version. When getting the latest version click **Merge** to merge the latest version and the version replaced with the backup. In the previous scenarios this would merge version 14 into version 12 avoiding the data loss situation.
7. After merging the files, *check in* the merged file.

These steps must be taken for each file that needs to be checked in safely when having the **Only allow checkouts of the latest version** option enabled. The alternative to this is simple—have this option disabled.

Only Allow Checkouts of the Latest Version Option Disabled

This configuration has the **Only allow checkouts of the latest version** option disabled. As a result, SourceSafe will be able to check out the local file versions and avoid the previous data loss situations by merging the local version with the latest database version.

In this scenario, for the current file that Visual Studio is trying to check out automatically there are two possible cases: the file may or may not be checked out.

File is Not Checked Out

When the file is not already checked out by someone else, Visual Studio is able to successfully check out the local file version automatically. The merge between the local version and the latest version is possible by manually issuing a **Get Latest Version** command after the checkout or when checking in the file. It is recommended to perform the merge by getting the latest version to be able to test the merged file version. After testing the merged file version we can safely check it in.

File is Checked Out

If, however, the file is checked out in the database by someone else, Visual Studio's attempt to check out the file can encounter the following two situations:

- Allow multiple checkouts option disabled
- Allow multiple checkouts option enabled

Allow Multiple Checkouts Option Disabled

This situation is characteristic to the exclusive check-out model. In this case, Visual Studio is not able to automatically check out the file and displays the following error dialog:

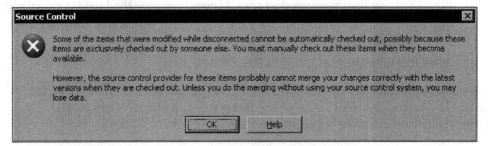

We will have to wait until the file is checked in by the other user before we can check it out. After the file is checked in by the other user we check it out manually using the **Check Out** command. When checking out, SourceSafe displays the following dialog because the file was marked as writable by Visual Studio while in the disconnected mode:

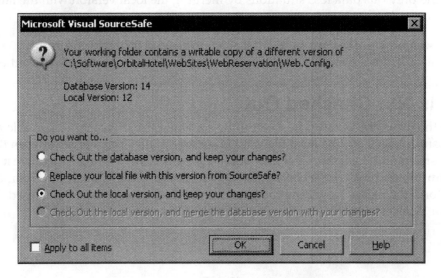

This time you can see the **Check Out the local version, and keep your changes?** option available and selected by default. This causes the check out to be performed against the local version instead of the latest database version. Click **OK** to check out the local file version.

To merge the local file and the latest database file version use the **Get Latest Version** command:

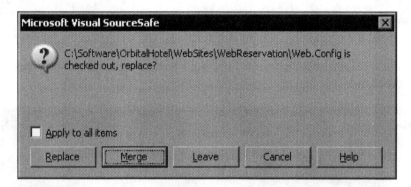

Click **Merge** to merge the two file versions and test the resulting merged file. After testing the merged file we can safely check it in.

Allow Multiple Checkouts Option Enabled

This situation is characteristic to the multiple checkout model. In this case, Visual Studio doesn't automatically check out the file and displays the following dialog because somebody else has the file checked out:

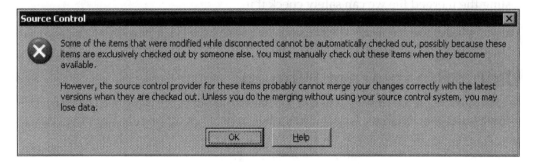

However, we are able to check out the file manually using the **Check Out** command:

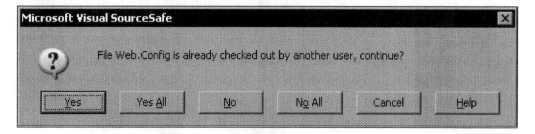

To merge the local file and the latest database file version use the **Get Latest Version** command:

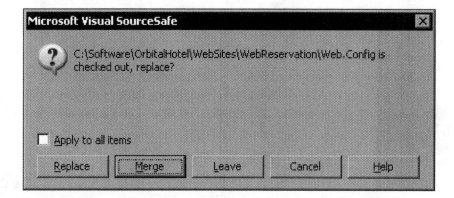

Click **Merge** to merge the two file versions and test the resulting merged file. After testing the merged file we can safely check it in.

This concludes the scenarios when using the SourceSafe LAN plug-in.

Using the Internet Plug-In

In the following scenarios we will use the SourceSafe internet plug-in to reconnect to the SourceSafe database. The internet plug-in behaves differently from the LAN plug-in because it always uses the local version checkouts when checking out disconnected versions, avoiding data loss.

For the current file that Visual Studio is trying to check out automatically when reconnecting there are two possible cases: the file may or may not be checked out.

File is Not Checked Out

When the file is not already checked out by someone else, Visual Studio is able to successfully check out the local file version automatically. The merge between the local version and the latest version is possible by manually issuing a **Get Latest Version** command after the checkout or when checking in the file. It is recommended to perform the merge by getting the latest version to be able to test the merged file version. After testing the merged file version we can safely check it in.

File is Checked Out

If, however, the file is checked out in the database by someone else, Visual Studio's attempt to check out the file can encounter the following two situations:

Allow Multiple Checkouts Option Disabled

This situation is characteristic to the exclusive checkout model. In this case, Visual Studio is not able to automatically check out the file and displays the following error dialog:

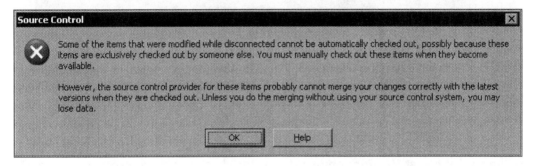

We will have to wait until the file is checked in by the other user before we can check it out. After the file is checked in by the other user we check it out manually using the **Check Out** command. When checking out, SourceSafe displays the following dialog because the file was marked as writable by Visual Studio while in the disconnected mode:

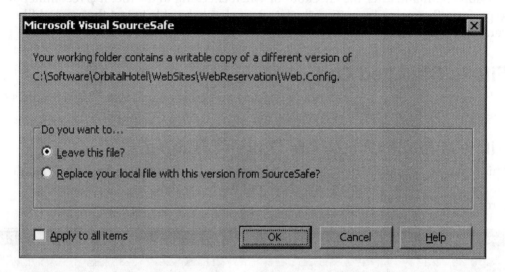

We must choose **Leave this file** in order to keep the changes made to the file in the disconnected mode or **Replace your local file with this version from SourceSafe** to *discard* the offline changes and replace the file with the original server version, *overwriting* them.

The merge between the local version and the latest version is possible by manually issuing a **Get Latest Version** command after the check out or when checking in the file. It is recommended to perform the merge by getting the latest version to be able to test the merged file version. After testing the merged file version we can safely check it in.

Allow Multiple Checkouts Option Enabled

This situation is characteristic to the multiple checkout model. In this case, Visual Studio automatically checks out the file and displays the following dialog because the file was marked as writable by Visual Studio while in disconnected mode:

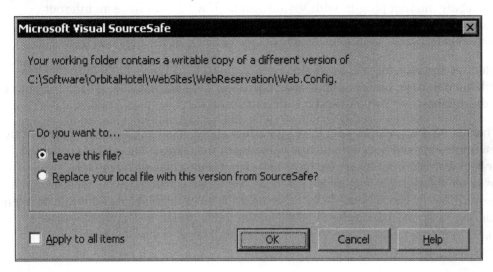

We must choose **Leave this file** in order to keep the changes made to the file in the disconnected mode or **Replace your local file with this version from SourceSafe** to *discard* the offline changes and replace the file with the original server version, *overwriting* them.

The merge between the local version and the latest version is possible by manually issuing a **Get Latest Version** command after the checkout or when checking in the file. It is recommended to perform the merge by getting the latest version to be able to test the merged file version. After testing the merged file version we can safely check it in.

This concludes the scenarios when using the SourceSafe internet plug-in.

Summary

In this chapter we explored working from remote locations using SourceSafe.

To work online and connect to the SourceSafe database remotely we can use the SourceSafe internet plug-in with Visual Studio. If we do not have an internet connection to the SourceSafe server, then we can work offline in the disconnected mode. Visual Studio simulates checkouts so we can edit the files we need.

Later, we can reconnect to the SourceSafe database and synchronize our changes with the database. Depending on the SourceSafe plug-in we have used to reconnect to the database, we can encounter different scenarios.

When using the LAN plug-in, the **Only allow checkouts of the latest version** option determines if there is a potential for data loss or not. When this option is enabled for backward compatibility, we have to be careful and take the necessary steps we've seen in the *Handling Data Loss Situations* section. This is necessary to avoid overwriting the changes made by other users in the revisions created while we were working disconnected on the same files. When this option is disabled, SourceSafe is able to merge the local version and the latest database version automatically, preventing data loss.

When using the internet plug-in, data loss situations are avoided as this plug-in will always check out the local file versions and merge them with the latest database versions.

7

Managing the Software Development Lifecycle

In this chapter, we are going to see how to manage the software development lifecycle using SourceSafe.

In the evolution of software products there are many milestones. We will see how to manage them using SourceSafe so that we can reproduce their specific configurations when needed. We will also talk about the build process and how a periodical build can catch integration problems early on.

Testing is important in ensuring the quality for the product. We will take a brief look at white-box and black-box tests and how they help in ensuring quality.

After releasing a product version, we have to maintain it while continuing development towards the next version. We will see how to conduct these efforts in parallel and fix the bugs found after the product was released, without affecting the current development effort. This allows us to release service packs. We will also see how to integrate these bug fixes into the current development code.

The Evolution of Software Products

The **Software Development Lifecycle** represents the process model used to organize and manage all the steps involved in the life of software products. Life-cycle models are used to control the evolution of software products starting with their conception and ending with their termination.

The first model created to address the problems of software development was the **waterfall** model. The waterfall model is a sequential development model in which the product evolves steadily (like a waterfall) through the phases of requirements, analysis, design, implementation, testing, and maintenance. Being sequential, the waterfall model requires that, in order to advance to the next step, all the previous steps must be fully completed. As a result, much time is spent early on to make sure that requirements and design are absolutely correct before advancing to the next phases.

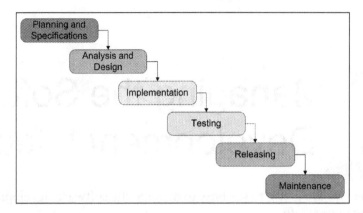

This model works even today for software products that have well defined and stable requirements. In a fast moving world, however, this is rarely the case. Requirements often change after the product's design is finished, invalidating more or less the initial effort put in analysis and design. Because of this, other models had to be created that do not rely on the steady downward evolution. Instead, these models use an incremental approach and are called **agile** models.

Agile models attempt to minimize the risk of requirements changing by developing software in short time boxes, called iterations. Each iteration includes all the tasks necessary to release the increment of a new functionality like planning, requirements, analysis, design, implementation, testing, and releasing a new version. As a result, the product comes to life earlier on and its customers can influence the future development.

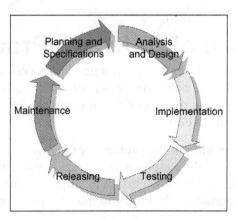

You can see that one way or another, the software development life-cycle models employ a set of common basic phases. Each phase affects the evolution of the software product in its own specific way.

The entire evolution of the software product must be supported through Software Configuration Management (SCM). SCM has to be able to adapt to any development model and ensure proper control over the development phases.

Milestones

A **milestone** (or checkpoint) is a point in time representing a key or important event in the life of a product like:

- *Product changes*: If we need to make some important product changes, we mark its state before beginning to make the changes, to have a snapshot of the latest configuration structure.

- *Product builds*: Just as with product changes, we want to keep track and identify project builds. This feature can be used by automatic building tools after getting the latest file versions from the database to mark the versions used in the build.

- *Product releases*: Releasing a project is a big event. We want to make really sure we know which file versions were used to build a certain project version in order to address potential problems.

Using Labels to Manage Milestones

Visual SourceSafe 2005 manages milestones using **labels**. Labels provide a way to associate a friendly name with a specific version of the entire solution, a project, or a single file. When reaching a milestone, the current configuration is marked using a new label. After it is applied, the new label identifies the specific configuration and can be used to recreate it later.

Creating Labels

The best way to create labels is by using the Visual SourceSafe Explorer.

In the OrbitalHotel example, I've reached the Beta1 milestone. I will label the current state of the solution as Beta1.

To create a new label, select the SourceSafe project (if you remember, SourceSafe refers to the folders in the database as projects) that contains the solution configuration specific to the milestone you want to label. In my example, this is the `$/OrbitalHotel.root/OrbitalHotel` project.

Do not select the root $/ or another project that is *above* the top project that contains the solution configuration you want to label. This is because the label will be inherited by all the sub-projects under the selected project. Select only the project that contains the configuration you want to label.

In the recommended case of hierarchical Visual Studio solutions (where all the projects are below the solution project) select the project that contains the solution's .sln file. This is the case for the Orbital Hotel solution.

After selecting the project, you can create the label using the Visual SourceSafe Explorer's toolbar **Label Version** command button.

Another way to create a new label is to right-click the selected project and use the **Label** command:.

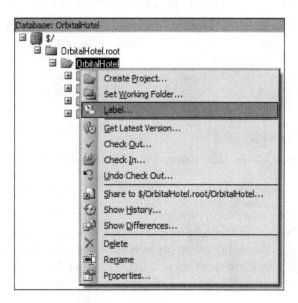

SourceSafe will display the **Label** dialog window:

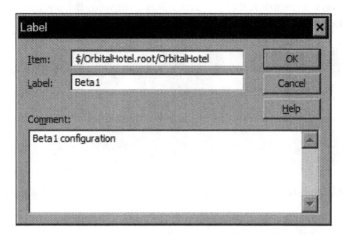

The **Item** text box contains the project you selected to label.

In the **Label** text box, enter the name for the new label. I will label the OrbitalHotel solution as **Beta 1**.

In the **Comment** text box, you can enter a comment about the label to help you identify later what the label contains.

To create the new label, click the **OK** button.

The label will be created and *attached* to the selected item (in this case the $/OrbitalHotel.root/OrbitalHotel project). All the sub-items (projects and files) will have a *reference* to the new label. If the label is removed, it will be removed from the sub-items too.

After it is created, the label will be a part of the history for the item and all sub-items.

Best Practice
Use labels as often as you can as they are an easy and efficient way to mark specific product configurations.

You cannot create a label twice with the same name for the same item. If you do so, SourceSafe will ask to remove the old label. For example, if I try to create a new label also named Beta1, SourceSafe will display the following dialog:

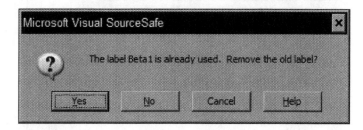

Clicking **Yes** will remove the old label and create the new one. Clicking **No** will abort the operation.

 You should never replace an old label with a new one because you will lose the configuration marked by the old one. That is, unless this is your intention.

Viewing Project Labels

Labels can be viewed using both Visual Studio and the Visual SourceSafe Explorer. However, choosing the item you want to view the labels for in Visual Studio is slightly different than in the Visual SourceSafe Explorer.

Because labels are part of the history, we can view them using the **History** dialog. For a complete reference about history see the *File Versions and History* section in Chapter 5.

To view the labels using Visual Studio, select the item in the **Solution Explorer** window and use the **View History** command.

In this case, we are interested in viewing the labels applied to the entire solution and in particular the Beta1 label created earlier. I've selected the solution node and used the **View History** toolbar command button.

Visual Studio shows the **History Options** dialog window:.

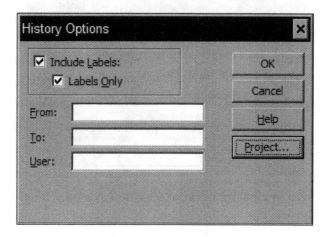

This window represents the difference between viewing the item history in Visual Studio and viewing it in the Visual SourceSafe Explorer. In the Visual Studio **Solution Explorer** window, you can only see the items in the solution and not the physical folders in which they reside. This is why in Visual Studio the **History Options** dialog has a **Project...** button.

If you want to view the history for the file selected in the **Solution Explorer**, click the **OK** button. In this particular case it will display the history for the OrbitalHotel.sln file.

If you want to view the history for the folder (called project in the SourceSafe database) that contains the file, click the **Project...** button. In this particular case, the folder that contains the OrbitalHotel.sln file maps exactly to the project I've labeled earlier.

In Visual SourceSafe Explorer you can see both the projects and the files. The history is shown depending on the selected item.

For projects, SourceSafe will display the **Project History Options** dialog window.

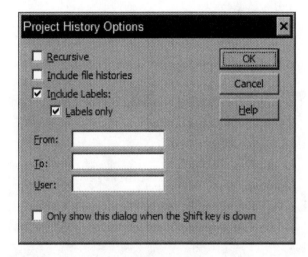

Because I'm interested in viewing the labels, I will check only the **Include Labels** and **Labels only** checkboxes.

Click the **OK** button to display the **History of Project** dialog window.

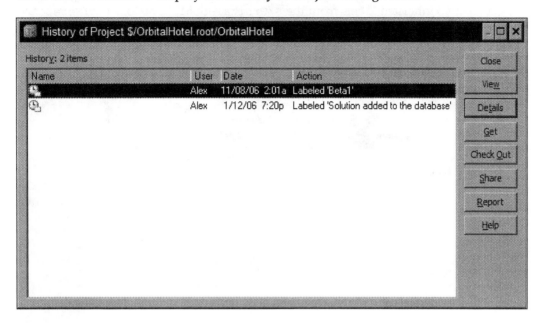

In the **History of Project** window, we can see the labels applied directly to the project and the inherited labels. The **Name** column is empty for labels that are applied directly to the current item and contains the name of the item for labels that are inherited. In this case there are no inherited labels.

Let's see how labels are inherited. I'm going to view the labels for the **BusinessLogic** project.

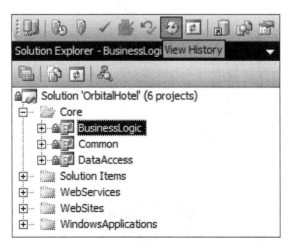

In this case if we look in the **Name** column, we can see that the **BusinessLogic** project has two inherited labels from the $/OrbitalHotel.root/OrbitalHotel project and another inherited label from the $/OrbitalHotel.root/OrbitalHotel/Core project. The Core project was labeled as **Core stable** before the Beta1.

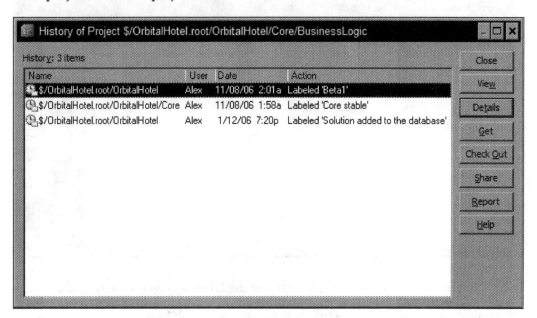

Viewing File Labels

To view the labels for a specific file, select the file in the **Solution Explorer** and use the **View History** command.

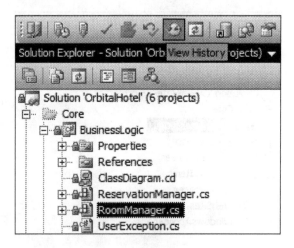

This will display the same **History Option** dialog window which we saw earlier.

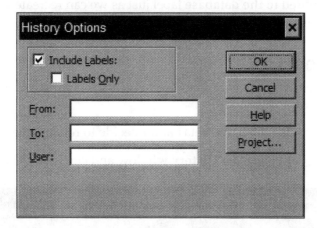

This time I will choose to display the entire file's history including labels. Click the
OK button to view the history for the file.

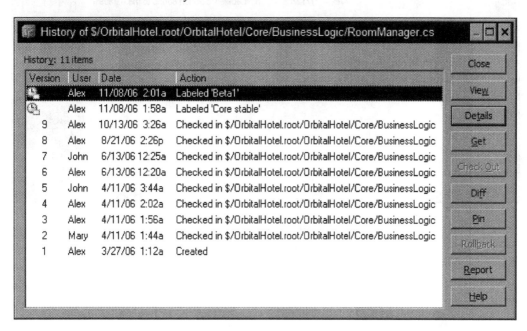

You can see that this file, although it is under the **BusinessLogic** project, does not
have the inherited **Solution added to the database** label. This is because the file was
created *after* the solution was added to the database and didn't exist when the initial
solution configuration was created and labeled.

We will see a little later that we can recreate the initial solution configuration based on the **Solution added to the database** label just as we can recreate any labeled configuration using its label.

Editing Labels

After creating labels, you can edit them to change their names or to add additional comments.

For example, I don't like the name Beta1 and I decide to rename the label Beta 1.

To rename a label, select it in the **History** window and click the **Details** button.

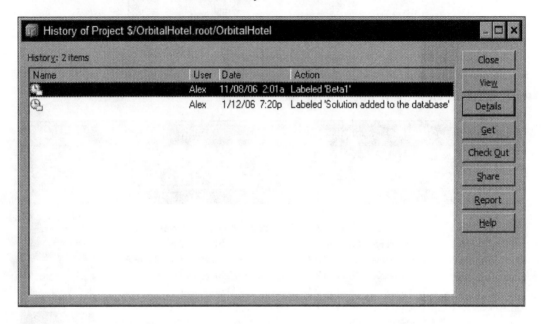

SourceSafe displays the **History Details** window.

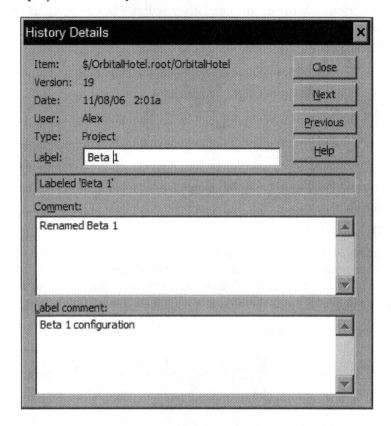

In this window, you can change the name of the label and add additional comments. When you finish, click the **Close** button. SourceSafe displays the following message dialog:

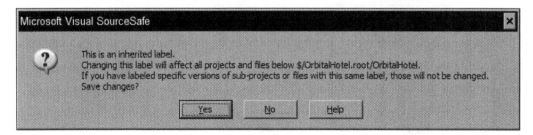

Because the label is inherited by all the sub-items (which have only a reference to it), changing the label will affect all the sub-items (which is what I want).

Also, the message specifies that if you have other labels created on sub-items that are named like the original name of this label, they will not be changed. In my case, even if other sub-items were individually labeled as Beta1, changing the name of this label will not change the names for those labels because they have been created separately.

Best Practice

Do not use the same label name to label individual hierarchical items. Instead, label just the root item. The label will be inherited by all the sub-items.

Click **Yes** to change the label, or **No** to cancel the changes.

Deleting Labels

Deleting a label will delete it from the item it is attached to and from all the sub-items that inherit the label. Although you should never delete a label, if you need to delete it for any reason, you can do so using the **History Details** dialog. The **History Details** dialog is displayed using the **Details** button in the **History** window.

To delete the label, delete the label's name from the **Label** text box.

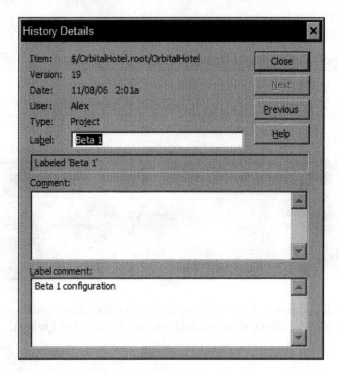

After deleting the name, click **Close** to remove it from the history. SourceSafe informs you that the label will be removed from all the sub-items that inherit the label.

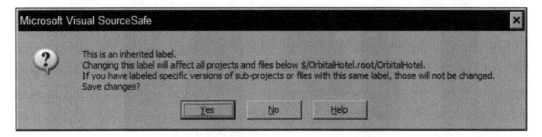

Click **Yes** to delete the label or **No** to cancel the operation.

Recreating Product Configurations

We've seen how to define specific product configurations using labels. All the effort is very useful later, when we need to see what has changed between milestones and perhaps recreate the configuration at a certain point.

For example, I've reached the Beta 2 for the OrbitalHotel solution. Things have evolved since Beta 1. Now the solution looks like this:

I want to see what has changed between Beta 1 and Beta 2.

I will look into the history for the solution in the `$/OrbitalHotel.root/OrbitalHotel` project, including the recursive file histories.

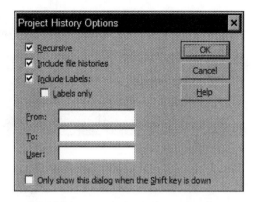

Additionally, we can filter the history using the **From** and **To** fields. We can enter the name of the first label in the **From** text box and the name of the second label in the **To** text box. This will only show the history between the two labels.

The **History** window displays all the changes that have occurred between the two milestone labels.

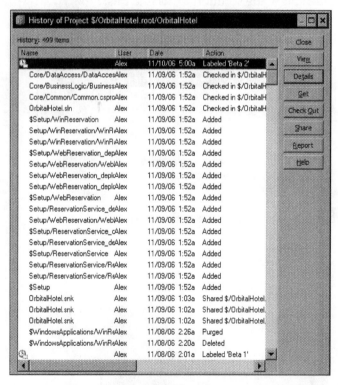

From a bird's eye view, I can see that some files were deleted, strong name keys were shared for the projects in the core section, and setup projects were added to the solution. All this provides a lot of useful information that we can use to identify configuration changes. But what if I want to recreate the solution configuration at Beta 1?

Using labels we can do just that. We can recreate any labeled configuration.

I'm going to recreate the configuration for Beta 1 in my local workspace.

Make sure you don't have any pending changes before you recreate another configuration in your workspace because the existing files are overwritten. Check in all the pending changes before getting another configuration.
A special case is represented by web projects. Because web projects don't have project files that contain the project's list of files, when getting different project versions it is possible for old files to remain in the project's folder. To overcome this problem, before getting different project versions, manually delete the local workspace files from the web project folder.

I will filter out file histories from the **History** window and show only the labels.

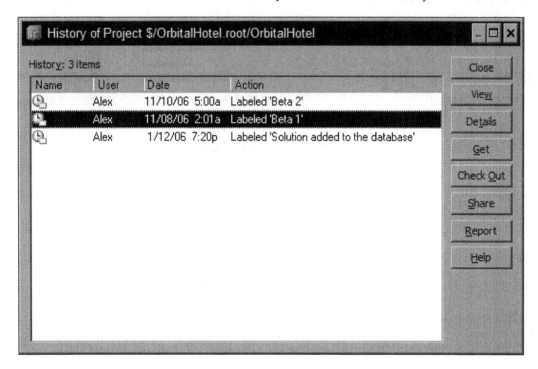

To recreate the configuration for Beta 1, I will select the Beta 1 label and click the **Get** button. This will display the **Get** dialog.

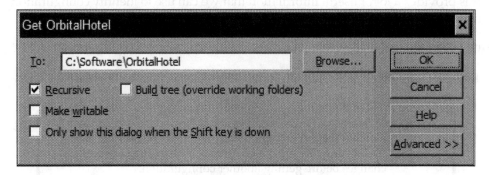

To get the files for all the sub-projects in the configuration, the **Recursive** option must be checked.

The **Build tree** option is enabled only if the **Recursive** option is checked. Checking this option will override working folders for sub-projects and build the exact structure from the SourceSafe database. This is relevant only if you have defined other working folder locations for sub-projects instead of the hierarchical solution structure. If you have followed the best practice of keeping the hierarchical structure, this option is not necessary.

If the **Make writable** option is checked, the read-only file attributes will be removed from the files that will be retrieved from the database. This option can be useful if you want to make experimental changes to the recreated configuration without checking in those changes. If you leave the files as read-only, every attempt to change them in Visual Studio will result in a check out for the latest version. If you get the configuration and make the files writable, when you want to get back in sync with the database you will have to get the latest configuration again and uncheck the **Make writable** option to make the files read-only again.

Click **OK** to start getting the files for the labeled configuration in your workspace. After getting the files, click **Close** in the **History** window. Visual Studio will reload the solution for the configuration.

> If you need to get a specific configuration and you want to make persistent changes to it, (such as fixing bugs and releasing service packs) then this is not the way. We will see later in this chapter in the *Parallel Product Development* section what the best way to handle such situations is.

Creating Persistent Configuration Snapshots

In the previous section we've seen how to get a specific configuration in our workspace using its label. It provides a simple and efficient way of going back in time and examining the configuration.

But what if I want to keep permanent snapshots for certain configurations? I could do this by getting the configurations locally and keeping them locally but this wouldn't be of much help if I wanted to see the differences between them. It would be better if I could keep them in the database itself.

SourceSafe allows us to keep persistent database configuration snapshots using the combination of the **share** and **pin** features.

[Using the Visual SourceSafe Explorer, create a new project under the *root* project to store snapshots. This ensures snapshots will not interfere with the other configurations.]

I will create a snapshot for the Beta 1 configuration in the OrbitalHotel database. Before creating the snapshot, I will create a new project under the **OrbitalHotel.root** project named **Snapshots** that will contain the future snapshots.

[Because the snapshots aren't part of the solution per se, but rather different solution configurations, the snapshots must be created outside the solution's hierarchy top folder. In my case, the **Snapshots** project that holds the snapshots is outside the $/OrbitalHotel.root/OrbitalHotel project that is the top folder for the entire solution. If your solution is not structured hierarchically (*not recommended*), create your snapshots folder outside the top solution folder that contains the solution and all the projects (that is most likely the [SolutionName].root folder).]

Sharing and Pinning Configurations

To create a persistent snapshot by sharing and pinning a specific configuration, use the Visual SourceSafe Explorer and open the **History** window for the project you want to create the snapshot for.

After opening the **History** window, select the labeled configuration you want to use for a snapshot and click the **Share** button.

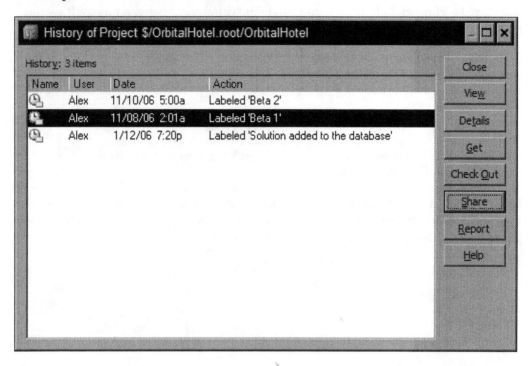

Clicking the **Share** button displays the **Share from** dialog.

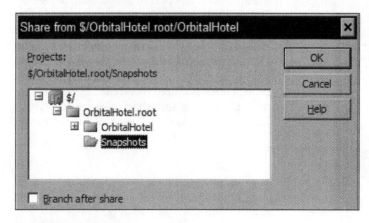

In the **Share from** dialog, select the project that will contain the snapshot. In my case I will select the **Snapshots** folder created earlier.

Leave the **Branch after share** checkbox unchecked.

Click **OK** to close the **Share from** dialog. This displays the **Share** dialog.

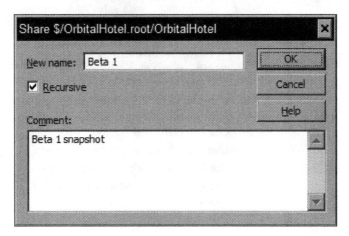

In the **New name** text box enter the name for the new snapshot. Check the **Recursive** checkbox to share all the files recursively. Optionally enter a comment about the new snapshot in the **Comment** text box. To start creating the snapshot, click the **OK** button in the **Share** dialog.

SourceSafe will *share* all the files that are a part of the selected configuration and *pin* them to the specific configuration version.

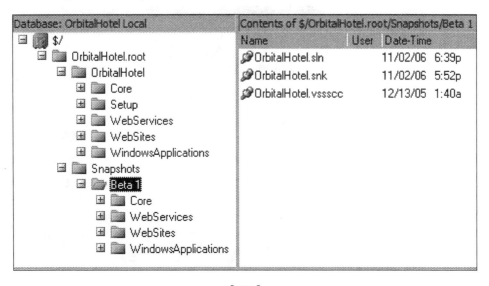

You can see that all the files have a **pin** icon. If you look at the history for each file, you can see the version where the file is pinned.

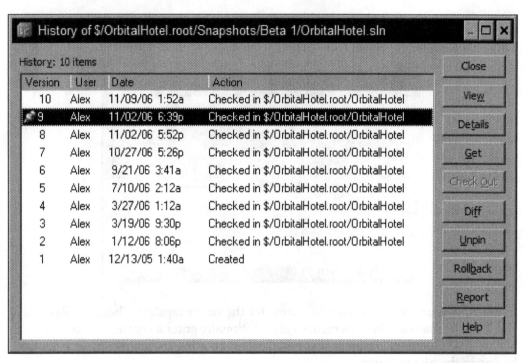

You can also look at the **Links** tab in the file's properties. Here you can see all the shared versions of the file and also the versions where they were pinned.

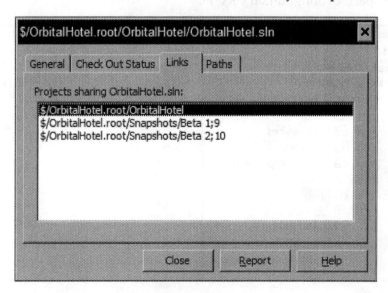

Now you have a persistent configuration snapshot in the database. The entire team can use Visual Studio to get the snapshot locally. Use the **Open Project** command and open the SourceSafe database. Browse to the project that contains the snapshots and open the solution.

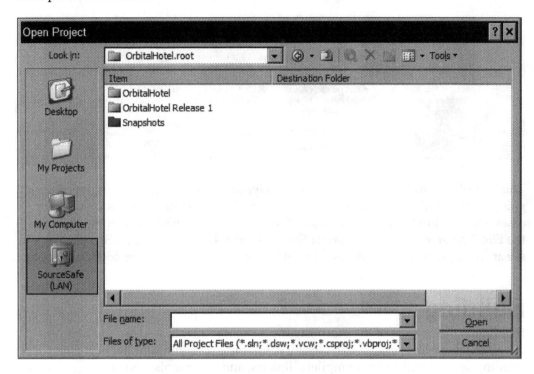

Because all the files are pinned, Visual Studio prevents the files from being checked out by mistake.

Also, if you have projects that rely on the solution's .sln file to store local configuration data (like website projects) or projects that store in their files the binding to the SourceSafe database, they will not be able to check out their files to refresh the configuration. In such cases you might see this message in Visual Studio.

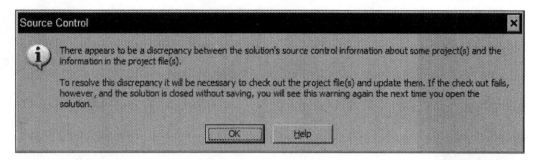

This is probably the only case when we can ignore this message because we are not going to further develop the solution as we are dealing with a snapshot. For other cases, we shouldn't ignore it and should verify the solution's bindings by opening the **File | Source Control | Change Source Control** dialog in Visual Studio. We will see an example on this a little later in the *Using the Maintenance Line* section.

Building

Building is the process of transforming the human-readable source code files into binary machine-level executable files by combining configuration items, using building scripts, make files, compilers, linkers, and other tools, and creating a version of a software program. Building can take from a few files to several hundreds or thousands of files, making it a delicate process.

While every developer must perform test builds in the workspace before checking in, to ensure the changes made do not break the repository state, when it comes to building the entire configuration and to releasing a project version, different policies have to be applied. If the workspace solution configuration is successfully being built in the local workspace, this doesn't necessarily mean that the repository configuration will successfully build also. This is because its state is changed every time a user checks in his or her changes.

Every once in a while someone will forget to check in a new file or a changed one, or will check in files that do not build, breaking the solution in the repository. This affects other team members, whose workspace contents will be broken after getting the latest solution version from the repository, affecting their productivity.

To avoid such situations, the "buildable" state of the repository must be checked regularly to address any situations that break it. Software that is not built regularly is difficult to release. For this purpose regular repository builds are scheduled and performed automatically. Depending on the build frequency, we can identify two major types of builds:

- Nightly builds
- Continuous integration builds

A **nightly build** is an automatic build that takes place at night on a special build machine, when no one is likely to be working. The results of the build are inspected the day after, when any issues that break the build must be addressed. The one day interval between builds is sufficient for traditional development models. However, for agile development models such as extreme programming, where the cycles are very frequent, this interval is too long.

Agile development models use **continuous integration** builds. A continuous integration server acts as a monitor to the repository. Every time a user performs a new check in to the repository, the server automatically gets the sources onto the integration machine, initiates a build, and notifies the user of the result of the build, usually by email.

Build Engines

The main build engines for .NET are:

- MSBuild
- NAnt

MSBuild is the new build engine for Microsoft and Visual Studio 2005. Until MSBuild, we had to build solutions and projects using Visual Studio itself. MSBuild is completely transparent with regards to how it processes and builds software, enabling us to build solutions and projects in build environments where Visual Studio is not installed. When opening projects created with previous Visual Studio versions in Visual Studio 2005, they are converted to the new MSBuild file format.

NAnt is an open-source .NET build engine. It is similar to Ant, the build engine from the Java world, developed initially by Apache. You can find the latest version at `http://nant.sourceforge.net/`.

Both MSBuild and NAnt use XML-based project configuration files that contain a series of *targets* (such as Build, Clean, and Rebuild). Targets are called to perform different tasks (such as calling the compilers or creating, moving, and deleting files and folders).

Both build systems come with a series of predefined tasks that handle the most common build operations. For particular uses we can also create custom tasks. For NAnt, we can find additional task implementations at `http://nantcontrib.sourceforge.net/`.

Testing

Testing is the process of identifying the correctness, completeness, security, and quality of software and it is very important in ensuring its quality. I will only scratch its surface as it is a subject for an entire book by itself.

There are two types of tests, depending on how we look at the software being tested:

- White-box testing
- Black-box testing

In **white-box** testing, we look from inside the tested software having an intimate knowledge of the source code.

In **black-box** testing, we look from outside the tested software dealing only with inputs and outputs with no knowledge of the internal structure.

Code Analysis

Code analysis is the analysis of software that is performed without actually running it, by looking only at its structure and/or source code. Software is analyzed for compliance with design guidelines and to locate potentially vulnerable code.

In the .NET world, one of the tools for code analysis is **FxCop**. FxCop checks .NET managed code assemblies for conformance to the Microsoft .NET Framework Design Guidelines. It uses reflection, MSIL parsing, and call-graph analysis to inspect assemblies for more than 200 defects in the following areas:

- Library design
- Localization
- Naming conventions
- Performance
- Security

FxCop includes both graphical user interface and command-line versions. For more information you can visit `http://www.gotdotnet.com/Team/FxCop/`.

Unit Testing

Unit testing is a black-box testing procedure used to validate that individual components or *units* of source code are working properly. The purpose of unit testing is to isolate each part of the software and ensure that the individual parts are correct.

Usually written unit tests are performed automatically by unit test frameworks. The most common unit test frameworks in .NET are:

- NUnit
- MbUnit
- csUnit
- Visual Studio Team System

NUnit is a unit-testing framework for all .NET languages. Initially ported from JUnit, the unit test framework in the Java world, it is now written entirely in C# and has been completely redesigned to take advantage of many .NET language features, such as custom attributes and other reflection-related capabilities.

For more information on NUnit you can visit `http://www.nunit.org/`.

MbUnit is an extensible unit-testing framework. As in NUnit, tests are created at run time using reflection and custom attributes. MbUnit differentiates itself from NUnit in its extensibility model. It contains a number of tests that go beyond simple unit testing, such as a greater assert range, pairwise testing, combinatorial testing, and data-oriented testing.

For more information on MbUnit you can visit `http://www.mbunit.com/`.

csUnit is a unit testing tool for the .NET framework. You can use it with all .NET languages including C#, Visual Basic .NET, J#, and managed C++. It also has an add-in for Visual Studio which makes it easier to run unit tests directly from the IDE.

For more information on csUnit you can visit `http://www.csunit.org`.

The **Visual Studio Team System** edition includes an integrated unit-testing framework with provision for automatic generation of unit tests and test projects.

For more information on Visual Studio Team System you can visit `http://msdn2.microsoft.com/en-us/teamsystem`.

Code Coverage

Unit test are as good as how we use them. **Code coverage** is another example of white-box testing and is used to see the degree to which the source code of a program has been tested and how thoroughly unit tests exercise the code base.

In .NET code coverage is provided by tools such as **NCover**. NCover provides statistics about the code, telling how many times each line of code was executed during a particular run of the application. After running the unit tests under NCover, you can easily pinpoint sections of code that are poorly covered and write unit tests for those portions. Code coverage measurement is a vital part of a healthy build environment.

For more information on NCover you can visit http://www.ncover.org.

Releasing

Releasing is an important software development event. When you reach a release version for the product, label the released configuration appropriately. If you use an integrated build tool, you can configure it to automatically label each built configuration. This will help identify correctly the configuration released into the production environment.

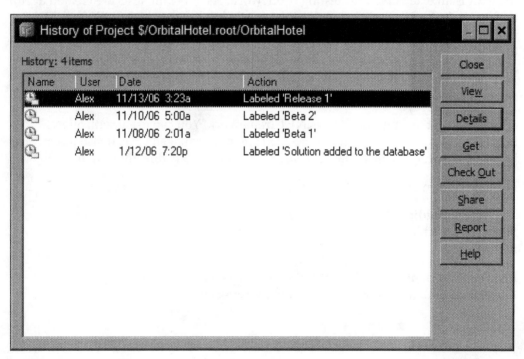

Parallel Product Development

After releasing a new version of the product, the development effort doesn't stop. The product will advance towards the next release while a separate effort will be made to maintain the current release and fix the issues found after the product is installed in the production environments. These efforts cannot be conducted on the same code base. They have to be conducted in parallel. This is where we introduce codelines.

Codelines

The **codeline** is the basic concept that represents the progression of the set of source files and other resources that make up the software product. It represents the development evolution across time, having a continuous history.

The first codeline is created when the development process is started and the initial files are added under source code management. This codeline is called the **mainline** or **trunk**.

If the mainline is used as the current development codeline it is also referred to as the **development line**.

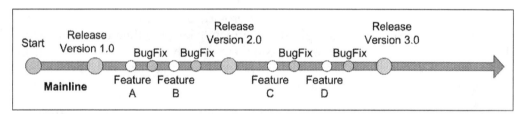

In the OrbitalHotel example, the `$/OrbitalHotel.root/OrbitalHotel` project represents the **mainline**. All the development effort until the first release (Release 1) was conducted on this codeline. But development doesn't stop here. The product will evolve towards the second release (Release 2) with additional features and improvements.

Meanwhile Release 1 will go into production and because you can never be 100 percent sure it is bug free, it will have to go through a maintenance process that will address the bugs discovered after the release. After the bugs are fixed, service packs will be built in order to fix the first release in the production environments.

You can see that after Release 1 the development effort will be split in at least two directions, with different policies, one to advance towards Release 2 and one to maintain Release 1. The maintenance effort policy will try to make the code as bug free as possible, while the development effort policy is to advance towards Release 2, which will add new untested features. If they were to use the same codeline, it would be practically impossible to release maintenance service packs for Release 1.

This is why the maintenance effort and the development effort must be conducted in parallel but separately, each on a separate codeline, effectively maintaining multiple product versions.

Maintaining Multiple Product Versions

Multiple product versions can be maintained on totally new and separate codelines.

In the OrbitalHotel product, I could do this by creating a new codeline and adding the Release 1 code to it in order to keep it separate from the development line. Then I could maintain Release 1 by fixing the bugs on this new codeline and release service packs from it. But these bugs still exist in the first codeline, the development line. I will have to remember, maybe by making notes about where the bugs are, and integrate the fixes in the development line too, file by file.

This is where SCM systems are helpful. They provide the flexibility of creating new codelines from base codelines by splitting them while keeping their common history. This way I can view the differences between them directly from the Source Control database making the integration much easier. These codelines are called **branches**, just like branches that grow from a tree trunk.

To maintain product releases while advancing to the next versions **maintenance lines** are created as branches from the mainline.

Creating Maintenance Lines

Maintenance lines provide the best way to keep product maintenance separate from the ongoing development by creating them as branches from the mainline.

Immediately after each release, a maintenance line is created for that release.

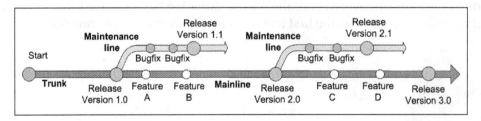

Bugs are fixed on the maintenance line while the development towards the next version continues on the mainline.

Visual SourceSafe provides support for creating branched codelines using the share, pin, and branch features. These features can be combined into two methods of creating maintenance lines:

- Share, Pin, and Branch
- Share and Branch

 Creating codeline branches is possible only in the Visual SourceSafe Explorer. All of the following techniques are performed using the Visual SourceSafe Explorer.

Share, Pin, and Branch

The **Share, Pin, and Branch** method is at the beginning identical to the method of creating persistent database snapshots that we've seen earlier in this chapter. Snapshots were created by sharing and pinning a specific configuration.

I'm going to create a Release 1 maintenance line for the OrbitalHotel example. It all begins in the **History** window of the project for which we want to create the branched codeline. In this case, the $/OrbitalHotel.root/OrbitalHotel project represents the mainline for the OrbitalHotel solution. The branch is created starting from the Release 1 configuration.

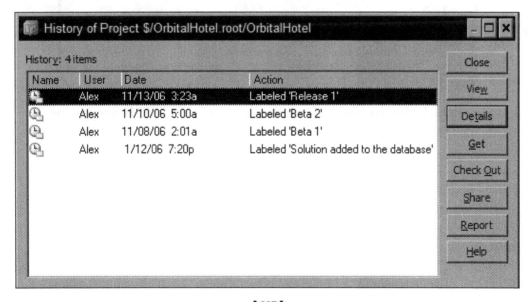

After selecting the configuration to be branched in the **History** window, click the **Share** button to share and pin this configuration to the new maintenance line. The **Share** button will show the **Share from** dialog, where we have to select the project that will contain the new branch.

In my case, I will select the $/OrbitalHotel.root project as the parent for the new maintenance line.

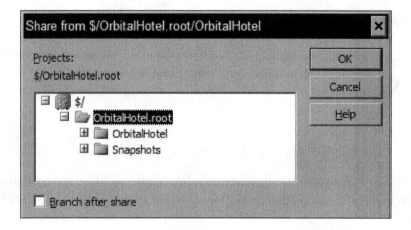

 The new braches must be created outside of the solution's hierarchy top folder. In my case, the project that holds the new branch is outside the $/OrbitalHotel.root/ OrbitalHotel project that is the top folder for the entire solution.

If your solution is not structured hierarchically (not recommended), create your branch folder *outside* the top solution folder that contains the solution and all the projects (that is most likely the [SolutionName].root folder).

Leave the **Branch after share** option unchecked. This option will be used in the second method of creating braches, covered later in this chapter in the *Branching the Maintenance Line on Creation* section.

After selecting the parent project for the new codeline, click the **OK** button. This will show the **Share** dialog.

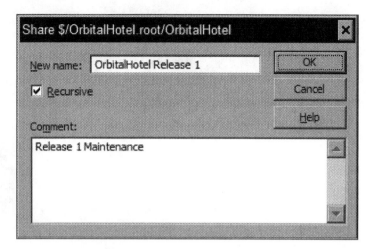

In the **Share** dialog, specify the name for the new project that will contain the new codeline in the **New name** text box. Also, you can specify a comment for the new project in the **Comment** text box.

Select the **Recursive** option to share and pin the project and files recursively.

Click **OK** to start creating the new codeline.

The newly created project contains the shared and pinned configuration for Release 1.

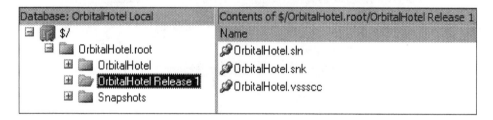

After the new project is created, apply a label to it that will help identify the initial configuration for the new codeline.

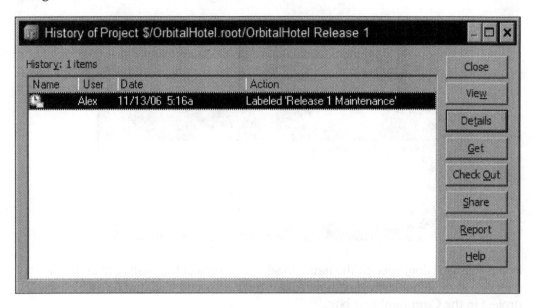

In the current state, the new codeline is nothing more than a snapshot of the Release 1 configuration. We can see, for example, if we look at the **Links** tab in the file's properties, the solution file is shared with the mainline and the Beta 1 and Beta 2 snapshots, but pinned at the last version.

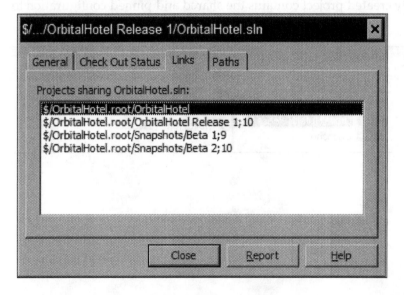

To be able to use the new maintenance line, we should be able to edit the files that we need. For this purpose we have to remove the pins from these files. If we unpin the files, they will become shared with the files in the mainline, which is not what we want. We want to continue from the pinned versions but in parallel with the files in the mainline. This is accomplished using the **Branch** command.

The **Branch** command will split the pinned file from its parent file in the mainline, creating a new file. The new file will have the same history as the parent file all the way until the branch is created. After the branch, the new file will have an independent history.

The first files we will want to branch are the solution and the project files. This is because these files must be updated by Visual Studio with the new bindings in the database.

The best way to find these files is to search for them using the Visual SourceSafe Explorer's **Search** function.

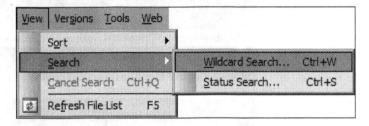

Open the **Wildcard Search** window and enter the extensions for the solution and projects you have in the solution such as `*.sln;*.csproj;*vbproj;*.vdproj;*. wdproj;` and for the files that maintain source code control bindings in Visual Studio such as `*.vssscc;*.vspscc`:

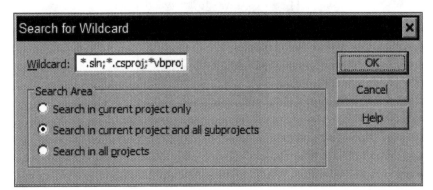

Select the **Search in the current project and all subprojects** option to search all the sub-projects and click the **OK** button to activate the search filter.

Then, select the project that contains the new codeline to search and filter the specified files. Make sure they are the correct files and click the **Branch Files** command in the toolbar to branch the files.

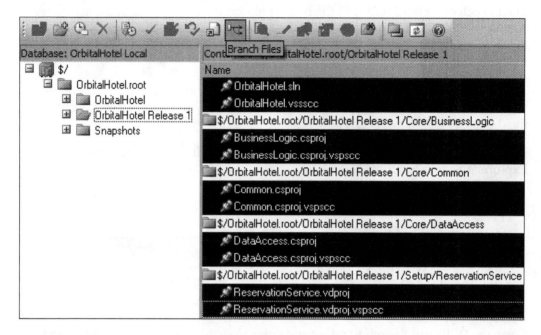

After the files are branched, cancel the search mode using the **Cancel Search** command.

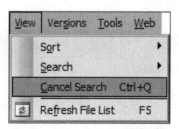

Now, if we look again in the **Links** tab of the solution file in the new codeline, we can see that it is no longer shared as it was before the branch. Now it is a stand-alone file.

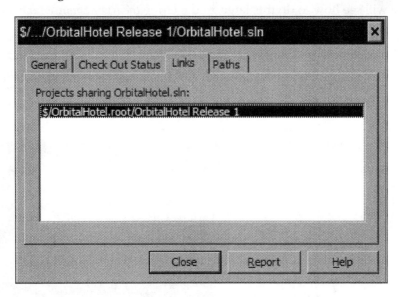

Looking at the **Paths** tab in the file's properties, we can see what happened. The file was branched at version 10 from the mainline and now it is evolving separately on the new codeline starting with version 11.

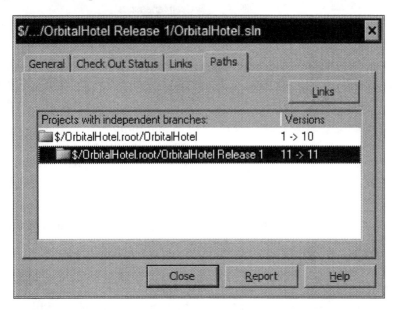

After branching the solution and the project files, we are able to start the maintenance process for Release 1 by opening the maintenance solution in Visual Studio. We will see how to do this later, in the *Using the Maintenance Line* section.

We are able to open the maintenance solution in Visual Studio. However, we are not able to check out any other file because they are still pinned in the SourceSafe database. To be able to modify any file, we will have to branch them as well. For example, if I need to fix a bug in the *Room Management* class, I have to branch its files first in the Visual SourceSafe Explorer before I can check them out in Visual Studio.

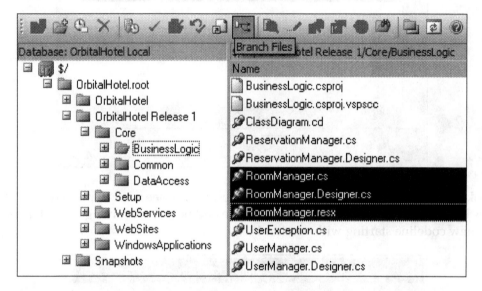

Using the Share, Pin, and Branch method can save database space because new files aren't created until you branch them. Also, it can be helpful in checking which files have been modified and which files are unchanged since the configuration was created.

This method has the disadvantage of having to manually branch the files in the Visual SourceSafe Explorer as needed. Another disadvantage is that if you accidentally unpin some files instead of branching them, they will become shared with the files in the mainline where development is being conducted. This can affect both the mainline and the development line.

The alternative is to use the **Share and Branch** method and branch all the files from the start, when creating the new maintenance codeline.

Branching the Maintenance Line on Creation

Using this method allows you to branch all the files from the start, when creating the new maintenance codeline.

Because branching creates new files, you will have to make sure, before branching, that enough space exists on the database drive. Also, it is recommended to analyze the database and to make a backup before creating the new codeline. Fore more information on analyzing and making a database backup, please see Appendix C.

To create the new codeline by branching all the files, select the configuration you want to branch from the main line's **History** window.

In my case it is the $/OrbitalHotel.root/OrbitalHotel project that represents the mainline for the OrbitalHotel solution. The branch is created starting from the Release 1 configuration.

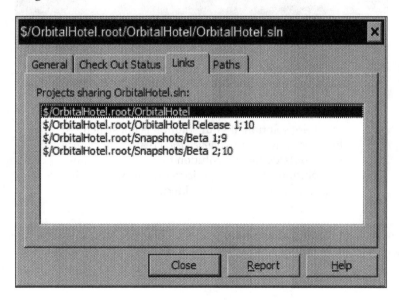

After selecting the configuration to be branched in the **History** window, click the **Share** button to share and branch this configuration to the new maintenance line. The **Share** button will show the **Share from** dialog where we have to select the project that will contain the new branch.

In my case, I will select the $/OrbitalHotel.root project as the parent for the new maintenance line.

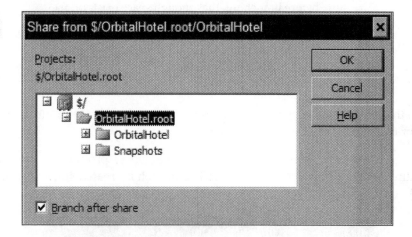

NOTE. The new branches must be created outside the solution's hierarchy top folder. In my case, the project that holds the new branch is outside the $/OrbitalHotel. root/OrbitalHotel project that is the top folder for the entire solution. If your solution is not structured hierarchically, (not *recommended*) create your branch folder **outside** the top solution folder that contains the solution and all the projects (that is most likely the [SolutionName].root folder).

This time, select the **Branch after share** option. This will branch all the files after sharing.

Select the parent project for the new codeline and click the **OK** button. This will show the **Share** dialog.

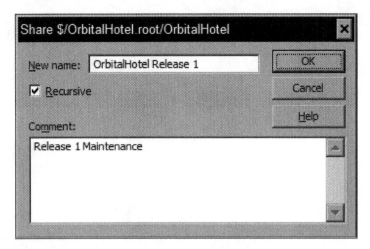

In the **Share** dialog, specify the name for the new project that will contain the new codeline in the **New name** text box. Also, you can specify a comment for the new project in the **Comment** text box.

Select the **Recursive** option to share and branch the project and files recursively.

Click **OK** to start creating the new codeline.

The newly created project contains the branched configuration for Release 1.

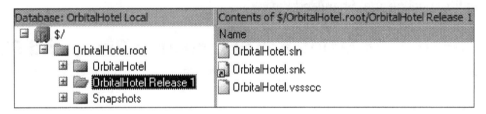

After the new project is created, apply a label to it that will help in identifying the initial configuration for the new codeline.

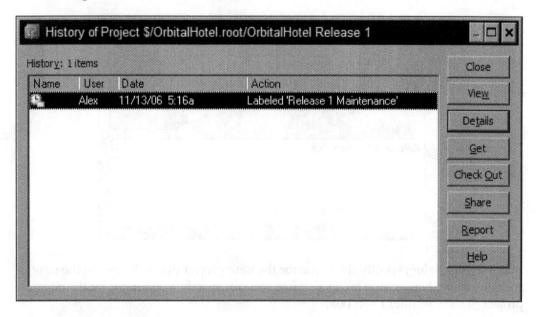

Now all the files are branched, and you can begin working immediately on the new maintenance line without having to branch the files manually as in the case of the Share, Pin, and Branch method.

If you used Share, Pin, and Branch when creating the codeline, you can still branch the entire codeline after Share and Pin.

Branching the Maintenance Line after Share and Pin

To branch the entire codeline after share and pin, you have two choices. One is to manually branch each file and the other is to branch them altogether.

Because branching creates new files, you will have to make sure before branching, that enough space exists on the database drive. Also, it is recommended to analyse the database and to make a backup before creating the new codeline. Fore more information on analyzing and making a database backup please see *Appendix C*.

To branch all the files at the same time, you can use the Visual SourceSafe Explorer's **Wildcard Search** function.

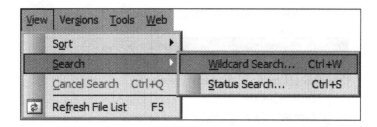

Use the command to display the **Search for Wildcard** dialog.

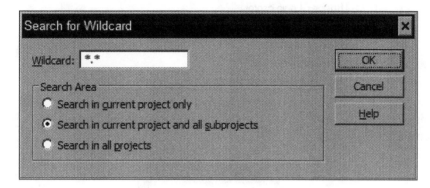

Enter the *.* filter in the **Wildcard** text box if not already entered, and select the **Search in current project and all subprojects** option to search in all the sub-projects. Click **OK** to activate the search filter and select the project that contains the codeline. This will display all the files recursively in the selected project.

Select all the files and click the **Branch Files** command in the toolbar.

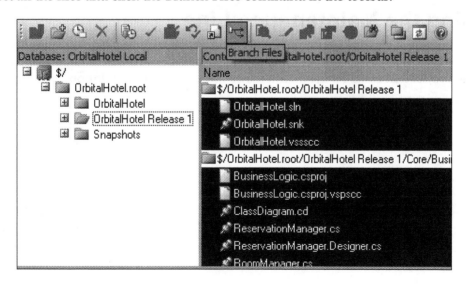

This will branch all the files that are not already branched.

After branching all the files, cancel the search mode using the **Cancel Search** command.

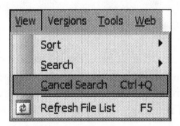

Using the Maintenance Line

After creating the maintenance line, you can open the maintenance solution in Visual Studio. Use the **Open Project** command and open the SourceSafe database. Browse to the project that contains the maintenance line and open the solution.

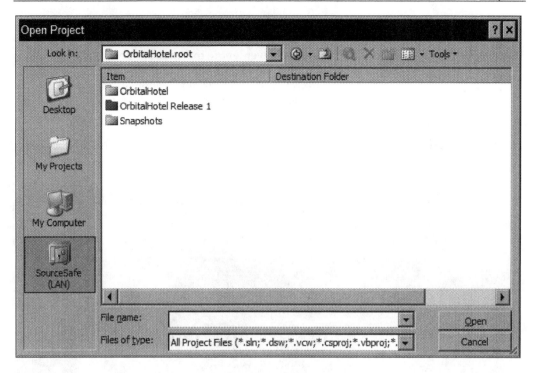

When loading the maintenance solution, if you have projects that rely on the solution's .sln file to store local configuration data (like website projects) or projects that store in their files the binding to the SourceSafe database, the first time you open them, their binding configuration will not be up to date because the solution and project now live inside another SourceSafe project.

In this case, Visual Studio will display the following information dialog:

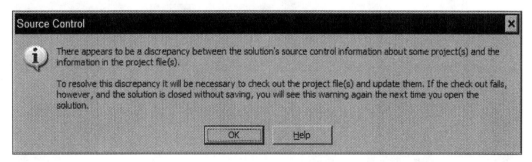

Click **OK** to close the dialog, and to resume the solution loading. Visual Studio will silently check out the required files and update the configuration.

After opening the solution from another branch, either
a disk or source control, never ignore this message and
always verify the project bindings are targeting the correct
branch. If some projects still target the old location, use the
Browse button and bind them to the new/correct location.

Failing to do this may cause you to start working on the wrong branch and check in
changes in the wrong project.

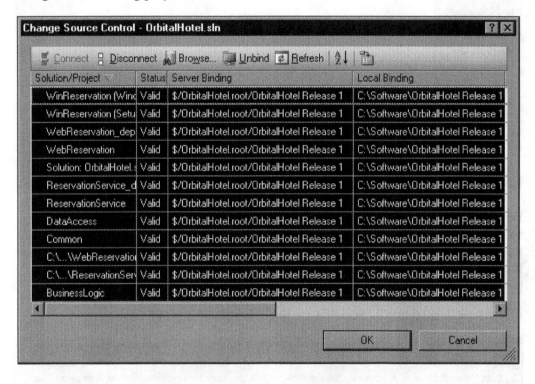

If you are curious to see what updates are being made, you can compare the new
versions with the previous ones. You will see changes regarding the binding to the
new project names.

Before:

```
SccProjectName = ""$/OrbitalHotel.root/OrbitalHotel", GDAAAAAA"
```

After:

```
SccProjectName = ""$/OrbitalHotel.root/OrbitalHotel Release 1", KVAAAAAA"
```

After the solution is loaded and the updates are made by Visual Studio, you can check in the new solution and project configurations to the database.

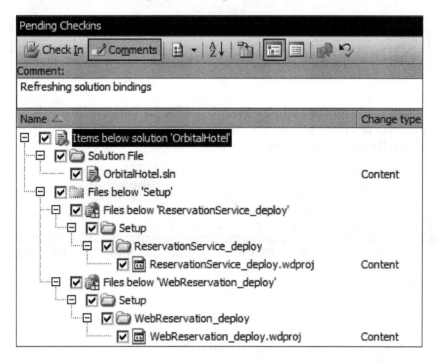

From now on, you are free to do all the maintenance required in this maintenance codeline, in parallel with the current development effort in the mainline. You can fix the bugs discovered after the release and build service packs that update the releases in the production environments.

However, at a certain point, all the bug fixes in the maintenance codeline must also be integrated into the mainline so the bugs are to be fixed here too. This is where we talk about codeline integration.

Integrating Codelines

We get a lot of benefits from parallel product development. We are able to keep efforts separate, ongoing development on the mainline and maintenance on maintenance codelines. The parallel efforts, however, need to converge at certain points. Work done in one place needs to be integrated in the other.

To integrate the work in different codelines we must merge the changes in one codeline with the other by merging branches.

Merging Branches

> Merging branches is available only in the Visual SourceSafe Explorer. All of the following techniques are performed using the Visual SourceSafe Explorer.

When changes made on one codeline branch need to be integrated into the parent branch, the branches must merge. The most common example is the integration of bug fixes from the maintenance line into the mainline.

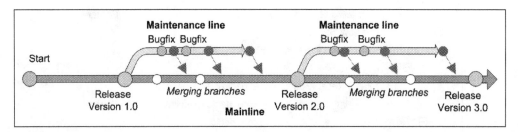

As bugs are fixed in the maintenance line, they need to be fixed in the mainline too.

Visual SourceSafe supports merging at the file level. Individual files are selected and merged separately.

In the following example, I will integrate the changes made in the maintenance codeline for Release 1 of the OrbitalHotel solution into the mainline.

The first step is to view the differences between the two codelines.

Viewing the Differences between Codelines

To view the differences between the projects that contain the two codelines, the **Show Differences** command is used.

I will view the differences between the mainline represented by the `$/OrbitalHotel.root/OrbitalHotel` project and the maintenance line for Release 1, represented by the `$/OrbitalHotel.root/OrbitalHotel Release 1/` project.

Start by selecting the mainline project and use the **Show Differences** command.

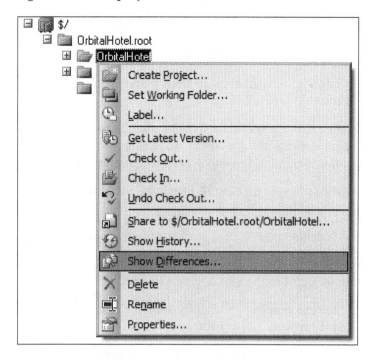

The **Project Difference** dialog is displayed.

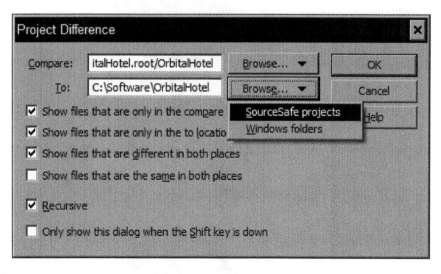

Select the **Show files that are only in compare location** option to view the files that exist in the **Compare** location but not in the **To** location.

Select the **Show files that are only in the to location** option to view the files that exist in the **To** location but not in the **Compare** location.

Select the **Show files that are different in both places** option to view the files present in both locations but that are different.

Select the **Show files that are the same in both places** option to view the files that are present in both locations and are identical. In this case, I will not select this option because I'm not interested in it. I'm only interested in files that are different.

Select the **Recursive** option to display all files in all the sub-projects.

By default, this window is set to show the differences between the SourceSafe database project contents and the local workspace contents.

Because the **Compare** location points to the mainline project location in the database, the **To** location must point to the maintenance line project location in the database.

Click the **Browse** button to select another location for comparison. You can choose between **SourceSafe projects** and **Windows folders**.

I will select **SourceSafe projects** to select the maintenance line project from the **Choose project from SourceSafe** dialog.

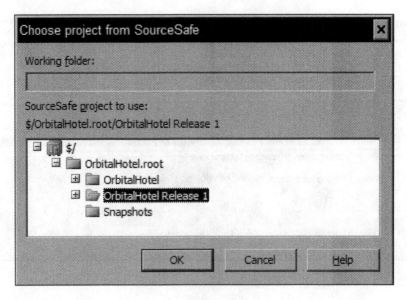

After choosing the project location, click **OK** to close the **Choose project from SourceSafe** dialog. Then, click **OK** in the **Project Difference** window to show the differences between the two SourceSafe projects.

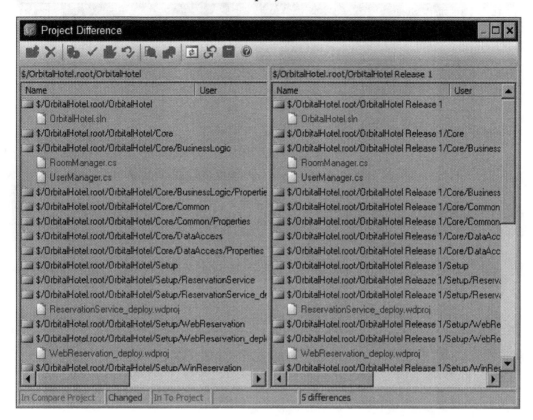

Now, the **Project Difference** window shows the differences between the two locations using the chosen filters. The status bar contains the legend with the different colors used for files **In Compare Project**, **Changed**, and **In To Project**.

We can see the differences between them using the **Show Difference** command in the contextual menu.

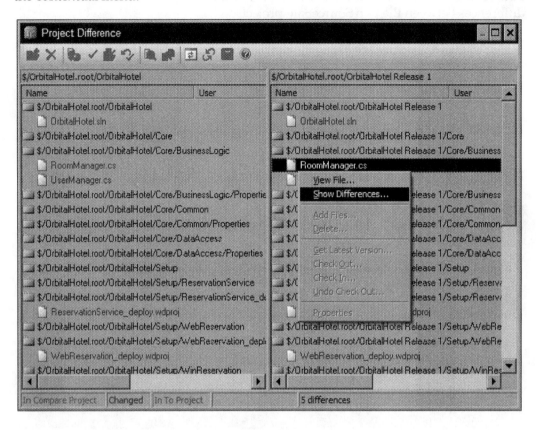

This will display the **Differences between** window as shown in the following figure:

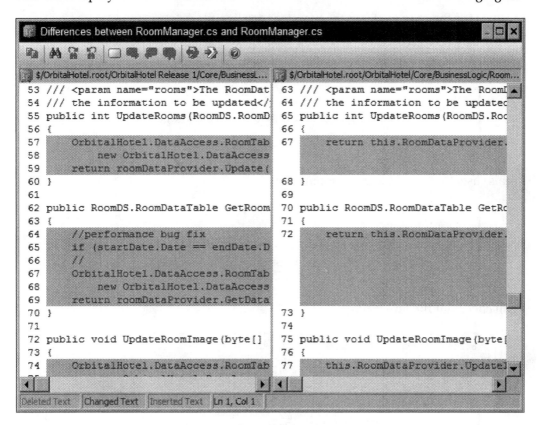

In the **Differences between** window, we can see the differences between the two files.

In the given example, we can see that things have changed quite a lot in the mainline (right side). The RoomDataProvider component is not created in each method anymore. It has been cached for performance reasons.

Things have changed in the maintenance line too (left side). A performance bug has been fixed so that if the startDate and endDate are the same, the database request is not made anymore because it makes no sense. You have to make a reservation for at least one night.

This bug fix must be included in the mainline too. This is done by merging these files.

Merging Files

I will merge the changes from the maintenance line file `OrbitalHotel.root/`
`OrbitalHotel Release1/Core/BusinessLogic/RoomManager.cs` into the mainline
file `OrbitalHotel.root/OrbitalHotel/Core/BusinessLogic/RoomManager.cs`.

 When merging files, we should select the **target** file first.

In this case, the target file is the mainline file.

 To merge the changes into the target file, first check out the
file into your workspace so you will be able to build and
test the new merged version locally before checking it in.

I will check out the target file.

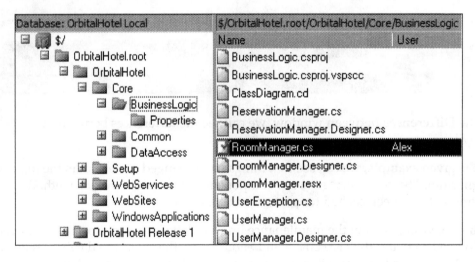

After checking out the target file, use the **Merge Branches** command form the **Versions** menu.

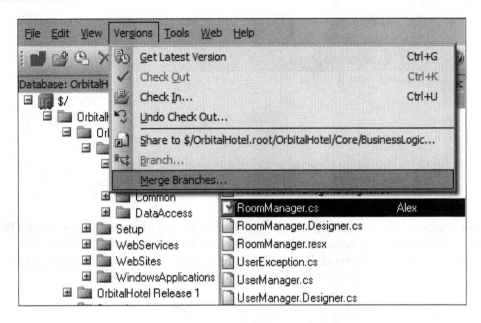

This will display the **Merge to** dialog.

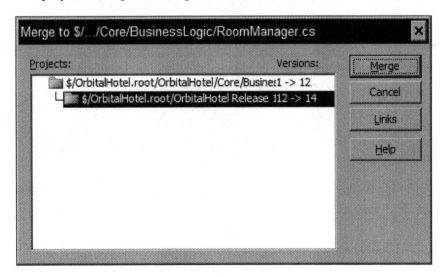

In the **Merge to** dialog, select the *source* file from which you are merging. In this case, I will select the Release 1 maintenance file.

Click the **Merge** button to start the file merge operation. This will display the **Comment for**...

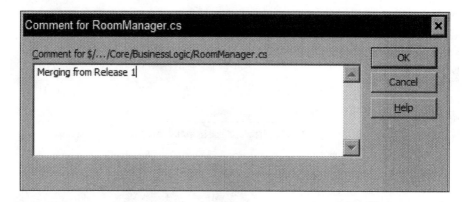

In this window, enter a description for the operation you are performing. Click **OK** to start the merging operation. If there are no conflicts between the two files, the merge operation will succeed. Before checking in the file, use Visual Studio to view, build, and test the merges to make sure everything is as it should.

Resolving Merge Conflicts

If there are conflicts between the two files, the three-way merge tool will be displayed to resolve the conflicts.

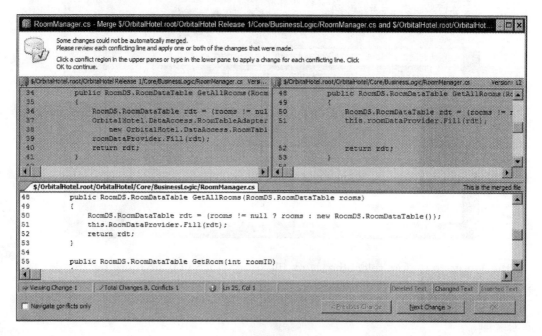

The merge tool shows the differences between the files in the two upper windows. The resulting merged file is displayed in the bottom window, which is editable.

To navigate conflicts only, make sure the **Navigate conflicts only** option is checked. Use the **Previous Change** and **Next Change** buttons to navigate changes.

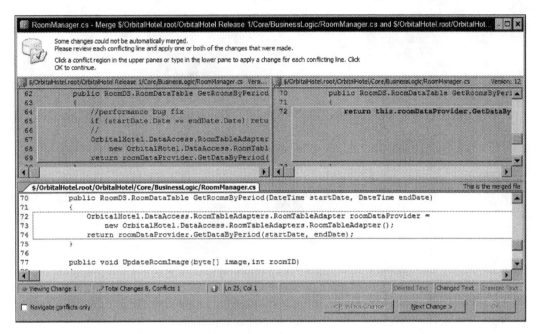

In this window, we can see the conflict between the files. The conflict has occurred because the same method (hence the same lines of code) was changed in both files. To resolve the conflict we have to reconcile the changes and create the final merged file.

In my case, I have to keep the changes made in the mainline where the component caching was added and also keep the bug fix from the maintenance line. To do that, I will select both changes and edit the result in the bottom window.

First, I will select the changes from the mainline by clicking on the changes in the right window. The bottom window will include only the changes in the right window.

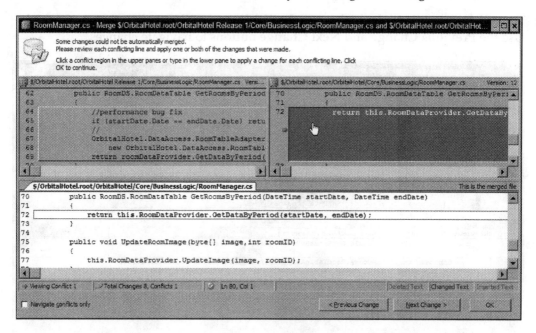

Second, I will select the changes from the maintenance line by clicking on the changes in the left window. The bottom window will include both changes.

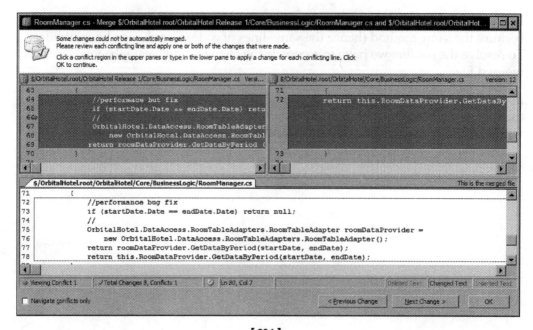

Now, I will edit the contents of the bottom window and make the necessary adjustments.

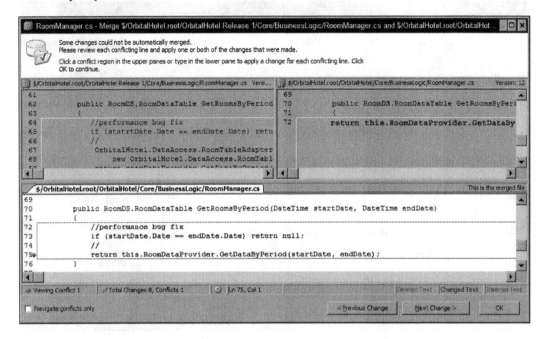

After editing, the conflict is resolved.

If there are no more conflicts that need to be resolved, click the **OK** button to close the merge tool. SourceSafe will ask if it is OK to save the new merged file.

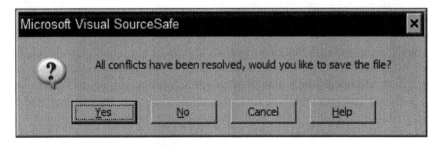

Click **Yes** to save the merged file locally in the workspace.

 After merging branches, use Visual Studio to view, build, and test the merges before checking in the files.

You can examine the changes in the merged files by opening Visual Studio.

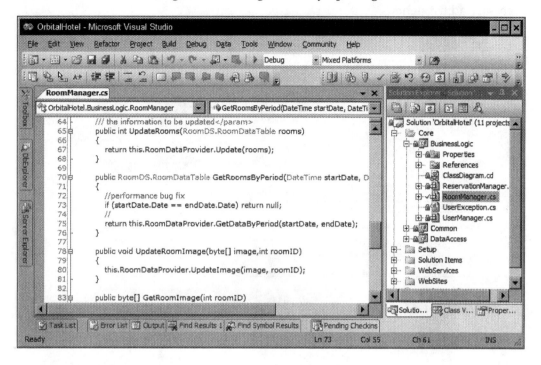

Summary

In this chapter we've seen how to manage the software development lifecycle using SourceSafe.

When developing a product we go through several milestones. A milestone is a point in time representing a key or important event in the life of a product. We mark milestones using labels so we can reproduce their configuration later when needed. We've seen how to create labels and how to get labeled versions and create persistent solution configuration snapshots in the SourceSafe database by sharing and pinning.

Then, we spoke about building either nightly or continuously, testing, and releasing a new product version. After releasing a new product version we have to maintain it while advancing development towards a new version. To be able to do this we have to conduct these efforts in parallel. We need to branch a new maintenance line for the maintenance effort while ongoing development is conducted in the mainline. After fixing bugs in the maintenance line we have to fix them in the mainline also. To do so, we have to merge the maintenance line changes into the mainline by merging the branches.

A

Installing Visual SourceSafe 2005

In this appendix, we will see how to install Visual SourceSafe 2005 and how to configure it for remote access using the internet plug-in. When installing Visual SourceSafe 2005 we have two types of configurations; the server and the clients.

 Installation of Visual SourceSafe 2005 on the Intel Itanium (IA64) is not supported.

Both installation configurations must be performed by a user with Windows administration privileges. The installation requires the .NET Framework 2.0 and the Microsoft Document Explorer 2005. If they are not already installed, they will be installed by the Visual SourceSafe 2005 Setup.

 If you have installed any previous versions of Visual SourceSafe, such as Visual SourceSafe 6.0d or any other previous version, then you *must uninstall* it before beginning to install Visual SourceSafe 2005.

SourceSafe 2005 should not be installed side by side with any previous version of SourceSafe, otherwise the correct operation of either version cannot be guaranteed. Furthermore, there is no need to keep previous versions of the product installed, because SourceSafe 2005 can operate against existing SourceSafe 6.0 databases.

Server Requirements

The Visual SourceSafe server hosts the SourceSafe databases, the LAN Booster Windows service, and the remote HTTP XML web service.

Although you can use Windows Professional editions to install SourceSafe as a server, to avoid connection limitations you must use a Windows Server operating system.

> Windows XP only supports a maximum of 10 concurrent client incoming sessions, which is sub-optimal if you plan to share your SourceSafe web service with other team members.

The server should have installed the network file sharing service (to enable shared folders), the TCP/IP protocol, an SSL Certificate (if you want to use remote access using HTTPS secure connections) and, for best security, a NTFS file system on the drives that will host SourceSafe databases. We will see how to create and install an SSL certificate in the *Configuring SourceSafe for Remote Access* section.

SourceSafe 2005 supports databases with a maximum individual file size of 4GB. While there is no limit for the database size, it is recommended to keep the database size to less than 4-5GB so that database maintenance tools like *Analyze* can run faster as well as often. The database drives must have enough disk space to accommodate database growth, especially when performing file operations like branching. To protect against disk drive failures, the server can have a **Redundant Array** of **Independent Disks (RAID)** configuration on the database drives.

Client Requirements

> When used as a source control provider for Visual Studio, the Visual SourceSafe 2005 client requirements fall into the requirements for running Visual Studio. Although administrator privileges are required for installation, after installation SourceSafe clients can run under normal user accounts.

SourceSafe Installation

The server installation is started by executing `Setup.exe` from the SourceSafe installation kit.

After loading the required components, the SourceSafe Setup displays the **Start Page**:

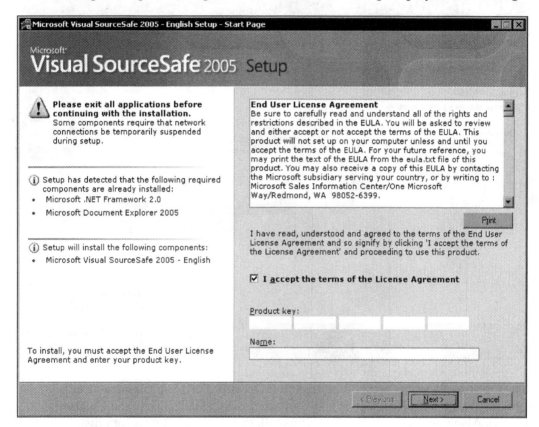

The **Start Page** asks for the product key, the user name, and the acceptance of the terms of the license agreement.

Every individual installation of SourceSafe requires a separate license. You can reuse the same product key on multiple installations but you must have a license for every one in order to avoid violating the copyright law.

After accepting the license agreement and entering a product key click the **Next** button to advance to the **Options Page**:

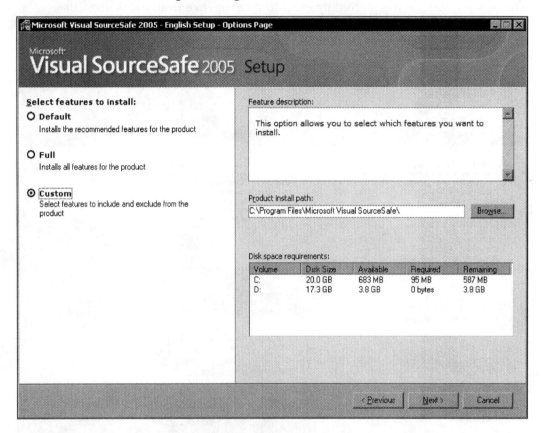

The **Options Page** lets you choose from the **Default**, **Full**, and **Custom** install options. To specifically select which components to install, choose the **Custom** option. Also you can leave the default installation path or set a custom installation path. Click **Next** to advance to the second **Options Page**:

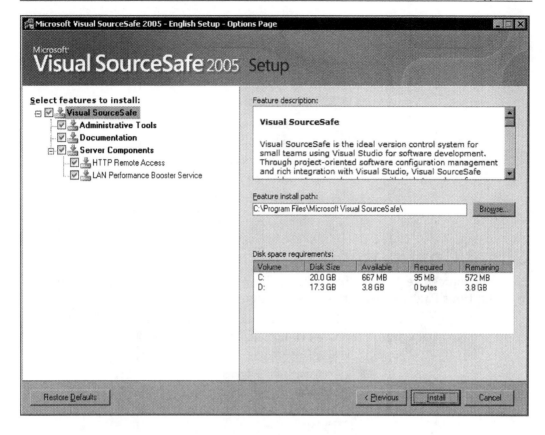

The second **Options Page** lets you choose the components you want to install.

- **Visual SourceSafe**: Installs the client components such as Visual SourceSafe Explorer.

- **Administrative Tools**: Installs the Visual SourceSafe Administrator and tools for database maintenance.

- **Documentation**: Installs the Visual SourceSafe documentation.

- **Server Components**: Installs the server components:
  - ○ **HTTP Remote Access**: Installs the HTTP web service components.
  - ○ **LAN Performance Booster Service**: Installs the LAN booster Windows service.

Server Configuration

To install SourceSafe 2005 on the server machine, select all the components.

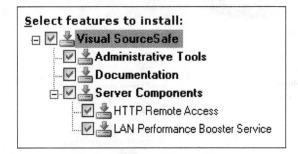

Client Configuration

To install SourceSafe 2005 on the client machines, select only the client components. In the **Options Page** uncheck the **Server Components** section.

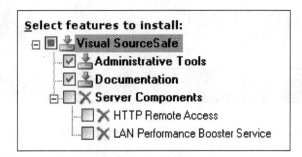

Finishing the Installation

After choosing the components to install, click **Install** to advance to the **Install Page** and finish the installation. After all components are installed, the Setup displays the **Finish Page**.

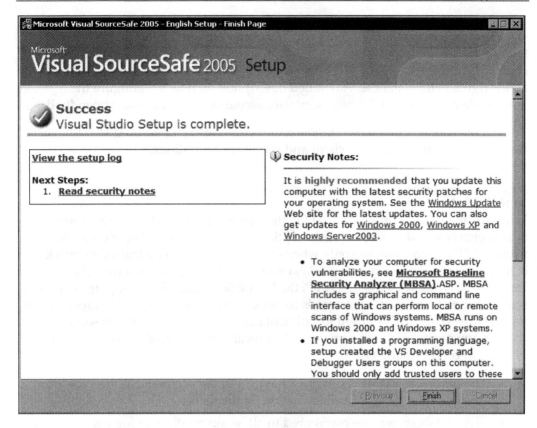

Click **Finish** to close the setup. .

Configuring SourceSafe for Remote Access

To be able to remotely access SourceSafe databases you must install the SourceSafe HTTP Remote Access components on the server machine. These components expose the XML web service used by the SourceSafe 2005 internet plug-in to perform source control tasks.

 You should make sure that the Internet Information Server (IIS) is installed on the SourceSafe server before configuring the SourceSafe web service.

When a remote user connects to the SourceSafe web service on the server, he or she authenticates using a Windows account. After authenticating successfully, the SourceSafe service impersonates that user account (performs operations in the user's context). For this reason, the Windows user account must be granted the necessary access rights in the database. A detailed description on how to configure the SourceSafe database and the necessary user accounts is provided in Appendix B.

The remote connection can use standard unsecured HTTP or secured HTTPS. These two methods require different client and server configurations.

Using HTTP

When using standard unsecured HTTP, the client requests and server responses are *not* encrypted, allowing data interception over the network. For this reason, using HTTP is recommended only when communicating over a trusted network connection (secured organization LAN or a secure VPN connection over the Internet). Even so, when using HTTP, the Visual SourceSafe internet plug-in doesn't send SourceSafe users and passwords to the server. Instead, because it impersonates the Windows user account used for authentication, the SourceSafe web service uses the Windows account's user name to automatically log in into the database. This brings two configuration issues:

- A SourceSafe user account must have the same username as the Windows user account used for authentication on the server.
- The database must be configured to allow automatic user log-ins.

For example, let's say John wants to access the SourceSafe database using the SourceSafe internet plug-in. If on the SourceSafe server he has the Windows *John* user account, his SourceSafe database user account must have the same username. A detailed description on how to configure the SourceSafe database and the necessary user accounts is provided in Appendix B.

On the client side, the SourceSafe internet plug-in must be configured to connect without using SSL.

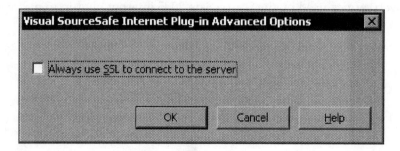

A detailed description of setting this option is provided in the additional material under the section *Advanced Options in the SourceSafe Internet Plug-In* provided online at http://www.packtpub.com/visual-sourcesafe-2005/book.

Using HTTPS

To secure the communication between the SourceSafe internet plug-in and the SourceSafe web service, you must use the **Secure Sockets Layer (SSL)** installed on IIS. SSL requires a server authentication certificate.

If you and all the teammates are part of the same Windows domain, it is likely that SSL certificates are already installed and everything should work without other configurations.

If not already installed, a local certificate can be created and installed using the **SelfSSL** tool provided in the IIS 6.0 Resource Kit (the easiest way available on both Server and Professional Windows editions) or the Certificate Services (available only on Windows Server editions).

On the client side, the SourceSafe internet plug-in must be configured to connect using SSL.

When this option is used, the SourceSafe Internet plug-in will send SourceSafe usernames and passwords to the server so the restrictions on user names as in the case of HTTP don't apply.

A detailed description of setting this option is provided in the additional material under the section *Advanced Options in the SourceSafe Internet Plug-In* provided online at http://www.packtpub.com/visual-sourcesafe-2005/book.

Setting up a Server Certificate using SelfSSL

To set up a server certificate using SelfSSL you must first install the IIS 6.0 Resource Kit Tools available at: http://www.microsoft.com/downloads/details.aspx?FamilyID=56fc92ee-a71a-4c73-b628-ade629c89499&displaylang=en.

During installation, make sure you select the SelfSSL 1.0 tool.

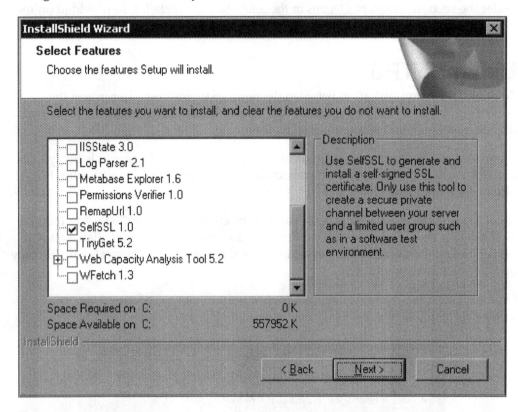

After finishing the installation, you can run `selfssl.exe` from the **Programs | IIS Resources | SelfSSL** start menu.

You can see all the command-line flags in the command window.

To generate a correctly configured certificate you must take into consideration the internet domain of your SourceSafe server. For example, my local computer name is ALEXS. Users on the local network can connect to it using this name. Users on the Internet, however, cannot connect to it using this name.

To be able to connect from the Internet, they must use the internet domain name address. By default SelfSSL generates a server certificate using the local name which is not correct in our case. To correctly generate the certificate you must use the internet domain address that will be used by the remote users to connect.

In my case, I have to execute the following command:

```
selfssl.exe /N:CN=vss.alexandruserban.com /T /V:365
```

The /T argument is used to automatically add the certificate to the Trusted Certificates list on the current machine (the server).

The /V argument determines for how many days the certificate will be valid. I created a certificate valid for one year.

The /S argument determines the IIS website on which to install the certificate. By default the certificate is installed on the website having the ID 1, which is the *default website*. On Windows Professional editions this is the only available website. On server editions you can create multiple websites. However, the SourceSafe web service is always installed on the web server having the ID 1. When configuring the certificate for the website that hosts the SourceSafe web service always use the ID 1 or use the default.

The /P argument determines the SSL port used. If you use a different port than the default 443, you can specify it using this argument.

Installing the Certificate on the Clients

After you install the certificate on the server using SelfSSL, it must also be installed on the client machines, because they need to trust it in order to use it for encrypting data.

The easiest way to install the certificate on the clients is to navigate to the SourceSafe server's website using *HTTPS* instead of HTTP.

For example, to install on a client machine the certificate I've created earlier, I will have to open Internet Explorer on the client and navigate to https://vss.alexandruserban.com.

Internet Explorer 6 will pop up a security alert because the certification authority (the server) is not trusted.

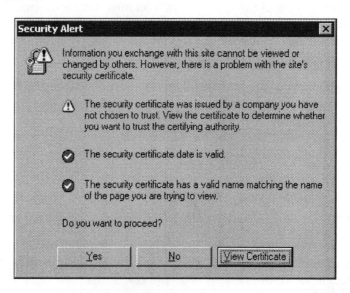

Internet Explorer 7 will show the following page instead:

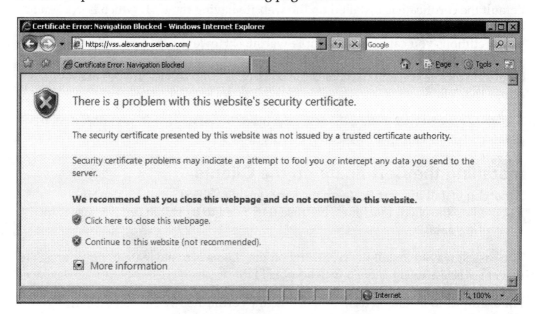

Click the **Continue to this website (not recommended)** link to continue and then click on the **Certificate Error** notification next to the address bar.

In order to trust the certificate we have to install it on the client. To do this, click **View certificates** either in Internet Explorer 6 or 7. This will display the following certificate:

We can use this installation method because the certificate created by SelfSSL is a root certificate. You can see that the **Issued by** and the **Issued to** fields are the same. Their value must be the server's internet address.

Click **Install Certificate** to install the certificate on the client. This will show the **Certificate Import Wizard**. Click **Next** until you finish the wizard. This will display a security warning similar to the following:

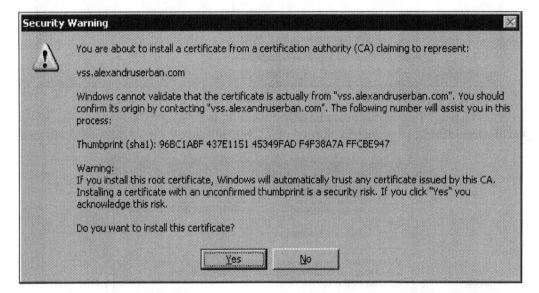

Click **Yes** in the security warning to install the certificate.

Restart Internet Explorer and navigate again to the same address. This time no security warnings should appear.

Repeat this procedure on all the clients.

Setting up a Server Certificate using Certificate Services

To create a server certificate you need to install the **Microsoft Certificate Services** on the server machine running a Windows Server operating system using the **Add/Remove Windows Components** section in the **Add/Remove Programs Control Panel**:

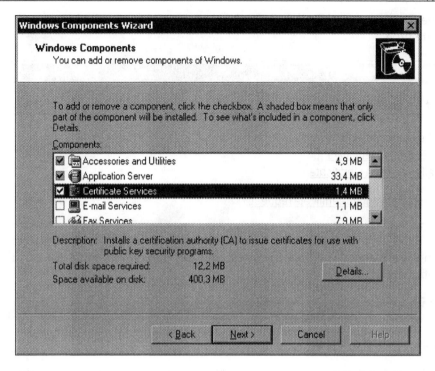

Use this wizard to install the Certificate Services if not already installed.

Requesting the Certificate

Open Internet Explorer and go to `http:/[your server name]/certsrv`. You will see a page similar to the following:

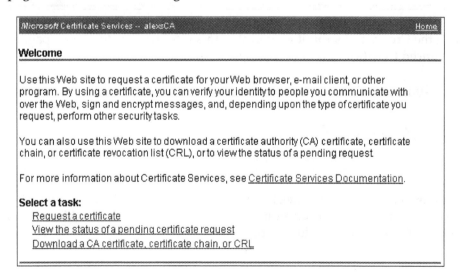

Click the **Request a certificate** link. In the next page you are asked for a certificate type.

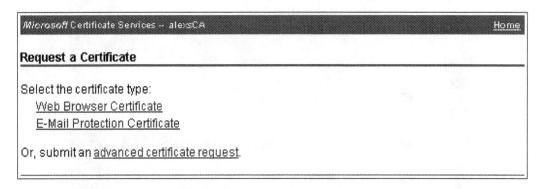

Click on the **advanced certificate request** link. The next page shows the certificate type options.

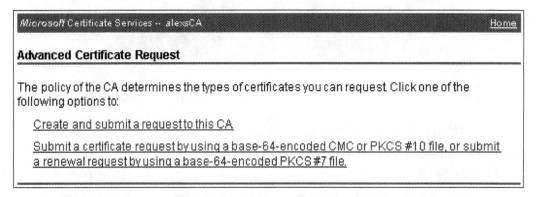

Click on the **Create and submit a request to this CA** link. The following page shows the **Advanced Certificate Request** options:

Advanced Certificate Request

Identifying Information:

Name: vss.alexandruserban.com

In the **Identifying Information** section you must enter in the **Name** textbox the internet domain name of the server machine where the SourceSafe XML web service is installed. The remaining fields are optional.

In this case I'm creating a certificate for the server whose domain is vss. alexandruserban.com. This is the domain that remote users will use to connect to the SourceSafe web service.

In the **Type of Certificate Needed** section, select **the Server Authentication Certificate** option.

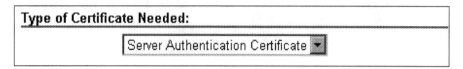

Under the **Key Options** section, select as the cryptographic service provider (CSP) the **Microsoft Enhanced Cryptographic Provider v1.0**. Also check the **Store certificate in the local computer certificate store** option to store the certificate in the local certificate store.

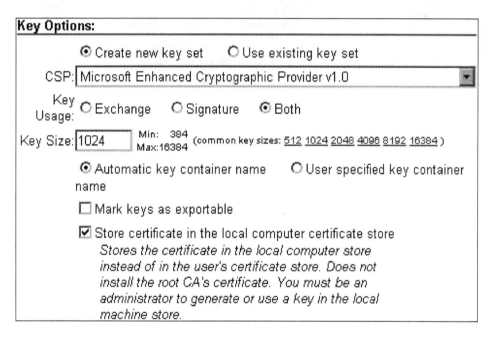

Click the **Submit** button to submit the certificate request and then click **Yes** in the warning message.

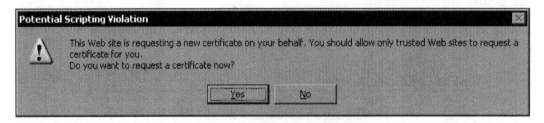

The certificate request is submitted to the certification authority, it is given a **Request Id**, and it is pending the approval to be issued.

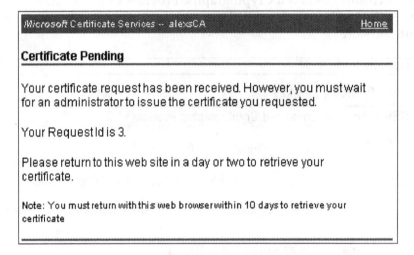

You must wait for the certificate request to be issued by the administrator, or, if you have administrator rights, you can issue it yourself.

Issuing the Server Certificate

To issue the server certificate, go to the **Certification Authority** section in the **Control Panel** under the **Administrative Tools**.

Expand your server name under the **Certification Authority** root node and click on the **Pending Requests** subfolder. In the right pane you can see all the pending certificate requests. To issue a certificate request right-click the request, choose **All Tasks**, and then click **Issue**.

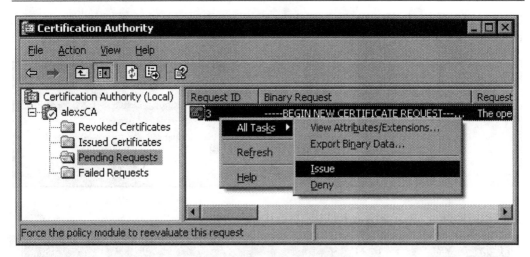

The certificate is issued and can now be installed on the server.

Installing the Certificate on the Server

To install the certificate open Internet Explorer and go to: `http:/[your server name]/certsrv`.

Click on the **View the status of a pending certificate request** link. The next page shows the statuses of pending certificate requests and issued certificates.

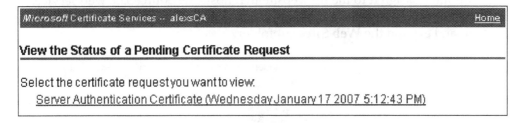

To view the certificate, click on the **Server Authentication Certificate** link. The next page allows you to install the issued certificate.

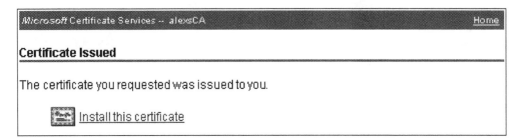

Click on the **Install this certificate** link and then click **Yes** in the warning message to install the certificate.

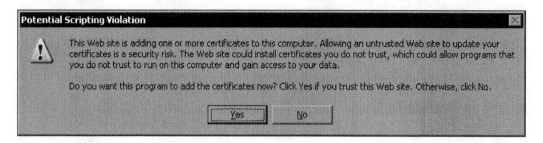

The certificate is successfully installed on the server.

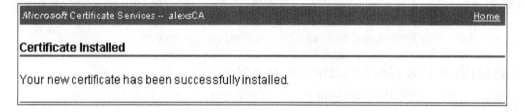

Assigning the SSL Certificate to the Website

Once you have the server certificate, (either created by you or issued by a third party) you must assign it to the IIS website that hosts the SourceSafe web service. To assign the certificate to the website, open the **Internet Information Services Manager**, and expand the **Web Sites** subfolder.

Right-click the **Default Web Site** (or the site having the ID of 1), and click **Properties**. Go to the **Directory Security** tab page. In this tab page, you can see the **Secure communications** section.

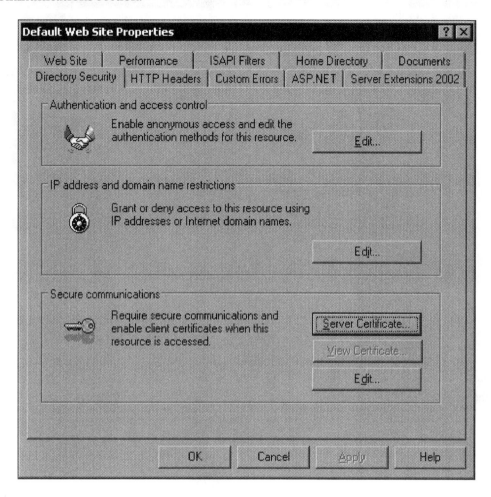

Click on the **Server Certificate** button to activate the **IIS Certificate Wizard**.

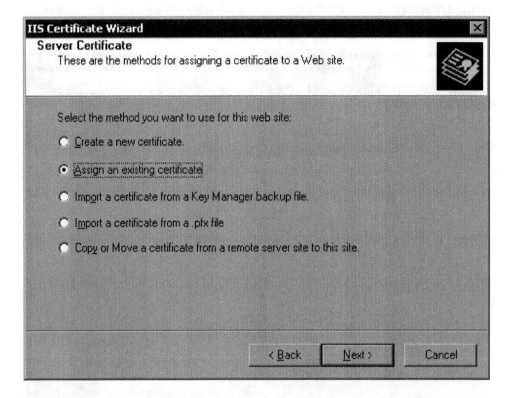

Select the **Assign an existing certificate** option and click **Next**. In the following page, select the server certificate.

In my case, I will select the certificate I created earlier:

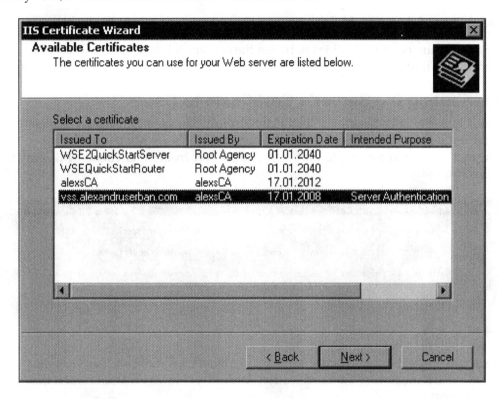

Click **Next** to select the certificate and advance to the **SSL Port** page.

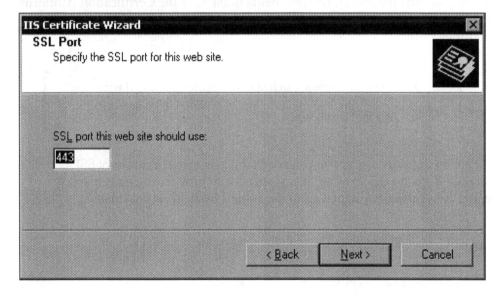

If you use another SSL port than the default 443 you can enter it here.

Click **Next** and then click **Finish** to assign the server certificate to the website.

Now the secure communications between the server and the clients will use the selected certificate.

Distributing the Server's Certificate to Users

If you choose to issue your own certificates, unless you are a globally recognized certification authority such as VeriSign, your certificates are not trusted by other machines. Trying to connect to the SourceSafe server from other clients will result in an error message.

To successfully establish a secure connection to the SourceSafe web service, the remote clients must trust the Certification Authority (the server) that issued the SSL certificate.

To be able to trust the server, remote clients must have the Certification Authority Root (CA Root) certificate installed into their local Trusted Root Certification Authorities store.

 Using the browser to install certificates generated with Certificate Services will not work unless the SSL certificate is a root certificate.

In the following screenshot, you can see that if you install a non-root SSL certificate on the clients using the browser, it will still not be fully trusted because the Certification Authority (displayed in the **Issued by** field) is not trusted.

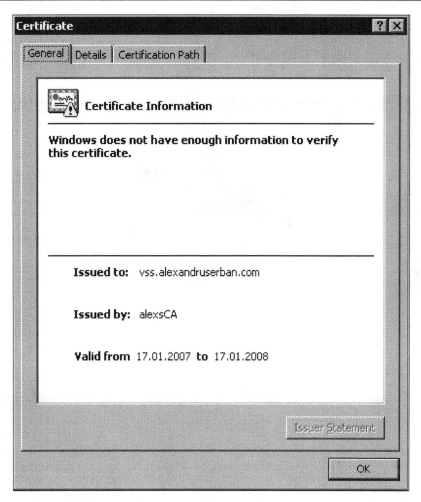

In this case you must export and distribute your server's CA Root certificate to users who will connect to the SourceSafe web service so the generated SSL certificates will be trusted.

To export the CA Root certificate, open the Microsoft Management Console (mmc.exe), and add the Certificates for the local computer snap-in to it. Go to the **Trusted Root Certification Authorities** store, right-click your server's root certificate and use the **All Tasks** menu to **Export** the certificate.

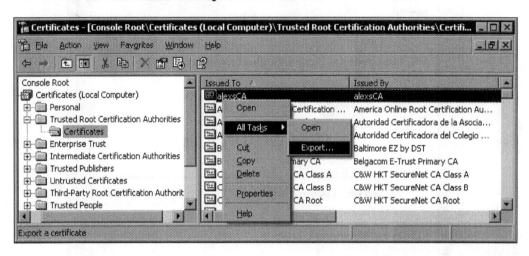

The **Certificate Export Wizard** will open. In the second page, choose not to export the private key and click **Next**.

Choose the format you want to use to export the certificate and click **Next**.

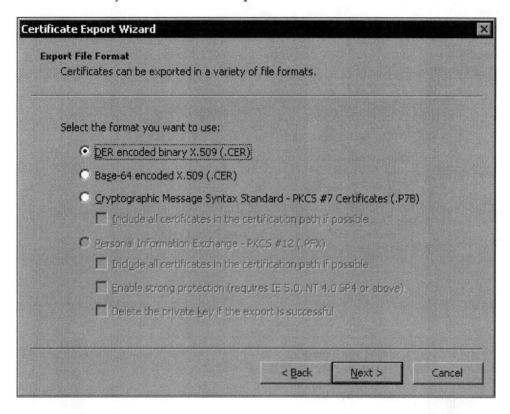

Enter the path for the certificate file to be created and click **Next**.

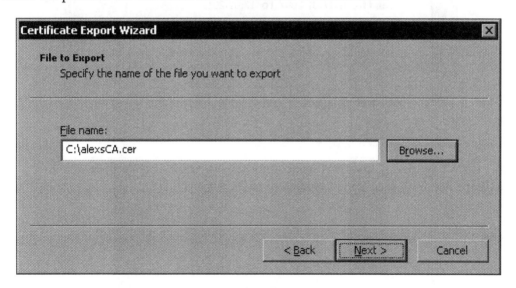

Click **Next,** and then **Finish** in the last page to export your CA Root certificate to the selected file.

Now you can distribute your CA Root certificate file to users who will connect to the SourceSafe web service. All they have to do is to double-click the file and click the **Install Certificate** button.

After installing the CA Root certificate, remote SourceSafe users will be able to successfully establish a secure connection to the server.

Summary

In this appendix, we've covered the SourceSafe 2005 installation. We've seen what are the requirements and the installation configurations for the server and the clients.

Then, we've seen how to configure SourceSafe for remote access using HTTP and HTTPS. You should use HTTP only on trusted networks to minimize the risk of data interception. If you connect remotely over the Internet, to secure the connection use HTTPS instead. You have to configure the server and the clients with an SSL certificate. You can create certificates using the SelfSSL tool or the Microsoft Certification Services. After creating and installing the SSL certificate on the server, you have to distribute it and install it on the client machines.

B

Creating and Configuring SourceSafe Databases

In this appendix, we will see how to perform SourceSafe database administration tasks such as creating and securing databases, managing database and Windows users, creating shadow folders, and configuring the services for the SourceSafe plug-ins in Visual Studio.

Creating Databases

To create a new SourceSafe database, we use the Visual SourceSafe Administrator application. After opening this application, to create a new database, use the New Database command by going to **File | New Database**:

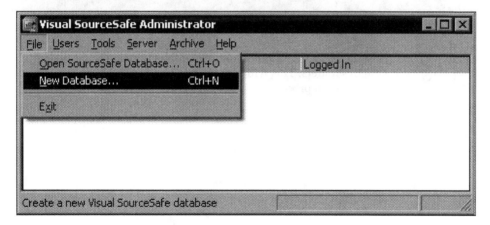

This will display the welcome dialog of the **Add SourceSafe Database Wizard**. To continue, click **Next** to advance to the second page. In the second dialog, we must specify a new empty folder to create the database in.

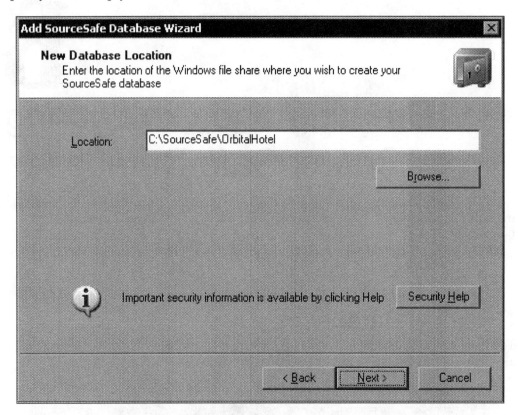

 Select a folder that is not under one of the operating system's folders. This will ease the database configuration process.

Click the **Next** button to advance to the next dialog. We can specify a friendly name
for the new database in this dialog.

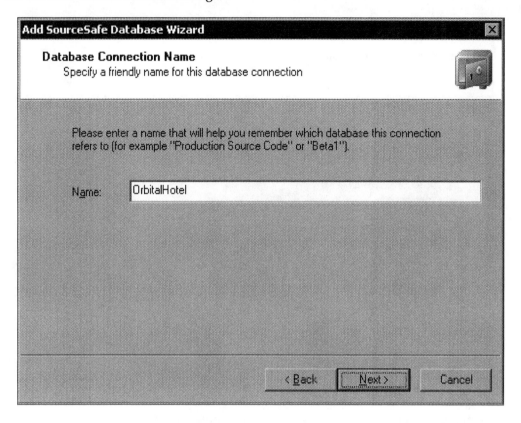

After specifying the friendly name for the database, click **Next** to advance to the **Team Version Control Model** dialog.

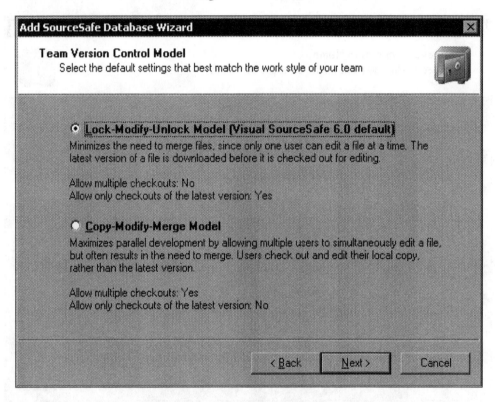

In this dialog, we must choose an initial version control model or checkout model for the database. Here we can choose between the two SourceSafe models:

- **Lock-Modify-Unlock Model** or the Exclusive Checkout Model
- **Copy-Modify-Merge Model** or the Multiple Checkout Model

This model can later be changed, if required, and we will see how in Appendix C.

After choosing the initial checkout model, the wizard has enough information to create the new database. Click **Next** to display the final summary dialog. If at this point you want to change any of the previous options, you can go back and make the necessary changes by clicking **Back**. To create the new database click **Finish**.

After the new database is created at the selected location, SourceSafe will display a security warning, informing about the necessary security settings that must be applied in order to secure the database.

Let's see how to enforce database security.

Securing the Database

The Windows security for a SourceSafe database is divided across two layers:

- Windows Shared Folder Security: applied to the shared folders, based on Windows user accounts.
- Windows NTFS Security: applied to the file system database folders, based on Windows user accounts.

The following diagram shows these layers:

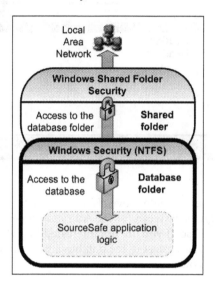

The most important layer in securing a SourceSafe database is the Windows NTFS Security layer applied to the database folder. This is the only way to assign strict access permissions to the users that must access the database files. The security of SourceSafe databases is determined by the security of the folder that contains them. To implement the necessary security, the database must be installed on an NTFS file system because you can grant permissions for individual files and folders.

In contrast, the **File Allocation Table (FAT)** file system applies the same permissions to the entire shared folder. Shared folder security is not restrictive enough and can be bypassed by users logged in locally on the database server.

In addition to these security layers, SourceSafe has its own mechanisms for account management and project rights, but they are not security measures. These mechanisms are applied at the application logic level and complement the operating system's security applied to the database folders and files. SourceSafe usernames and project rights assignments can be bypassed by malicious users; therefore, it is important to secure your database using Windows integrated security.

Every user that will access the SourceSafe database will have a Windows user account for the database server and a SourceSafe user account for the database.

After a new SourceSafe database is created, its initial configuration contains three SourceSafe users, the **Admin** user, the **Guest** user, and a third user named after the Windows user account that created the database, in my case **Alex**.

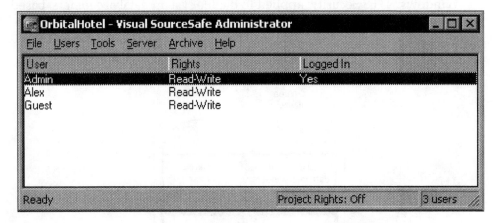

 These users initially have *blank* passwords. Do not forget to assign a password for the Admin user before sharing the database. If you are not interested in giving access to someone as a guest in the database, you can delete the Guest account.

The SourceSafe Admin User

The SourceSafe *Admin* user is a special user account. This is *the only* account name you can use to administer a SourceSafe database and cannot be edited or deleted. When opening the Visual SourceSafe Administrator application to log in to an existing database, you can see that the **User name** is always set to **Admin** and it cannot be changed.

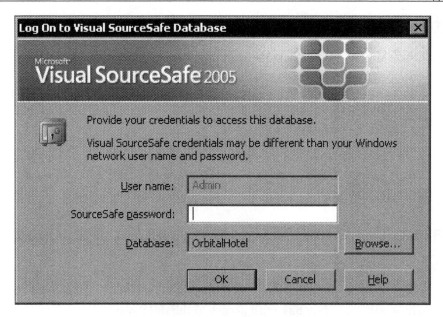

As a result, if there are several database administrators, they will all have to log in to the database using this built-in **Admin** account.

To set the Admin user password use the **Users | Change Password** command.

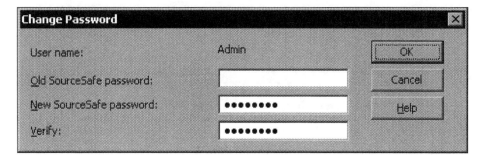

Do not choose the same password as your Windows account password because if your Windows password is weak, the SourceSafe password may be used as leverage in a dictionary attack in an attempt to guess your Windows password.

If third-party tools are used to access the SourceSafe database, they may not secure the SourceSafe passwords enough and may accidentally disclose the Windows passwords this way.

Setting the Windows Security for the Database

Every SourceSafe database user will have a Windows user account on the database server for authentication in addition to the SourceSafe user account. This can be a domain user if the database server and the user's machine are part of the same domain, or a local Windows user on the database server.

The best way to simplify user administration on the database server is by creating Windows **user groups** to which the database users will be assigned depending on their role.

Creating the Windows Groups for the Database Users

There are two user roles for a SourceSafe database:

- Administrators: they have full access to the database
- Users: they have restricted access to the database

As a result, the database's users will be assigned to one of these two user groups.

For the OrbitalHotel database, I will create two groups using the **Local Users and Groups** snap-in in the **Computer Management** console, one for the administrators, named **OrbitalHotel Admins** and one for the users, named **OrbitalHotel Users**.

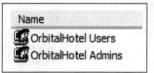

When adding users or administrators to the database, all that is required to manage the Windows security for the database is adding their Windows user accounts to one of these groups.

Setting the Security Permissions for the Database

After creating the two groups of users, we have to configure the NTFS security permissions for the database folder.

In my case I will configure the `C:\SourceSafe\OrbitalHotel` folder I used to create the OrbitalHotel database in.

The default security for a Windows folder is inherited from its parent folder and looks something like this:

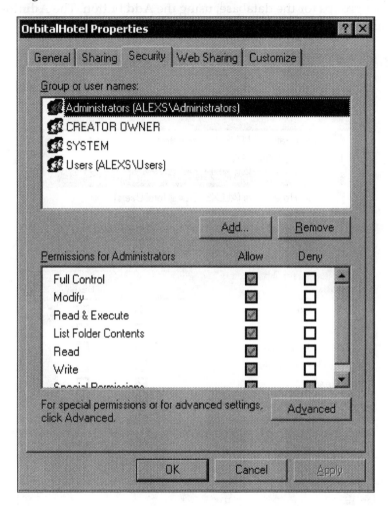

Because we don't want all the default users to be able to access the database folder, the inherited security must be removed. Before doing that, we must add the two Windows user groups for the database, using the **Add** button. The **Admins** group will have **Full Control** security permissions on the database folder.

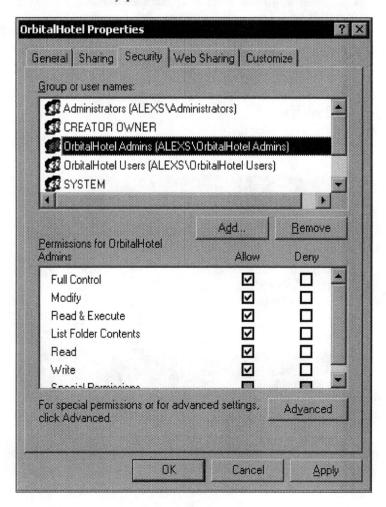

The **Users** group will only have the **List Folder Contents** and **Read** security permissions on the database folder.

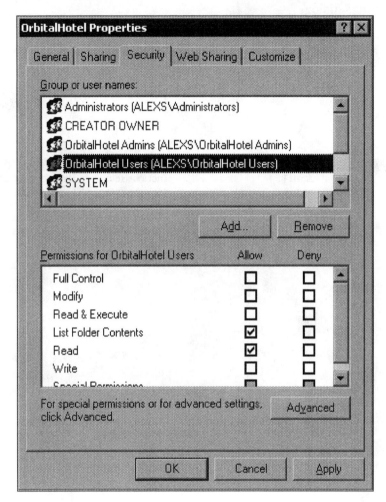

This is because the database folder contains files like the `srcsafe.ini` that contain the database configuration information and should be modified only by administrators. As a result, several security permissions must be added individually to the other folders under the database folder. To ease this task let's first remove the inherited security permissions.

To remove the inherited security permissions, we have to go to the advanced security settings by clicking the **Advanced** button. This will display the **Advanced Security Settings** dialog.

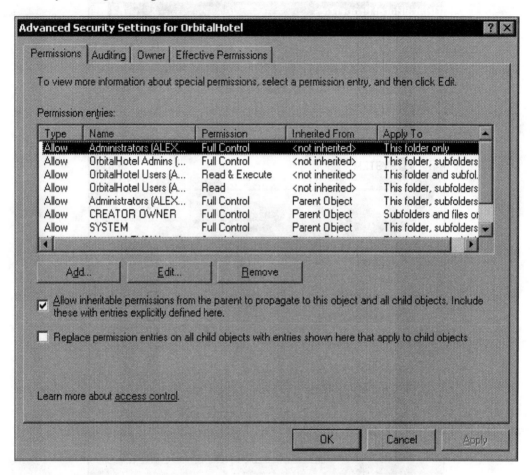

To remove the inherited security permissions we must uncheck the option allowing permission inheritance. This will display a question dialog asking whether to copy the inherited permissions or to remove them.

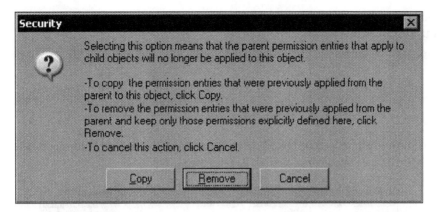

Click the **Remove** button to remove the inherited security and then click **OK** to close the **Advanced Security Settings** dialog. Now, the security permissions for the database folder contain only the two required user groups.

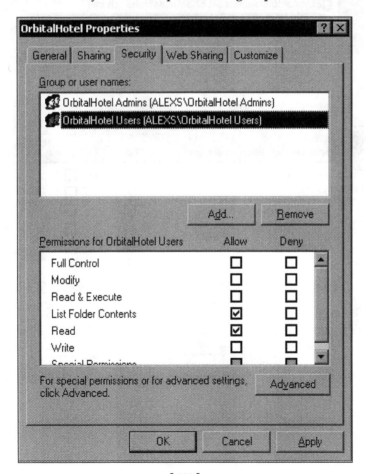

After removing the inherited security we can continue to assign permissions for the folders under the database folder.

All the folders under the database folder (except for the `users` folder) must be granted **Modify** permissions for the *Users* group.

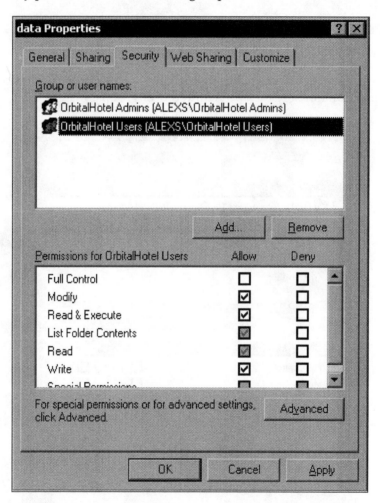

As you already know, the `users` folder contains a folder for each database user that stores individual customizations and configurations. Each user must be allowed to modify only his or her personal folder. This will also ensure that each user can log in into the database only using his or her username. For each user folder we must grant **Modify** permissions for the user Windows account.

In my case, I will add the Windows user Alex in the security for the `users/alex` folder and give it permissions to modify its contents.

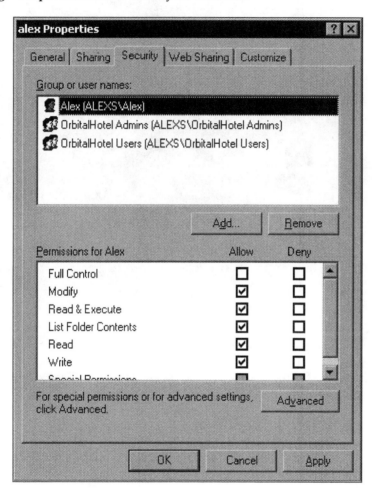

Setting the Time Zone

If the database will be used by a geographically distributed team, it is important to set the database time zone to avoid time problems with resource, time stamping, and logging.

To set the time zone for the database, open the **Option** window in the Visual SourceSafe Administrator using the **Tools | Options** menu command and select the **Time Zone** tab page.

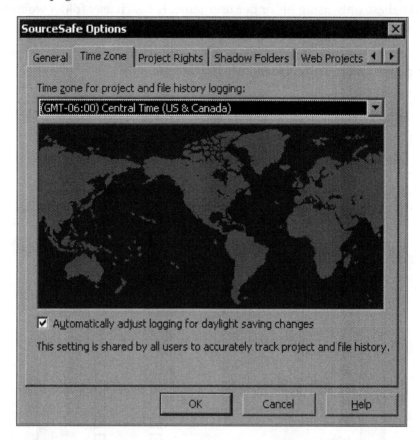

Specify the time zone for the SourceSafe server by using the **Time zone for project and file history logging** combo box.

 The time zone should not be changed once the database is used, to avoid data loss due to overlapping time stamps.

Sharing the Database

After setting the Windows security permissions for the database, we can share the database on the local network.

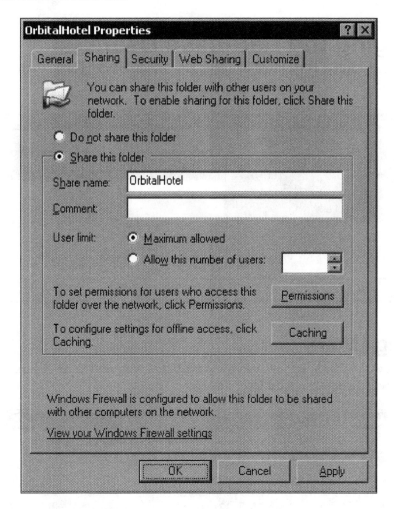

You can hide the shared folder by appending the $ character at the end of the share name. For example, if I want to hide the OrbitalHotel shared folder so that it is not visible on the local network, I would have to name it OrbitalHotel$. If you hide the shared folder, you will have to inform all the users about the correct name.

The default sharing permissions are set so that everyone can read the contents of the shared folder. We have to change that by clicking the **Permissions** button. Remove the **Everyone** group from the **Permissions** dialog and add the two groups of users for the database.

You must give **Full Control** permissions to the **Admins** group and **Change** permissions to the **Users** group.

Now the database is ready for use.

Managing the Database Users

User administration is performed by using the commands available in the **Users** menu.

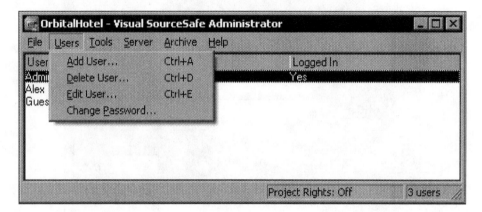

Adding Users

To add a new database user, we use the **Add User** command in the **Users** menu. This command will display the **Add User** dialog.

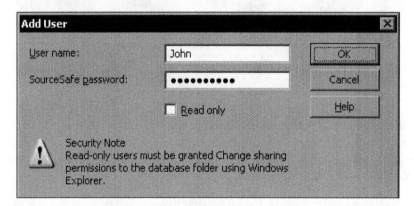

Specify the new username and an initial SourceSafe password for the user. The user will later be able to change the password using the Visual SourceSafe Explorer application.

The best practice for naming SourceSafe users is to give them the same names as their Windows account names used to access the database. This ensures that automatic user login is possible, especially when accessing the database remotely over simple HTTP.

You can give certain users read-only access to the database by checking the **Read only** option. These users will only be able to see the contents of the database without being able to change, add, or delete files in the database when using the SourceSafe applications. These restrictions are only enforced at application logic level.

The **Security Note** warns about the fact that these read-only users will still need **Change** sharing permissions on the database shared folder. Because we used the two Windows groups to manage the user security permissions and we have given the required permissions to these groups rather than managing users individually, we are covered.

To allow a new user into the database, we have to create a Windows account for this user if he or she doesn't already have an account, and add his or her account to either the *Admins* Windows group or the *Users* Windows group, depending on the role of the user. In my case I will add John to the *Users* group for the database.

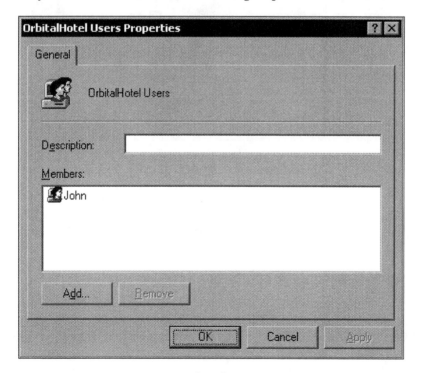

To enable the user to log in, we have to grant **Modify** permissions to his or her personal folder under the database users folder. In my case, I will grant **Modify** permissions to John's Windows account for the users/john folder.

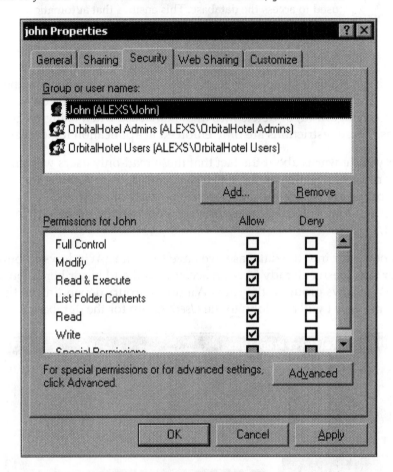

Now, John can log in to the database successfully.

We've seen that we can set read-only permissions for users who wouldn't have to change anything in the database. However, a better way to deal with users that require read-only permissions is by using **shadow folders**.

Setting Shadow Folders for Read-Only Users

A shadow folder is a special folder that contains copies of the most recently checked-in files for a specific project. Each time a check in is performed on a shadowed project the latest versions for the modified resources are copied to the shadow folder.

The latest file versions are copied to the shadow folder by the user's client SourceSafe application, and not by the server.

You will most often use a shadow folder in a team environment to allow users to view, but not modify files. Another use for the shadow folder is for the compilation of the latest project version, for example in a nightly build.

Because shadow-folder users don't have access to the database, it is not recommended to set the shadow folder under the database folder. Instead, the shadow folder must be set to a different shared folder.

Shadow folders are created using the **Options** dialog in the Visual SourceSafe Administrator application. To display this dialog use the **Tools | Options** menu command.

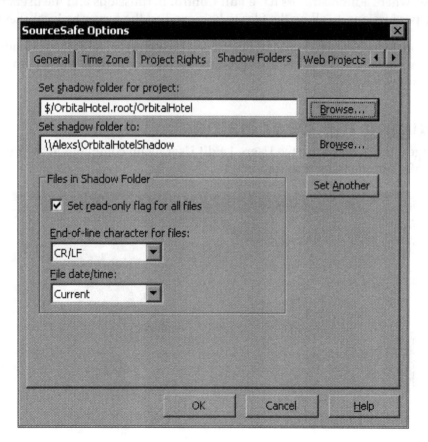

Select the database project you want to shadow using the first **Browse** button and the shared shadow folder using the second **Browse** button.

> When setting shadow folders, always use the server's (UNC) network path to the shared folder designated to hold the shadow copies. If you set local paths, because files are copied to the shadow folders by the SourceSafe client applications, when users check in files they will be copied into the local folder *on their machines*. Use the network name to identify the server folder correctly.

You can set more than one shadow folder for a project. To do that, use the **Set Another** button.

The security permissions for the shadow folders must be the same as for the database, where administrators have **Full Control** permissions and the users have **Modify** permissions, to allow the files to be copied on the server by local clients.

In addition, to manage the read-only users you can create an additional Windows group that contains these users. This group must have only **Read Only** permissions to the shadow folder.

Changing the User Name

To change a user's name use the **Users | Edit User** menu command in the Visual SourceSafe Administrator application.

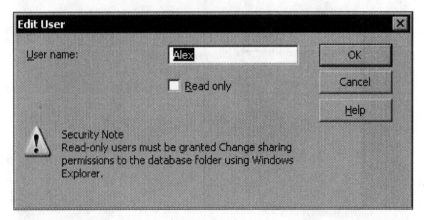

Enter the new user name in the text box and click **OK**.

After changing the user's name you have to reapply the Windows security for the user's new folder name in the `users` folder.

Changing the User Password

To change a user's password use the **Users | Change password** menu command in the Visual SourceSafe Administrator application.

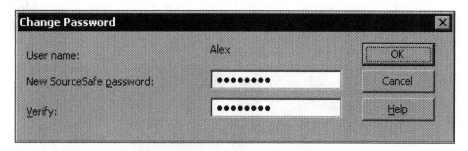

Enter the new user password in the text box and click **OK**.

Users can change their passwords using Visual SourceSafe Explorer.

 Instruct the users not to choose the same password as their Windows account password so that SourceSafe passwords cannot be used as leverage in attempts to crack the Windows password. The Windows security assures that only authorized users can access the database.

Allowing Automatic User Logins

You can choose not to use the SourceSafe passwords and rely only on Windows security. Users will log in to the database without the need to specify their SourceSafe password as long as their Windows account used to access the database has the same name as their SourceSafe user account name.

When using remote access using simple HTTP, you have to always allow automatic user logins. This is required because the SourceSafe internet plug-in doesn't send SourceSafe usernames and password to the server when not using a secured HTTPS connection. The SourceSafe Web Service will try to automatically log in to the database using the SourceSafe username that matches the Windows account's username used for server authentication.

To enable automatic user logins, open the Visual SourceSafe Administrator **Options** window and select the **General** tab page. Select the **Use network name for automatic user log in** option.

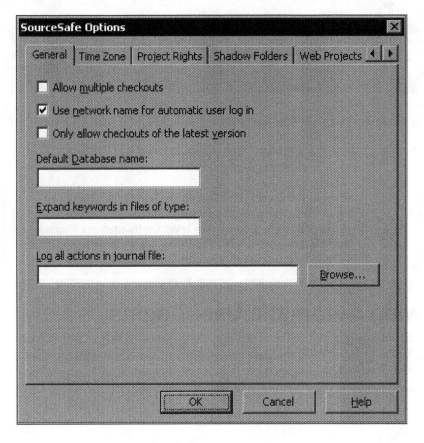

Setting Project Rights for Users

You can set different rights for SourceSafe users on projects. This can be useful if each user works on specific projects where he or she needs to have full access, while having restricted access on the other projects.

By default project rights are disabled for a new database. To enable project rights, we have to go to the **Options** dialog in the Visual SourceSafe Administrator. Use the **Tools | Options** command to display this dialog and select the **Project Rights** tab page. Click the **Enable Rights and Assignments commands** option to enable project rights.

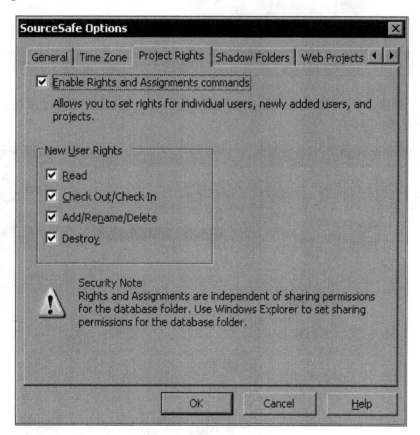

After enabling project rights, you can also set the rights assigned for new users when they are first added. By default all the rights are assigned to a new user. To restrict the default rights, uncheck the rights that shouldn't be assigned to new users. For example, you can set **Read** permissions to new users, and then assign **Rights by Project**.

Project rights are assigned using the first three commands in the **Tools** menu. After enabling project rights, these commands will be enabled.

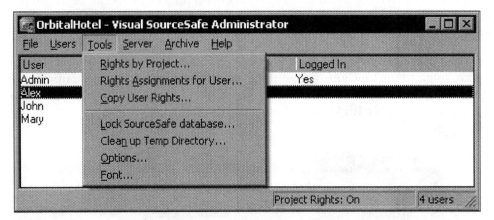

To assign rights by project, use the **Rights by Project** command. This will display the **Project Rights** dialog.

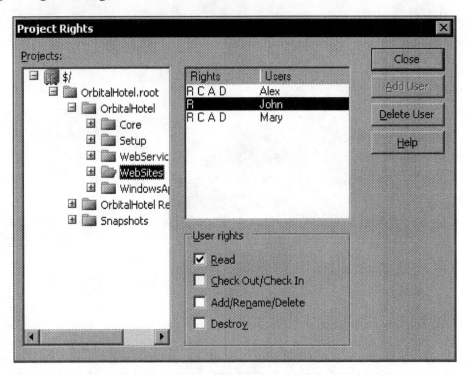

To assign the rights a user has for a specific project, select the project you want to assign rights for in the **Projects** tree. Then, select the user to assign the rights for in the user list. Assign the rights for the user using the **User rights** group under the user list. In my case, because John is not assigned to work on the **WebSites** project, I will only give him **Read** rights, to prevent him to make accidental modifications to that project.

At any time you can see and edit the rights assignments for a user by selecting the username in the Visual SourceSafe Administrator main window and using the **Rights Assignment for User** command. This will display the **Assignments** window.

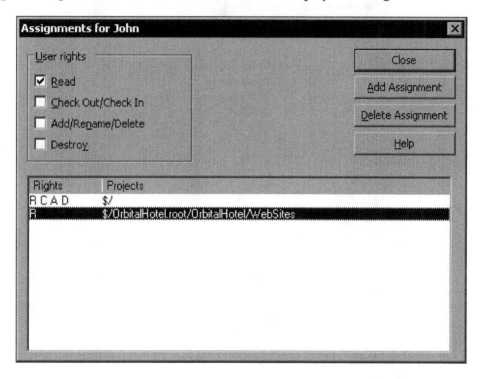

In the **Assignments** window you can see all the assignments for the selected user with the possibility to add, edit, or remove them.

To add new assignments use the **Add Assignment** button.

To edit the rights for an assignment, select the assignment in the list and use the **User rights** group box to edit the rights.

To delete an assignment, select the assignment in the list and click the **Delete Assignment** button.

You can also copy rights assignments form one user to another. This allows you to use a user as a template for another user. To copy the rights form one user to another, select the user you want to copy the rights to in the Visual SourceSafe Administrator main window and use the **Copy User Rights** command in the **Tools** menu.

For example, I will give Mary the same rights as John by copying the rights from John.

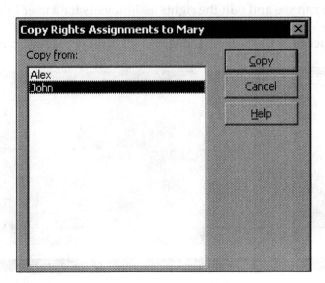

 Copying the rights from another user will delete any previous assignments the target user had.

Auditing User Actions with Journal Files

To monitor the actions of database users, you can set up a journal file. A journal file is a text file that records any action by a user that generates a history entry for a file or project in the database.

To set up a journal file, create a text file in the database folder, for example `journal.txt`.

 Entries in the `journal.txt` file are created by local SourceSafe applications, and not by the server.

As a result, to be able to write to this file, give members of the **Users** group **Write** permissions to the journal file.

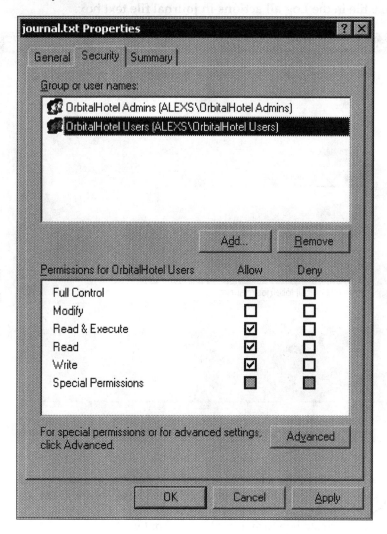

To set the file as a journal file, open the **Options** dialog in the Visual SourceSafe Administrator and select the **General** tab page. Enter the network path for the journal.txt file in the **Log all actions in journal file** text box.

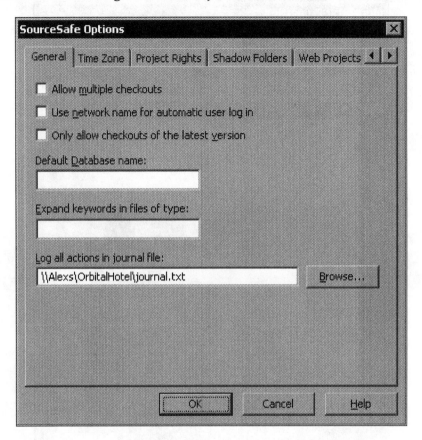

 Do not use a local path for the journal file because the path is used globally by all the clients to write entries in the journal. If you use local paths, the journal.txt file is created on each user's local computer.

The entries in a journal file look like this:

```
$/OrbitalHotel.root/OrbitalHotel/Core/BusinessLogic/RoomManager.cs
Version: 8
User: Alex              Date:  8/21/06  Time:  2:26p
Checked in

$/OrbitalHotel.root/OrbitalHotel/WindowsApplications/WinReservation/Program.cs
Version: 4
User: John              Date:  8/21/06  Time:  2:31p
Checked in
```

Deleting Users

Before deleting a user, make sure he or she has all the files checked in first. To delete a user from the SourceSafe database, select the user in the Visual SourceSafe Administrator main window and use the **Users | Delete User** menu command. A question dialog will be displayed to confirm the user deletion.

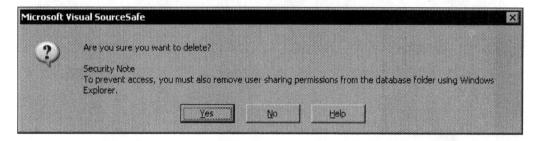

Click **Yes** to delete the user from the database. This will delete the personal user folder under the `users` database folder.

You will also have to prevent the user from having access to the shared database folder by removing the user's access permissions. Because the user is part of one of the two user groups that control access to the database, all you have to do is remove the user from the Windows groups he is assigned to.

> If the user still has checked out items, you must undo the checkouts by logging in to the Visual SourceSafe Explorer using the Admin account and using the **Undo Checkout** command.

Configuring the Services for Visual Studio

Visual SourceSafe 2005 contains two server components used by the Visual Studio SourceSafe plug-ins:

- Local Area Network booster service: this accelerates operations on the local network using the Visual Studio SourceSafe LAN plug-in.

- Remote Internet access service: the enables access to the SourceSafe database from the Internet using the Visual Studio SourceSafe internet plug-in.

These services are configured using the Visual SourceSafe Administrator on the database server with the **Server | Configure** menu command.

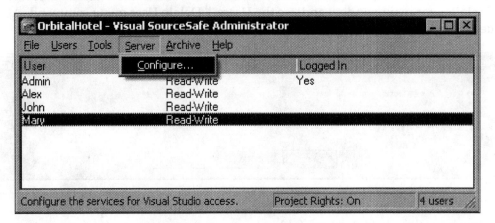

Configuring the Local Area Network Service

To configure the Local Area Network booster service, select the **LAN** tab in the **Server Configuration** dialog.

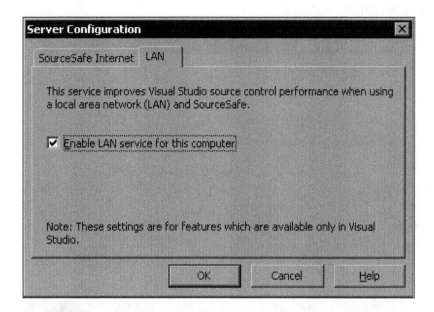

To enable or disable the service, use the **Enable LAN service for this computer** option.

Configuring the Remote Internet Access Service

To configure the remote internet access service, select the **SourceSafe Internet** tab in the **Server Configuration** dialog.

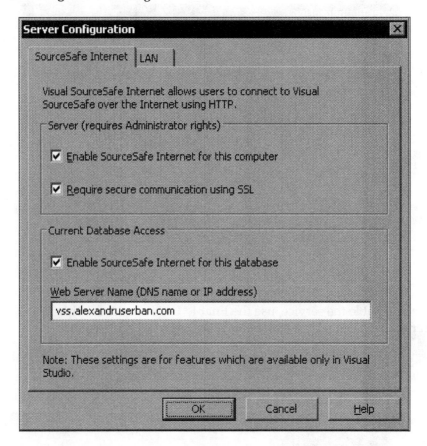

To enable the SourceSafe internet service for the local database server computer, select the **Enable SourceSafe Internet for this computer** checkbox. This will install an XML web service named *SourceSafe* in the **Internet Information Services (IIS)** on the local database server computer.

The service is always installed in the **default website** (or the website having ID 1) in IIS.

Check the **Require secure communication using SSL** option to enable secure communications over Secure Sockets Layer.

To enable SSL you must first install an SSL certificate in IIS. For more information on creating and installing an SSL certificate consult Appendix A.

To enable internet access for the current database, select the **Enable SourceSafe Internet for this database** option. You must specify the Internet domain name for the server or its IP address in the **Web Server Name** text box.

When using SSL you must specify the same name used in the SSL certificate otherwise you will see the following error message:

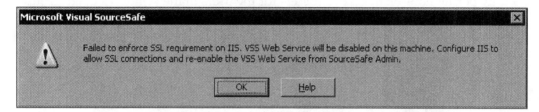

To apply the configuration, click **OK** in the **Server Configuration** dialog.

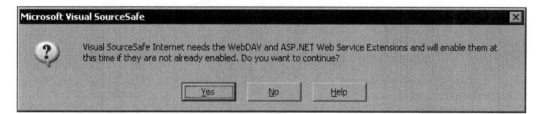

Click **Yes** to configure the required server components.

After the configuration is applied, the *SourceSafe* web service will be configured to access the SourceSafe database. Two new folders are created in the database, **VssWebDownload** and **VssWebUpload**.

These folders are used to download and upload files over the Internet. They are configured as virtual folders in the SourceSafe web service.

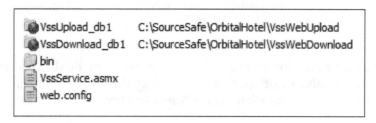

As a result, to allow remote users to use the internet service, you must grant **Modify** security permissions on these two folders for the users in the Windows **Users** group.

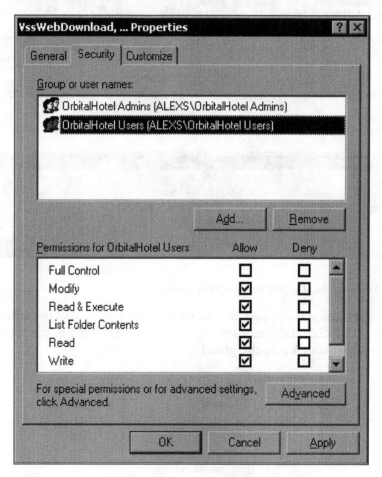

After setting the security permissions for these folders, remote users can log in to the database using the SourceSafe remote internet service.

Summary

In this appendix, we've seen how to create and configure SourceSafe databases. After creating a new database we have to set the necessary Windows security. The best way to manage security is to create two Windows user groups, one for the administrators and one for the normal users. These groups make it easier to manage the Windows permissions for the database folders.

We also saw how to add, edit, and delete SourceSafe database users, how to set shadow folders, and how to set database project permissions. We've also seen how to configure the two server components used by the SourceSafe plug-ins in Visual Studio.

C

Database Maintenance

In this appendix, we will see how to perform maintenance tasks on SourceSafe databases such as undoing user checkouts, changing the team version control model, locking, archiving, restoring, and running database maintenance tools.

Undoing User Checkouts

Sometimes, there are cases when users forget to check in files for a long period of time. If the database is configured not to allow multiple checkouts (exclusive checkout model) and other users need to modify the file, they are unable to do so. In these cases you, as database administrator, can resolve the situation by undoing the checkout on the file.

To do so log in to the database using the Visual SourceSafe Explorer using the **Admin** account.

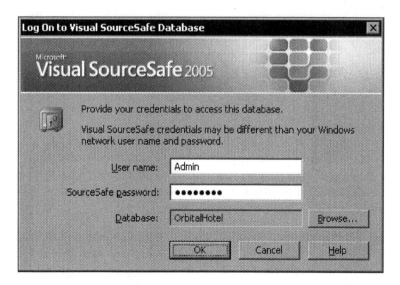

Then, right-click on the file left checked out and use the **Undo Check Out** command.

If the user has many files checked out you can use the search by status function to search for the files checked out to that user. To be able to perform this operation, you must have a working folder set for the project that contains the file.

Changing the Team Version Control Model

We examined the team cooperation checkout models in Chapter 5. If during development you decide to change the checkout model for the database, you can do so by using the **Option** window in the Visual SourceSafe Administrator.

To enable the multiple checkout model, (enabling multiple users to check out a file at the same time) select the **Allow multiple checkouts** option. To restrict the checkouts only to the latest versions, (force a get latest operation) select the **Only allow checkouts of the latest version** option.

The **Only allow checkouts of the latest version** option is new in Visual SourceSafe 2005 and it is designed especially for disconnected scenarios as we've seen in Chapter 6. It controls the file version that will be checked out as a result of a checkout operation.

If it is enabled, only the latest database file version can be checked out. This is for compatibility with older SourceSafe versions and can lead to data loss.

If it is disabled, local file versions can be checked out also. The ability to check out local file versions is critical when reconnecting to the database after checking out files in disconnected mode because it avoids manual file merges and possible data loss.

To avoid data loss keep this option disabled.

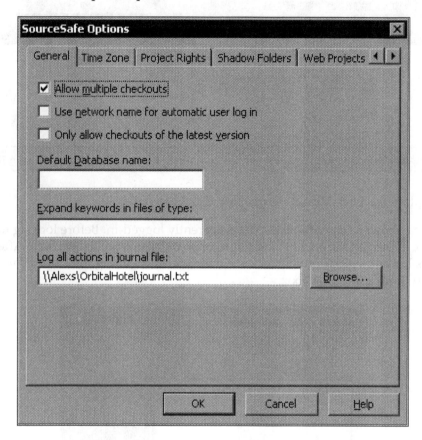

 Because initialization and customization data is read by SourceSafe clients only while starting up, these options will take effect only after the logged-in users restart any opened SourceSafe client and Visual Studio.

Locking the Database

When performing database-wide operations, (such as archive and restore) it is necessary to keep users from logging in and making changes to the database. You can do this by locking the database while performing these operations.

To lock the database, use the **Lock SourceSafe database** command in the **Tools** menu.

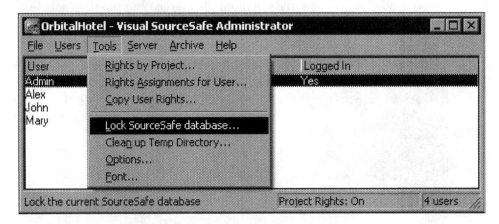

This displays the **Lock Visual SourceSafe Database** dialog.

The dialog shows a list with all the users currently logged-in. Before locking the database, inform all the users to log out to prevent them from losing data. After all the users log out, you can safely lock the database by checking the **Lock all users out of Visual SourceSafe** checkbox.

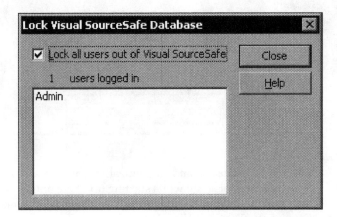

While the database is locked, no one is allowed to log in until you finish your task and uncheck the checkbox.

Archiving the Database

You will want to archive a Visual SourceSafe database or individual projects periodically for backup purposes.

 Before you start the archiving operation, make sure no users are logged in and lock the database to prevent users from logging in and making changes during archiving.

If you use Visual SourceSafe Administrator from a client computer or from the server using the network path, you will see the following message:

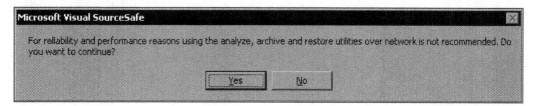

For maximum performance, you should use it directly on the SourceSafe server and log in to the database using a local path rather than a network path. For this purpose you can add the same database to the database list but by using the local path.

To start the archive wizard, use the **Archive Projects** command in the **Archive** menu.

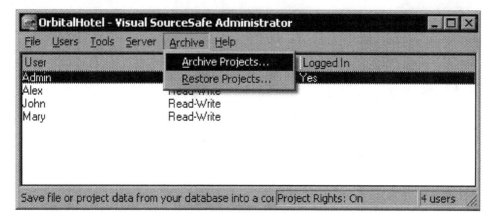

In the first step of the **Archive Wizard** you must specify the database projects to archive using the **Add** button.

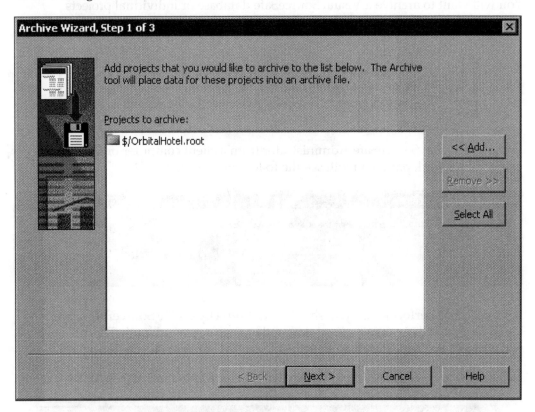

> If you select the root folder $ for archival you will only be able to restore it later as a sub-folder with the name of the archive, like $/OrbitalHotel.ssa. This may not be what you want, in which case you may choose to select individual projects for archival.

Click **Next** to advance to the second step.

In the second step you have to choose between three archiving options.

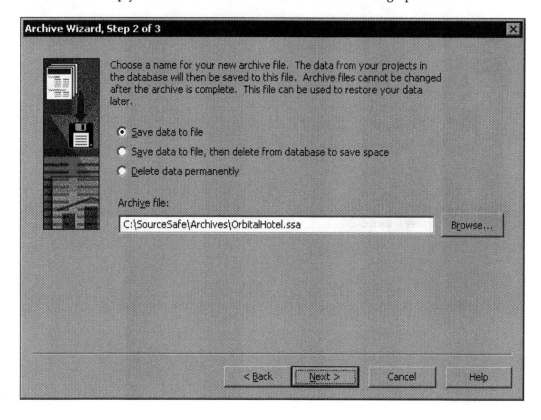

Archive Wizard, Step 2 of 3

Choose a name for your new archive file. The data from your projects in the database will then be saved to this file. Archive files cannot be changed after the archive is complete. This file can be used to restore your data later.

- Save data to file
- Save data to file, then delete from database to save space
- Delete data permanently

Archive file:

C:\SourceSafe\Archives\OrbitalHotel.ssa   Browse...

< Back   Next >   Cancel   Help

The first option archives the database to a file.

The second option archives the data and then deletes it from the database. This option is useful when the database becomes large and allows you to save space.

The third option deletes the data permanently and you can use it to delete a project that you don't use anymore.

In this case I will choose to save the data to a file for backup.

Click **Next** to advance to the third and final step.

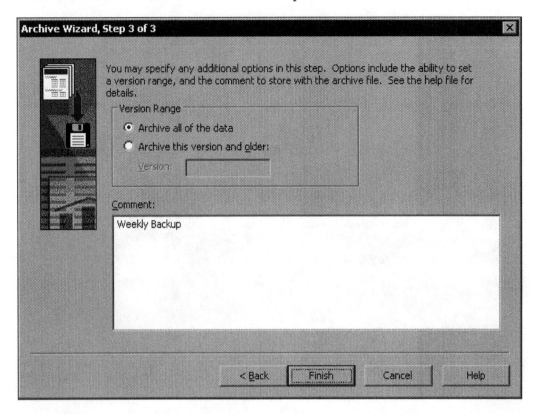

At this point you can specify the file versions you want to archive. You can choose to archive all the data in the database, or archive the contents from a particular version and older. Combined with the second option in the previous step, you can archive old file versions and then delete them from the database to free space and speed operations. Later you can restore them using the restore function.

In the Version text box you can specify:

- Project versions using the version number format **N** (for example **5**)
- Project dates using the date format **MM/DD/YY** (for example **1/25/07**)
- Project labels using the string format (for example **Beta1**)

All the versions including the specified version and below will be archived.

You can also specify a comment for the archive in the **Comment** text box.

To start archiving the selected projects click **Finish**.

Restoring the Database

The restore function allows you to restore a previously archived project over the original project, to a new project in the same database, or to a new project in a different database.

 Before performing the restore operation, make sure no users are logged in and lock the database.

If you use Visual SourceSafe Administrator from a client computer or from the server using the network path, you will see the following message:

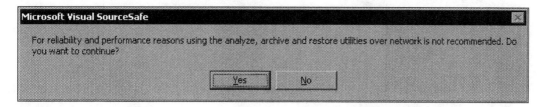

For maximum performance, you should use it directly on the SourceSafe server and log in to the database using a local path rather than a network path. For this purpose, you can add the same database to the database list but by using the local path.

To start the restore wizard use the **Restore Projects** command in the **Archive** menu.

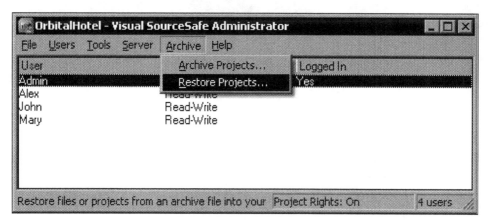

This will display the first step of the **Restore Wizard** where you must select the archive file that contains the previously archived project.

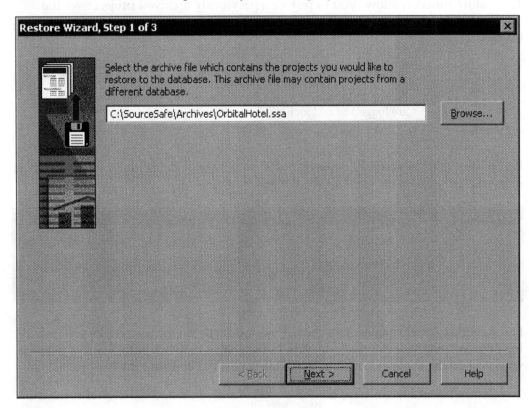

Use the **Browse** button to select the archive file. Then, click **Next** to advance to the second step.

The second step shows the projects in the selected archive file.

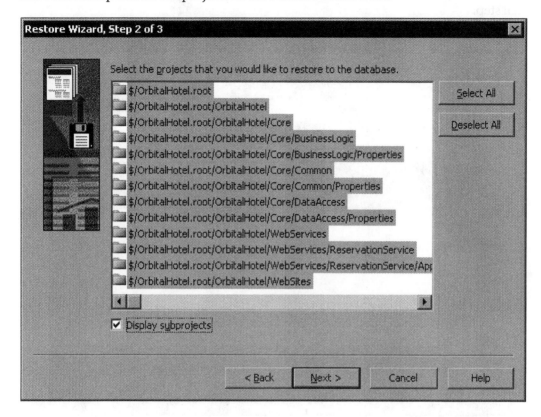

You can choose to restore only a subset of the projects by selecting them using the *Shift* and *Ctrl* keys. To display the subprojects, check the **Display subprojects** option.

After selecting the projects you want to restore, click **Next** to advance to the final step.

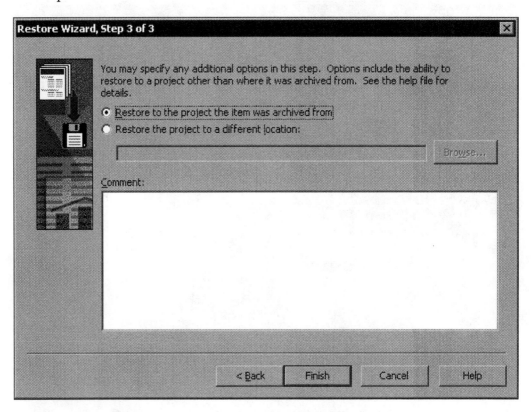

The final step allows you to select where to restore the selected projects.

The first option will restore the projects using the original project path. If restoring to the original database, this will restore the project versions contained in the archive file. If the archive file contains a full project archive, the project will be restored to the state found in the archive. If the archive file contains a project version range, the archived project range will be restored to the database.

If restoring to a different database, you cannot restore a project version range; you can only restore a full project archive.

The second option allows you to specify a different location to restore the project. Use the **Browse** button to select a new location or to create a new location in the target database.

You can specify a restore comment in the **Comment** text box.

To start restoring the archived project click **Finish**.

Analyzing the SourceSafe Database

To keep the database in good shape and to ensure it is running as fast as possible, SourceSafe uses the **Analyze** utility, which looks out for the following problems:

- Parent-child mismatch: Possible situations include those in which a parent (project) assumes it has a child (file or subproject) but the child disagrees; a child assumes it has a parent but the parent disagrees; or child and parent don't reference each other, but the child counts are off.

- Corrupt database files: Files that can contain corrupted data include `Names.dat`, which stores file names longer than 34 characters; `Rights.dat`, which stores relationships between users and project rights; `Status.dat`, which contains checkout status information for files; `Um.dat`, which stores all users of a Visual SourceSafe database; and `Version.dat`, which stores the Visual SourceSafe version.

- Removal of unused items from the database.

It is recommended to run the **Analyze** utility every week. If you don't run this utility for more than 30 days, when logging in to the Visual SourceSafe Administrator or the Visual SourceSafe Explorer using the Admin account you will be prompted to run it.

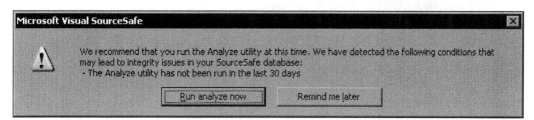

 Before starting the **Analyze** utility, make sure no users are logged in and lock the database.

The utility is located in Visual SourceSafe installation folder and it is represented by the analyse.exe file. While running, it will display the progress in its main window as shown in the following figure:

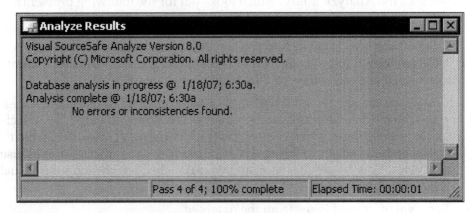

Analyze has the following command-line options:

```
Usage: analyze [options] [@<response file>|<List of files>]
<SourceSafe data path>
    -? or -h  Display this message.
    -b<folder> Specify the folder to use for backup.
    -c        Compress unused space.
    -d        Delete unused items.
    -db       Delete backup.
    -dc       Disable common messages (bad case in physical file
names).
    -df        Disable free space check.
    -dw        Run SourceSafe 2005 reference checking only.
    -f         Automatically fix files with corruptions.
    -fl        Automatically fix files with corruptions and re-build
the label cache.
    -fp        Automatically fix files with corruptions and remove
invalidly named physical files.
    -i-        When the analysis is complete the program exits.
    -refv6     Run SourceSafe 6 reference checking instead of
SourceSafe 2005 reference checking.
    -s         Slow project rebuild (slower but more rigorous scan for
child items).
    -x         Do not attempt to lock the database when analyzing. If
-x is specified, -c, -d, and -f are not allowed.
    -v1        Show only critical errors.
```

```
-v2          Show only significant errors.
-v3          Show all errors and inconsistencies.
-v4          Show errors, inconsistencies, and informational notes.
```

You can display these options by executing `analyze.exe -h`.

Summary

In this appendix, we've examined the database maintenance tasks. We've seen how to undo user checkouts, how to change the checkout model, and how to lock, archive, and restore the database. We've also seen how to run the Analyze maintenance tool to fix any database issues.

Index

Thank you for buying
Visual SourceSafe 2005 Software
Configuration Management in Practice

About Packt Publishing

Packt, pronounced 'packed', published its first book "*Mastering phpMyAdmin for Effective MySQL Management*" in April 2004 and subsequently continued to specialize in publishing highly focused books on specific technologies and solutions.

Our books and publications share the experiences of your fellow IT professionals in adapting and customizing today's systems, applications, and frameworks. Our solution based books give you the knowledge and power to customize the software and technologies you're using to get the job done. Packt books are more specific and less general than the IT books you have seen in the past. Our unique business model allows us to bring you more focused information, giving you more of what you need to know, and less of what you don't.

Packt is a modern, yet unique publishing company, which focuses on producing quality, cutting-edge books for communities of developers, administrators, and newbies alike. For more information, please visit our website: www.packtpub.com.

Writing for Packt

We welcome all inquiries from people who are interested in authoring. Book proposals should be sent to authors@packtpub.com. If your book idea is still at an early stage and you would like to discuss it first before writing a formal book proposal, contact us; one of our commissioning editors will get in touch with you.

We're not just looking for published authors; if you have strong technical skills but no writing experience, our experienced editors can help you develop a writing career, or simply get some additional reward for your expertise.